Social Relations and Social Exclusion

Social Relations and Social Exclusion sets out a new approach to understanding society, based on rational choice theory.

Starting from a few simple assumptions about the nature and context of human action, this book provides a complete reinterpretation of our major social institutions. Its central aim is to see how far social relations can be explained on the basis of human beings acting in their own interests rather than as helpless puppets of wider social forces.

The institutions examined by the book include households, communities, workplaces, social classes and the state. In each case, it is shown how the institution forms a context within which social interaction can be explained in terms of the rational decision taken by the actors involved.

A key question in the book is why people choose to enter into social relations in which they are exploited, and the question is answered mainly by reference to established forms of rule that lead people to believe they have no choice. The book criticises the current form of such rule in Britain, arguing strongly that it does not have to be like this. It argues for a rethinking of social policies, based on sound principles of universal human liberation.

Peter Somerville is Professor in Social Policy at the University of Lincolnshire and Humberside. He has published widely on issues of housing, social exclusion and community empowerment.

Routledge Studies in Governance and Public Policy

1 **Public Sector Ethics**
   Finding and implementing values
   Edited by Charles Sampford and Noel Preston with Carol-Anne Bois

2 **Ethics and Political Practice**
   Perspectives on legislative ethics
   Edited by Noel Preston and Charles Sampford with Carol-Anne Bois

3 **Why Does Policy Change?**
   Lessons from British transport policy 1945–99
   Jeremy Richardson and Geoffrey Dudley

4 **Social Relations and Social Exclusion**
   Rethinking political economy
   Peter Somerville

Social Relations and Social Exclusion
Rethinking political economy

Peter Somerville

London and New York

First published 2000
by Routledge
11 New Fetter Lane, London EC4P 4EE

Simultaneously published in the USA and Canada
by Routledge
29 West 35th Street, New York, NY 10001

Routledge is an imprint of the Taylor & Francis Group

© 2000 Peter Somerville

Typeset in Garamond by
Exe Valley Dataset Ltd, Exeter
Printed and bound in Great Britain by
University Press, Cambridge

All rights reserved. No part of this book may be reprinted or
reproduced or utilized in any form or by any electronic,
mechanical, or other means, now known or hereafter
invented, including photocopying and recording, or in any
information storage or retrieval system, without permission in
writing from the publishers.

British Library Cataloguing in Publication Data
A catalogue record for this book is available
from the British Library

Library of Congress Cataloging in Publication Data
Somerville, Peter.
  Social relations and social exclusion: rethinking political economy / Peter Somerville.
    p. cm.
  Includes bibliographical references and index
  1. Social institutions. 2. Rational choice theory. I. Title.
HM826.S65 2000
306–dc21   00–042220

ISBN 0–415–24040–9

Contents

List of tables vii
Preface ix
Acknowledgements xi

1 Introduction: a theory of social relations 1

2 Households and families 13

3 Communities and community development 48

4 Contractual relations and social divisions 88

5 State–citizen relations and social justice 112

6 Policy implications: the case of housing 144

7 Conclusion 165

Bibliography 183
Index 205

Tables

2.1	Distribution of household financial management systems	26
3.1	Types of social relations	51
3.2	The relative power of locals and newcomers	64
6.1	A typology of housing regimes	145

Preface

This book came to be written as a reaction against the widespread view that sees human beings as the creatures of impersonal social forces such as the market, the state and class struggle. While not wishing to deny the powerlessness of so many individuals in the face of the overwhelming might of mass organisations, this book argues uncompromisingly that we are not victims of such powers except insofar as we choose to be so. Our choices are constrained by the contexts within which we act, but these constraints do not enslave us. Far from it: contexts themselves provide opportunities for action and therefore make liberation possible. The message of this book is that freedom in this sense is personally and politically achievable.

Peter Somerville
University of Lincolnshire and Humberside

Acknowledgements

I am very grateful to Paul Watt, Tricia Emptage and several anonymous referees for their constructive and helpful comments and criticisms.

I am particularly grateful to my wife Sue for her support at a crucial stage in the proceedings of completing this work.

1 Introduction

A theory of social relations

In social science as in natural science there is no shortage of people who make fundamental assumptions about what human beings are 'really' like. This in itself is not a problem so long as the assumptions are falsifiable and not beyond the influence of all possible arguments. The real mistake is to elevate what should be only working hypotheses into exclusive claims about the essential nature of humanity; that is, claims to some kind of unique and ultimate truth about the human condition. This book argues that what we can know is basically the 'text' and 'context' of humanity and the interaction between them; that is, the autobiographical narratives of individual human beings communicated through third parties, the social relations in which they are embedded, and the observable dynamical processes in which these individuals act upon and are acted upon by specific contexts.

The concern of this book is primarily with social theory. There is a sense in which human interaction and organisation represent a specific level of evolution where individual organisms adopt patterns of behaviour which 'best fit' the environments in which they operate. Some sociologists have used the term 'strategies' to describe such patterns (Pahl 1984; Crow 1989; Edwards and Ribbens 1991; McCrone 1994), although the limitations of the concept have been pointed out by others (Wallace 1993). The basic point is that what could be called an evolutionary approach serves to focus attention on three key features: the individual human being (known through their autobiographical texts), their natural/social environment (conceptualised as their 'context'), and the courses of action by individual human beings which determine their comparative advantage or disadvantage in different environments (processes of text–context interaction).

Some of the assumptions of this evolutionary approach are shared by what is known as the 'public choice' or 'social choice' or 'rational choice' perspective (Olson 1965; Buchanan 1965) and by the related theory of 'human capital' (Becker 1981). It is this perspective which will inform much of the argument in this book. According to this perspective, derived from neoclassical economics, each individual acts or tends to act to maximise his or her utility, and this is primarily what determines their orientation to their environment. Co-operation among human beings is then achieved mainly through the social construction of group advantage, and understanding how such construction occurs lies at the root of explaining social relations generally.

In common with all perspectives deriving from the 'Enlightenment', including marxism and feminism, rational choice theory makes one key assumption about the nature of human beings, namely that they are capable of self-determination; that is, critical reflection through developing their own autobiographical narrative (Drover and Kerans 1993: 6) which enables them to make up their own minds about the values they wish to maximise. Sen (1987) argues that human beings have 'basic capabilities' which they should be able to develop and exercise as a condition for 'participation autonomy' (Doyal and Gough 1991). This assumption is not fundamental in the sense of being assumed to be true *a priori* for all human beings: it is of course recognised that some human beings will not be capable in this sense (a failure or absence of 'text'). The status of the assumption is rather more transcendental, in that it is required in order for rational choice theory to have substantive applicability. It is still only a working hypothesis, but it is one that lies at the root of the theory itself.

Rational choice theory holds that in general individuals are responsible for their own self-determination. Any form of external compulsion tends to undermine that sense of personal responsibility and is therefore to be minimised. In some circumstances, however, it is necessary to have rules or regulations which are binding on individuals in order for the basic capabilities of those individuals to be developed. In such cases, acceptance of the rule or regulation should be achieved by means of reasoning and negotiating among the individuals concerned. Essentially, rational choice takes place within a system of constraints by means of a negotiated balance between the desires of the individual and those with whom that individual relates (their 'community'). If negotiation fails, there are only three possible outcomes: the rule or regulation is removed (effective 'voice'); the individual chooses to obey the rule ('loyalty'); or the individual leaves the group ('exit') (Hirschmann 1970). Where an individual is unable to exercise the exit option, and where the rule remains in place, that individual can be said to be constrained to act against their will, for example through the application of effective sanctions if they fail to comply with the rule. This represents a failure of 'context', in that external conditions effectively deny the exercise of rational choice to the individual.

The general approach adopted in this book is along the lines of: what are the rational courses of action in any given context and, if it is assumed that individuals follow such courses of action, how far can this explain the consequences? This approach therefore does not assume that individuals always do act rationally or in their own interest, nor does it assume that individuals will necessarily agree on whether a given course of action is rational or not. It argues more modestly that an assumption of rational behaviour can explain a good deal that would otherwise appear puzzling about social relations and social action. The theory also has a normative dimension, in that it suggests that people ought to act rationally and that an increased commitment to rational action within a context of appropriate norms and rules is essential for human dignity and human progress.

Rational choice approaches have frequently been criticised on the grounds that people do not and indeed should not always act in a rational or self-centred or goal-oriented way (Morris 1990; for a more detailed critique, see Zey 1998). It is indeed true that some writers in this tradition appear on occasions to lack an appreciation of the fact that utility itself is socially constructed and that this necessarily conditions individual behaviour. This book, however, takes the view that utility or value is essentially context-dependent; that is, it varies according to the nature of the social institution in which it figures. This view is shared by those identified with the perspective of New Institutional Economics (North 1990). It is also consistent with the approach of those writers who talk in terms of a 'bounded rationality' (Simon 1982; Conlisk 1996).

The rational individual is therefore one who has a capacity for self-determination or autonomy, who adopts a strategy which selects the course of action that most effectively (that is, at least cost and risk) fulfils their desires (Laver 1997: 20). This apparently simple notion, however, is in fact extremely complex. It can be unpacked in terms of three assumptions. The first is that individuals act in such a way as to maximise value (either in a specific monetary sense or in some other context-defined sense) through the restraint of competition with other individuals by means of compulsion and selective incentives (Olson 1965). The concept of value is a difficult one, but essentially it involves the object of human desire, the means towards the enjoyment of the good life as determined on the basis of the individual's own critical reflection. The second assumption is that individuals act so as to minimise their costs by sharing them with other individuals. Again, costs can be interpreted in either a financial sense or some other sense – social, emotional or psychological and the measurement of costs is also self-determined. The third assumption is that the milieu within which co-operation among individuals takes place is defined by access to a common resource (Ostrom 1990); that is, it is the common resource which determines the context or environment within which value is constructed (and this context can be social or institutional as well as spatial). The rational individual is therefore one who weighs value in the balance against cost and risk as part of their calculus for self-determination within a framework of their knowledge of the contextual possibilities of action. The rational course of action is the one based on the best obtainable knowledge of text and context, and on the most plausible analysis of the repertoire of likely outcomes of text–context interaction.

The importance of each of these three assumptions can be explained as follows. In the first case, the action of 'free' individuals results in the creation of mutual obligations within a group in return for a comparative advantage for the group as a whole. By reducing the waste involved in competing with others, every individual maximises value for herself or himself. The drawbacks, however, are that each individual has to accept a certain level of regulation in order to sustain the arrangement (for example by preventing individuals from 'free-riding'), that inequalities of power within the group may be reinforced (because weaker individuals have less value to contribute to the pool), and that the creation of group norms and regulations inevitably means the drawing of a boundary between members and non-members of the group.

For the purposes of this book, a norm is a rule that guides how an individual is to act in a generality of cases. Here, the norm involved is a utilitarian one; that is, it says: 'I will co-operate with the others if and only if my co-operation makes a positive contribution to the collective good.' But why should a rational individual follow such a norm or any other norm for that matter when they can take an occasional free ride on the backs of the efforts of others? After all, if a person is acting in accordance with a norm, then he or she is not necessarily proceeding on the basis of a rational analysis of the situation. The general answer to this question is to point to processes of 'normalisation' which occur very early on in the lives of individuals and organisations through rituals of interaction (Goffman 1969), processes of routinisation (Giddens 1984: 15, 21, 90), habits of cooperation or trust (Coleman 1990: 177–80; Hardin 1992: 505–7; Putnam 1993: 167), or techniques of domination (Foucault 1977, 1980; Luke 1990). Rational choice theory, however, declares that we are not hapless victims of our early socialisation, but can choose to act differently if we wish. If a rational individual decides to follow a norm, their decision will be based on a rational appraisal of the costs of non-co-operation (for example in terms of sanctions imposed by others) as against the benefits to be derived from access to a common resource. A decision to free-ride incurs costs for an individual which may not at first be open to calculation but may become clearer as time goes on, for example in terms of the damage thereby caused to that individual's reputation or to the esteem in which they are held by others.

In the case of the second assumption, the sharing of costs involves an element of redistribution which may benefit the weaker members of the group. It also defines what individuals are entitled to enjoy by virtue of being members of the group: these could be described as membership rights. Essentially, each individual co-operates conditionally in return for improvements in their own situation. The form of co-operation is said to be governed by this principle of reciprocity. For the stronger members, the benefit could simply be the co-operation of the weaker members themselves. Again, the creation of rights which include people in membership by the same token excludes others from membership.

The norm involved in this case is that of reciprocity, which says: 'I will co-operate if and only if a substantial number of others co-operate' (Elster 1989: 48–9, 187, 192, as derived from Bengtsson 1998b: 12). This is more clearly rational in its avoidance of being taken for a ride, but if it were followed by everybody it is difficult to see how co-operation could ever get off the ground. In strictly rational terms, co-operation should arise only where there is 'balanced reciprocity'; that is, where the act of one individual in benefiting another is 'balanced' by a reciprocal act from the other individual. Such 'balanced reciprocity' is based on a relationship of trust between the two individuals concerned: one individual takes a risk in co-operating, but if his or her trust in the other individual is broken or misplaced, then further co-operation may not be forthcoming. Trust is therefore the key to the normalisation of personal relationships. Trust also involves more than strictly balanced reciprocity or conditional obligation: it encompasses mutuality (Gould 1988: 292) or 'complementary reciprocity' (Benhabib 1988 1990), that is mutual recognition and communicative competence (Habermas 1987). Basically, the exercise of autonomy by one individual depends (among other things) upon respect and understanding from other individuals. This involves a readiness to affirm not only their essential humanity, but also their individuality, with different needs, talents, capacities and points of view (Drover and Kerans 1993: 261). The extension of this principle to larger social groups, however, where the individuals are strangers to one another, is problematic (see Chapter 4).

The third assumption essentially defines the arena or context in which a set of rights and responsibilities operates. The existence of a common resource of some kind is what provides the basis for community. In this sense, a household is perhaps the most basic kind of community, but the term could probably be applied to any form of 'free' association of human beings. The context is always present as the embodiment of dead labour (that is, the product of past actions of human beings), but it is also a continually moving reference point for action and interaction. The importance of this assumption is that it provides a concrete form in relation to which the highly abstract concept of value can be measured; that is, in terms of the benefit to be gained from the consumption of the common resource. Here too, however, access to the common resource is unlikely to be equal, so this can give rise to new forms of inequality of wealth and power.

Maximisation of value therefore leads to the creation of obligations while minimisation of costs creates individual rights. Jordan (1996) has rightly concluded from this that rights and obligations are not necessarily linked within the practice of any particular individual, as is claimed by neo-conservatives and some neo-labourites — that is to say, for any given individual right there does not *necessarily* exist a corresponding individual responsibility, although this can be artificially induced through morality or law. This is because they are linked only in the context of the group as a whole and specifically through their access to the common resource.

In this book the postulates of rational choice theory will be used in order to make sense of key institutional contexts in modern society: households, local communities, workplaces and political institutions. In each case, it will be shown how rational choice theory can throw light on how such institutions work and on how they can be changed. This is not to say, however, that rational choice theory provides anything like a full explanation of social relations. For example, as Zey (1998) points out, it lacks an adequate theory of power and of the contexts within which rational choice takes place. More generally:

> The limits of [rational choice theory's] explanations show that it is an incomplete theory of social action and that it can remain vital only by incorporating other theories at different levels of explanation. Rational choice theory itself should remain narrow . . . if it is to retain its explanatory power.
> (Bohman 1992: 225, cited in Zey 1998: 111)

For this reason, other theoretical concepts will be introduced.

Rational choice theory is not able to explain how power in society came to be unequally distributed. As Zey (1998: 57) says: 'The explanation of cause is at the heart of a social theory of power and cannot be reduced to the economic exchanges of rational choice theory'. We therefore need separate theory, not derived from rational choice theory, for this purpose. In this book, I use a form of marxist-feminist theory based on a concept of exploitation. Exploitation can be defined as a social relation in which the value produced by the labour of one individual is appropriated, at least partly, by another (Delphy and Leonard 1992). Exploitation in this sense occurs in a variety of social contexts, but the two main ones to be considered in this book are the family and the labour market. An important distinction exists between exploitation in which the labour is forced and that where it is free. Forced labour is characteristic of social systems based on slavery or totalitarian state rule. Free labour, however, is typical of capitalism which is the globally dominant economic system today, and it is also typical of the household economy with its own system of labour relations. Under both capitalism and the household economy, exploited individuals labour on behalf of others in return for remuneration which is less than the value of the product of their labour. In capitalism, a propertyless individual hires out his or her labour power in return for a wage or a salary, and in domestic production a sexually subordinated individual commonly (though not always) performs labour for other household members and receives some payment in kind such as provision of shelter and material goods (Apps 1981). In both cases, the value of the payment received is always less than the value produced by the labour in question.

The importance of the concept of exploitation for the purposes of this book is that it helps to explain not only enduring patterns of inequality among individuals but also how these patterns appear to be freely chosen by the individuals concerned. This serves to counteract the common liberal assumption among rational choice theorists concerning the sovereignty of the individual; that is, that each individual has supreme power to determine his or her own fate. In reality, individuals exist within social contexts which are structured by patterns of exploitation. These contexts do not merely constrain people but shape the very freedom of their individual choice. It is not merely the rationality of human beings which is 'bounded', but their whole physical and emotional being.

Exploitation needs to be distinguished from oppression. Under forced labour, the two are intertwined in a single system of domination. Where labour is free, however, the relation between exploitation and oppression is less direct and more complex. Under capitalism, the working class is typically subordinated to a 'dominant political coalition' (Mollenkopf 1989), so that workers are both exploited and oppressed, but there is no necessary relationship between the two. In the domestic system also, the exploited woman is typically oppressed by the man, but not necessarily so, and the nature of the oppression is subtle and difficult to establish. All this suggests that the social bases of power inequality need to be rethought.

Another general consideration is the distinction between closed or exclusive groups and open or inclusive groups. Whether a group becomes exclusive with restricted membership, or inclusive with unrestricted membership, broadly depends upon whether the costs (or risks) of recruiting new members outweigh the benefits. This consideration leads to a theory of social policy according to which social exclusion and inequality among groups can in principle be tackled through sanctions and incentives to ensure that the benefits of recruiting new members exceed the costs (or risks), or that the costs (or risks) of *not* recruiting new members exceed the benefits. This argument suggests that an explanation of social exclusion is derivative from a more general dynamic theory of social relations based on the marginal utility of particular (new) members to a dominant group.

A final general consideration is that given the assumptions outlined above, the mechanism by which groups operate and develop can be identified as one of 'structural selection'. This idea is analogous to that of natural selection. Essentially, co-operation within a group occurs in order to gain advantage for members of that group in comparison with other groups. Co-operation among individuals is therefore indissolubly associated with competition among groups. Since capitalism is based on this principle, that of individuals co-operating 'freely' within competitive markets, this helps to explain why it has been such a successful system for its participants. The group which succeeds is the one that best 'fits' with its social environment and this involves the production of what are known as 'virtuous circles' (Putnam 1993). This should not be taken to imply, however, that the history of capitalism is one of unilinear and even development. This is because of the unlimited differences and diversity among human beings and the contingencies and uncertainties associated with their interactions, both as individuals and as members of different groups.

An important, and indeed vital, question to consider is how diverse individuals with radically different autobiographical narratives come to recognise the advantages of their participation in groups, to accept their rights and responsibilities, to trust their fellow group members, and to commit themselves to those groups on a long-term basis. This essentially anthropological and psychological question has not as yet been satisfactorily answered. Goffman (1969) suggested that human communication is embedded in ritual exchanges of value between people who recognise each other as members of the same group and that children learn these basic reciprocities unconsciously. Without value exchange within groups, therefore, involving restraint of competition, human communication would be impossible. A common language might exist but there would be no common understanding. This does not explain, however, how a common understanding based on such reciprocity can arise in the first place.

This issue of how exactly socialisation takes place is not examined in depth in this book. The tenor of the argument, however, would tend to favour a dynamical approach (Leisering and Walker 1998). This approach relies on a concept of the 'life course' (Leisering and Walker 1998: 9) as the expression of text–context interaction for a given individual. Each individual is viewed as following specific trajectories consisting of sequences of states and transitions. During their life course, each individual then makes rational choices in the light of the values they have internalised, their knowledge of the context at any given time, and the life chances they anticipate enjoying in the future. This conceptualisation is then close to that of Giddens (1991: 53, 80, 145ff.) who sees individuals as existing in a process of continual reflexive ordering of their autobiographies, but is different in its way of attempting to make sense of the contextualisation of that reflexivity.

Although the book does not consider socialisation processes in depth, it does touch upon them in relation to the question of why individuals acquiesce in their own exploitation and why they accept the authority of others. Here the argument draws upon Foucauldian concepts of monarchical and disciplinary power in order to supplement theories of rational choice and exploitation. This additional element of theory is required in order to explain the character of hegemonies and hegemonic change. Hegemony (Gramsci 1971) is a form of disciplinary power in which 'free' citizens consent to, and even actively reinforce, their own oppression. There have been attempts to explain the effects of hegemony in marxist terms (for example, in terms of 'false consciousness'), but such explanations conflict with rational choice theory which assumes precisely that individuals do act in their own interest. Such conflict needs to be resolved, by means of deeper rational explanations of apparently irrational behaviour.

The theory developed in this book is therefore a form of political economy modified by Foucauldian theory. It is a form of rational choice theory grounded within a theory of exploitation and supplemented where necessary by Foucauldian approaches. The political economy is required in order to explain the dynamics of collective action in different social contexts, and Foucauldian theory is needed to explain the overall governmentality of that collective action. Political economy on its own can explain the formation and maintenance of rights and obligations but it cannot explain, for example, their unconditional character within kinship networks. Similarly, the boundaries to kinship networks are drawn in a way which cannot be fully explained on the basis of rational choice, although the latter can throw some useful light on the process. Also, a sense of identity with or commitment to a group cannot be explained entirely in terms of the benefits that membership of the group brings.

The structure of the book is as follows. Chapter 2 considers households as a social context or institution within which individuals interact. It considers two types of relationships in particular, namely those of gender and generation, which are arguably the most important ones in this particular context. With regard to gender, the chapter concentrates on two issues: the division of labour within the household and the management and control of household finances. In relation to generation, the discussion focuses on why people choose to have children and the processes involved in children leaving the parental home. The approach of rational choice theory to these relationships involves the application of two models, the Exchange Model and the Chicken Model. The literature on domestic relations is extensively reviewed and it is shown how the bulk of the findings can be satisfactorily explained on the basis of these two models. One interesting implication of the argument is that rational choice theory, far from contradicting feminist theories of patriarchy, actually adds to our understanding of how patriarchy is maintained, reproduced and reinforced. The chapter notes that rational choice theory is not capable of explaining everything about domestic relations. In particular, phenomena of intimacy, attachment and unconditional obligation are highlighted as being beyond the range of a rational choice approach. Nevertheless, it is emphasised that these phenomena are not irrational, and may actually be produced by the routinisation of complex combinations of past rational choices. It is suggested that unconditional obligations in particular, both to sexual partners and to children, arise from the rational desire to ensure the continuity of the individual's primary social group. In contrast, conditional obligations, which govern most interactions among individuals, can be explained more straightforwardly in terms of a rational norm of reciprocity. The chapter concludes with a discussion of the double exploitation that gender and generational relations give rise to, and the implications of this for policy reform.

Chapter 3 considers the interactions of individuals beyond their own households. A distinction is made between different types of social relations produced by such interactions: relations within informal groupings such as local communities; voluntary contractual relations such as in market exchanges between vendors and purchasers; bureaucratic relations, for example between managers and managed, which involve contractualised compulsion; and relations between a state and its citizens, which involve non-contractual compulsion. Each of these types of social relation is explored further in subsequent chapters. In Chapter 3, it is communities and the development of communities that are the subject of examination. The literature in this area is comprehensively reviewed and analysed from a rational choice perspective. Essentially, communities are seen as arenas in which individuals interact and rational choice theory is used as a means to shed light on the outcomes of the interactions involved. It is shown that much, though not all, of what happens can be explained on the basis of the assumption that the individuals concerned are acting rationally. However, the context within which rational choice is exercised is less clear than in the case of households, and this inevitably makes the analysis more complex and more tentative. For this reason, the chapter explores a number of different possibilities, but nevertheless comes to the conclusion that rational choice theory on its own, even without the support of a theory of exploitation, is sufficient to explain both the basic functioning of communities and the advantages and problems with different approaches to community development. Rational choice theory at this level, however, is not adequate to explain why specific forms of community action succeed or fail. For this it is necessary to go beyond the context of local communities and consider the wider impact of market, organisational and political forces.

Contractual relations are the specific subject of Chapter 4. This chapter does not attempt to review the literature in this area (this would be a book in itself), but confines itself to highlighting the general nature of these relationships, explaining why they have been favoured by rational choice theorists and pointing out the problems that can arise from contractualisation in practice. The chapter argues that class divisions arise largely on the basis of contractual relations deriving from the labour market. This possibly contentious argument is supported by research evidence on class formation and social mobility. This research draws attention in particular to the phenomenon of social exclusion which arises directly or indirectly from the process of increasing contractualisation. Current theories relating to social exclusion are then reviewed and criticised for taking insufficient account of the views and practices of the socially excluded themselves. In this respect, the superiority of rational choice theory is demonstrated, because the latter theory incorporates the autonomy of individual agents as a fundamental premise, even though this autonomy is bounded by the context of contractual regulation and the laws of market operation. In combination with a theory of exploitation, rational choice theory is then used in order to explain the general character of labour processes under capitalism, and from there, processes of social reproduction. It is argued that by these means a more convincing explanation of social exclusion is produced. The chapter concludes with a discussion of how in general terms contractual relations might be changed so as to be liberating rather than exploitative, leading to the abolition of social exclusion. Controversially, the option of liberation through an expansion of non-contractual relations (e.g. socialism) is rejected as incompatible with individual freedom. This does not rule out, however,

Introduction 11

the prospect of the exploited taking collective control of exploiting organisations within a changing framework of contractual relations. Foucault's concepts of monarchic power and disciplinary power are used in order to try and make sense of the processes involved in this potential transformation.

Chapter 5 evaluates rational choice in the arena of political action. The context within which choices are made is defined as a 'hegemony' (Gramsci 1971) and the chapter attempts to analyse the changes in hegemony that are currently taking place in Britain. It is argued that a new hegemony is emerging, in which state power is increasingly dispersed to a growing variety of power centres, in the process empowering but at the same time disciplining a wider constituency of individual citizens. The process is simultaneously inclusionary and exclusionary, but the boundary between included and excluded is both unclear and unstable. At this stage, therefore, it is not clear what position a rational choice theorist should adopt in relation to the new hegemony. For this reason, the chapter reconsiders the theory of rational choice and derives a number of principles which can enable a more coherent evaluation be be made. The basic argument is that different individuals should not be subject to different degrees of constraint and that real freedom of choice is incompatible with exploitation. From this, principles of democracy, partnership and citizenship follow, which are then applied in an attempt to construct an ideal system of state–citizen relations from the bottom up – that is, from the level of local communities through local government up to central government. At the latter level, the three principles are interpreted in terms of the prevailing hegemonic discourse, and the new hegemony is then evaluated through the application of these principles. Rational choice theory therefore makes possible an important clarification of the advantages and limitations of the new hegemony.

In order to illustrate the arguments in Chapter 5, which tend to be at a highly abstract level, Chapter 6 considers housing policy in particular as an example of a field of state–citizen relations. Each area of policy has its own unique history which affects its position within the current hegemony, so the chapter briefly summarises the history of housing policy in Britain and relates this to the discussion of changing hegemonies in Chapter 5. It is shown how housing policy not only exemplifies in many ways the processes described in Chapter 5, but also how the theoretical framework developed in that chapter provokes new thinking about housing policy change and suggestions about the likely direction of future courses of events. In particular, the theory promotes a clearer and more focused critique of current government policy on housing and the setting out of proposals that would be more consistent with the principles of non-exploitative rational choice.

The book concludes with a defence of rational choice theory against a range of criticisms and misunderstandings, citing the arguments used in different chapters in order to demonstrate the cogency and relevance of the theory. Some of these criticisms are understandable, such as the failure of the theory to yield predictions, but others seem to arise from prejudice, for example allegations that it must be right-wing. A particularly recurrent misunderstanding is that rational choice theory is a 'Grand Theory' like marxism, liberalism or feminism. These latter theories, however, are not really theories at all but perspectives that guide the formation of theories. Rational choice theory is a theory, not a perspective, which means that it consists of a set of postulates that directly explain phenomena of different kinds. This final chapter continues with a statement of the arguments and developments of each of the preceding chapters and ends with a list of the achievements of the book as a whole.

2 Households and families

This chapter aims to explore the extent to which key processes within households can be explained on the basis of the theory outlined in Chapter 1. A distinction is made between relations of gender and generation and, for the sake of convenience, the two sets of relations are considered separately. Gender relations which have been most extensively examined in the literature include the domestic division of labour, the management and control of household finance, the determination of responsibility for making important decisions within the household, and the formation and long-term maintenance of heterosexual ties. Generational relations discussed in the literature include the determination of parental responsibility, historical changes in fertility rates, the nature of parent–child reciprocity, and the transition to adulthood for young people. In this chapter, rational choice theory will be used to cast light on all these phenomena, showing how the decisions of individual human beings, based on their perceptions of how to fulfil their desires most effectively in given contexts, determine to an unexpectedly high degree the outcomes for the households of which they are members.

This chapter does not examine all aspects of domestic and familial relations by any means – this would be a book in itself. Its purpose is the rather more limited one of assessing the effectiveness of rational choice theory for explaining interactions among household members. It focuses particularly on heterosexual couple households because, in spite of a certain erosion in the dominance of this family form in recent years, it continues to be the main institution through which gender and generational relations are reproduced. The nuclear family may be declining in statistical terms, as a proportion of the total number of households, but it remains of key importance in social reproduction (Somerville 1994).

A particular difficulty in analysing domestic relations early on in this book is that they tend to be seen as removed or abstracted from their economic and social context. The household appears as an isolated, self-contained entity, rather than as reflecting rational choices made by its individual members within a more complex, multi-layered environment of constraints and opportunities. A certain degree of abstraction, however, is inevitable in order to identify and explain the key patterns of interaction that occur in households. These patterns of interaction will be contextualised in detail in Chapters 4–6, so the reader who finds themselves dissatisfied with the lack of context in this chapter is advised to refer to these later chapters in order to avoid any possible misunderstanding.

Gender relations

Households and families of course do not live in isolation but within a context of socially and historically formed sets of relationships. They are outcomes of complex processes of normalisation. Two norms produced by these processes are of particular importance for this chapter: the norm of female domestic responsibility and that of the male 'breadwinner'. These are utilitarian norms (see Chapter 1) in the sense that they say: 'I will act in a particular fashion (assuming responsibility for the home or for supporting it financially) if and only if such action makes a positive contribution to the common good (of the household).' Both of these norms are products of a long historical process associated with the separation of 'home' from 'work' which originated with the Industrial Revolution. These historical origins have been well explored by a number of writers (Middleton 1979; Tilly and Scott 1978; Daunton 1983; Davidoff 1986; Davidoff and Hall 1987; Dyhouse 1986; Blumin 1989; Coontz 1988). The resulting fundamental division of responsibilities has also been the subject of analysis and debate by a huge variety of academic commentators, most notably prominent feminist historians and sociologists such as Saegert (1980), Gershuny (1982), Martin and Roberts (1984), Gregson and Lowe (1993, 1994), Vogler (1994) and Purcell (1996).

Essentially, what happened was that a person's workplace became identified as something set apart, both spatially and institutionally, from their dwelling-place, whereas traditionally the two had been indistinguishable. Production became separated from reproduction, and the separation assumed a gendered form. In the context of this separation, a division of responsibilities is arguably rational on the grounds that it promotes the maximisation of benefit to the household as a whole. By having one household member focus their activity on paid work while the other concentrates on the domestic sphere, the houschold ensures that both production and reproduction are achieved most efficiently. Abstracted from history, however, this would not explain why it should always be the man (rather than the woman) who goes out to work while the woman (rather than the man) looks after the home. The rational choice explanation has to be set in the social context where males dominated (and still dominate) the organisation of production. In Foucauldian terms, new techniques of domination were created which secured the normalisation of male breadwinning and female domestic responsibilities. This chapter attempts to show how rational choice theory can enrich certain feminist explanations of household dynamics by constructing women not as victims of external social forces but as potential authors of their own destiny.

In exploring the role of rational choice in explaining how households work, it is not denied that other perhaps non-rational factors may play a part. For example, writers have pointed to the importance of the exchange of gifts, particularly on special commemorative occasions, in achieving ritual order in a small social world (Cheal 1988: 104), and even to the role of housework in the ritual creation of social order (Martin 1984). Our understanding of such processes is likely to be improved by empirical investigations of the dynamics of households, revealing more clearly the significance of such phenomena as rites of passage in the trajectories of individual life courses (Wallman 1984; Wight 1987).

The application of rational choice theory to relationships within the household has actually been rather limited. The main text attempting to do this (Becker 1981) has been criticised for portraying the household as an undifferentiated decisionmaking unit (Berk 1985). Becker's work has also been criticised for assuming that wage labour can straightforwardly substitute for domestic labour in the allocation of time by household members (Horrell 1994: 220). These criticisms, however, do not invalidate rational choice theory as an approach to explaining domestic processes, and this will be demonstrated later in this chapter.

The main alternatives to rational choice theory in explaining domestic relations are forms of structural explanation. Most work in this field can be broadly characterised as feminist, but for the purposes of this book it is important to distinguish between what could be called 'structural feminism' and approaches which explicitly recognise the fundamental character of human agency such as liberal or libertarian feminism. The argument followed in this book is one of critical support for the latter and supportive critique of the former. An example of structural explanation is one in terms of patriarchal structures (Walby 1990). According to this theory the long-term historical reproduction of unequal power between the sexes constrains individual men and women against their will into relationships based on unequal exchange. A number of writers, and in particular Morris (1990), have emphasised the lack of fundamental change in this pattern of gender relations within the household over the past hundred years or more. Morris suggests that this is due to three major factors: institutional constraints in the functioning of the labour market and the welfare state; normative constraints reinforcing and maintaining established gender roles; and inequitable distributions of power within households which enhance male power to resist change (Morris 1990: 190). Another example of structural explanation is Murgatroyd (1985), who argues that the socio-economic process selects and allocates individuals to culturally approved and assigned roles.

There is a general problem with structural explanation which is discussed further in Chapter 4. The main point is that by assigning primary causal power to impersonal economic and social forces, it makes it virtually impossible to explain how conscious social change can be achieved and, as a result, runs the risk of reinforcing the very lack of fundamental change which it bemoans. In this case, it does not allow for the possibility of a theoretically informed female challenge to male power. For this reason alone, there is a need to consider alternative explanations.

Gershuny (1998: 37) has suggested a rather different model of explanation which he calls 'recursive determination'. This is essentially a behavioural model, rather reminiscent of Wilson (1987), in which individuals act mainly out of habit according to more or less well-established routines modified from time to time by more or less rational choices (Gershuny 1998: 40). The problem with this model, from a rational choice point of view, is that it prioritises socialisation over rational choice. For example, by emphasising the socialisation of children into gender roles in order to explain the gender division of labour in their later adult life, this model suggests that people may not actually be fully responsible for the choices they make. This ignores or glosses over the rationality of the decisions made by adults to follow gender norms. A rational choice theorist would not disagree that people act mainly out of habit, but would argue that on the whole they choose to follow certain routines because they are useful to them – the choice to adopt a routine, and then to follow it, is, after all, a rational one.

There is a certain tension, as Bengtsson (1998b) has noted, between thinking of households as institutions, where actions are routinised and performed out of habit, ritual, or according to rules which have been set down at some point in the past, and thinking of them as groups of free agents who act rationally in accordance with their interests and objectives. The routinisation of human action, however, can be seen as the product of attempts by rational actors to make sense of their world (in this case, the 'home'). What might be described as non-rational features of human behaviour can then be explained by reference to the effects of *past* rational choice. Such choice produces the whole patterning of social relations which then becomes the ever-changing and developing context that forms the backdrop against which new rational choices take place.

An approach which is more compatible with rational choice theory is to be found in anthropology. Here, there is a widespread recognition that 'women can and do bring about social and political change through their influence in the private domestic sphere' (Emptage 1994) (see also Rosaldo and Lamphere 1974; Hirschon 1983). Much of this, however, is hidden from the male-dominated public world. It is accepted that the 'structural' circumstances of individuals have a major influence on how they organise their reproductive strategies and manage their lives, but their own consciously determined interactions within households are also capable of working transformative effects. As Emptage (1994) has said: 'The choices made by individual women in overcoming constraints and adopting strategies to ensure their own and their children's survival and well-being can and do bring about changes in the structure and the culture of society as a whole.' If rational choice theory can throw light on how such choices come to be made, then it will have served a most useful purpose.

Two key processes for domestic relations are those of household formation and household dissolution. The issue of young people leaving the parental home is specifically considered from a rational choice point of view later in this chapter. As far as gender relations are concerned, a rational individual will not choose to set up home with another unless the benefits of the new arrangement are seen to outweigh the costs. The determination of the costs and benefits in any given situation, however, is typically extremely complex and varies from one individual to another. It is possible to make general analyses only because the context (for example, late capitalist society) is the same, or at least very similar, for different individuals and because these individuals have similar desires and aspirations in relation to these contexts. This is why so many people in modern society adopt common norms such as those of breadwinning and domesticity. The gendered character of these norms, however, is a product of historical processes of industrialisation interacting with rational choices of household members, in a pattern of mutual reinforcement (see Chapter 4).

With the advent of deindustrialisation and the creation of a so-called 'post-industrial' society, with all that this means in terms of flexible working (including home-based employment), the feminisation of labour, and long-term mass unemployment, the old stereotypes of male breadwinner and female homemaker have been challenged and have lost a good deal of the power that they used to wield. The purely economic incentive to commit oneself to marriage or long-term cohabitation is therefore less than it used to be, at least for those men who are not in full-time paid employment and for those women whose opportunities for sexual partnership are restricted to such men. Consequently, for these individuals, the pattern is likely to be one of unstable domestic relations (Kempson *et al*. 1994; Kempson 1996). It should be noted, however, that for men who are in full-time paid employment, so long as the pay is not too low, and for women who can find partners at least as well off as themselves (whether the woman is unwaged or not, the man must be in reasonably well-paid employment), long-term cohabitation may still be an economically rational choice. This is because the man gets the benefit of cheap domestic service, and the woman gains access to a major source of income (providing of course that the man is prepared to share it). These issues are explored in detail in the following sections of this chapter.

The domestic division of labour

This section is concerned with evaluating the available evidence on the division of labour within households, to see how far it can be explained in terms of rational choice theory. It is argued that the theory is capable of providing new understanding of how gender relations in this area are formed, maintained and broken.

Carling (1991) has argued that rational choice theory is necessary but not sufficient for explaining the division of labour between men and women in households. He outlines two models of rational choice, which he then tests in the light of available research evidence. The first model, the Exchange Model, draws upon traditional neo-classical economics (including Becker) and the domestic labour debate of the 1970s (Humphries 1977; Beechey 1987). The second model, the Chicken Model, derives from the work of Taylor and Ward (Taylor and Ward 1982; Taylor 1987; Ward 1987), and relates specifically to the way in which rational (male) actors can gain comparative advantage from the sexualisation of domestic responsibilities.

Under the Exchange Model it is assumed that there are two kinds of good, money (and credit) and household use-values, which are initially appropriated by the producer. In a household consisting of a married or cohabiting couple, the two actors can bargain with each other using their own money and/or use-values as bargaining chips. A household will be established if a mutually advantageous deal (an exchange of use-values for money) can be concluded by the two parties on the basis of their initial private possession of the respective goods (Carling 1992: 108). Such a deal is obtainable only if the external wage rates of the two actors differ. The higher earner will then subcontract the lower earner to do some housework, and thus free the higher earner to work extra time to pay for it. In order for the deal to be beneficial for both parties, the shadow wage for housework needs to be lower than the payer's external wage rate but higher than the receiver's external wage rate (Carling 1992: 109). Carling shows that the Pareto-superior deal is where at least one of either waged work or housework becomes the exclusive preserve of one partner, because the trade-off between the two continues to the optimum or Pareto frontier (Carling 1992: 111–12).

Perhaps the earliest variant of the Exchange Model is to be found in Blood and Wolfe (1960), who argued that husbands' low contribution to domestic labour is the result of a rational distribution of resources. Men have greater strength in the labour market and women have the time. Sharing of domestic work would therefore be incompatible with efficient use of resources. Blood and Wolfe found that power was closely related to levels of earnings, with high-earning husbands being most powerful where their wives contributed no income at all. This so-called 'resource theory of power' can in fact be regarded as a 'political' consequence of the exploitation inherent in Carling's Exchange Model. Other studies since Blood and Wolfe have found that higher-earning husbands do less housework (Eriksen *et al.* 1979; Pahl 1984).

The Exchange Model can be used to make sense of much of the evidence on the domestic division of labour. Where the external wage rates of the two parties differ, it follows that the extra time worked by the higher earner to pay for the work of the lower earner will be less than the time expended by the latter in order to earn the same amount of pay. The lower earner will therefore tend to work longer hours overall than the higher earner (in order to achieve an equivalent benefit), and this is confirmed by nearly all studies, both in Britain and in the USA (Eriksen et al. 1979; Gershuny 1982; Geerken and Gove 1983; Martin and Roberts 1984; Berk 1985; Pleck 1985; Gershuny et al. 1986; Hochschild 1990; Gershuny et al. 1994; Laurie and Rose 1994 – but note Horrell 1994: 213). In addition, because the higher earner is paying the lower earner only for their time, not for the use-values which they are producing, the relation between the two parties is one of exploitation (Somerville 1994).

Other factors which can be explained on the basis of the Exchange Model include the following:

1 the sexual specialisation of tasks at an early stage in a heterosexual relationship (Hunt 1980; Jowell and Airey 1984; Jowell et al. 1989; Gershuny et al. 1986; Ashford 1987; Witherspoon 1988; Brannen and Moss 1987; Mansfield and Collard 1988; Vogler 1994: 259). The general pattern here is that even when couples start out by sharing household work, they tend to adopt more stereotypical roles in anticipation of parenthood (Henwood et al. 1987) as a rational response to the organisation of the labour market and child care. This is explicable in terms of men's higher earnings relative to women's and the greater likelihood of continuous waged work for men compared with the typically interrupted labour market career for women (Martin and Roberts 1984).

2 When wives increase their participation in the labour market, they tend to reduce the time which they spend on household work (Pleck 1985; Berk 1985; Bryson et al. 1994; Horrell 1994: 220 – but note Gershuny 1982). The reduction is particularly significant where the wife enters full-time employment (Gershuny et al. 1994: 165; Horrell 1994: 207). This can be explained in terms of the existence of an optimum amount of time available to the woman for work (both domestic and waged). She may choose to reduce her standards and/or let her husband free-ride. So long as she works only in part-time jobs, the pressure to reduce her domestic work may not be so great. The transition to full-time employment, however, is a true test for the rationality of the sexual division of labour.

3 In general, the extent of husbands' contribution to household work depends upon the significance of their wives' employment and earnings (Jowell and Witherspoon 1985). Where husband and wife have equal employment and income status, for example, the husband has been found to increase his domestic work (Laite and Halfpenny 1987). The gap between the higher and lower earner in such situations is small or non-existent, so the sexual division of labour is negotiated on a different basis, with greater sharing of domestic work.

4 In dual-career families, the husband's occupation has been found to take precedence (Pahl and Pahl 1971; Rapoport and Rapoport 1971; Edgell 1980). This is easily explained as the product of a rational strategy in the

light of the man's more typical continuous employment career compared with the woman's more typical career 'breaks' to have children. Where the couple decide to employ other people to carry out domestic tasks, however, new considerations come into play (Gregson and Lowe 1994), which are discussed further below.
5   Wives with independent income exert more power within the household (Ostrander 1984; Luxton 1980; Blumstein and Schwartz 1983; Hunt 1980; Pahl 1983). This accords with the resource theory of power, which is a consequence of rational choice theory.
6   Increased participation by wives in paid work over a long period of time leads to greater participation by husbands in domestic work (Fielding and Clift 1991), a process known as 'lagged adaptation' (Gershuny et al. 1994: 182) which is more pronounced where the wife is in full-time employment (Horrell 1994: 211–12). This process is very slow, however (Lewis and O'Brien 1987; Hewlett 1987; Cowan 1989), and this presents a problem for rational choice theory, which is discussed further below.

Evidence from a variety of sources in different countries suggests a number of patterns which appear to contradict rational expectations concerning the domestic division of labour. Some of these, however, can be explained by invoking the Chicken Model as an alternative to the Exchange Model of rational behaviour. According to the Chicken Model, it is assumed that there is only one good for the household and whatever is produced is shared by both household members, with the benefit being distributed according to some distributive norm (Carling, 1992: 108). This model is in fact a variant of the prisoner's dilemma (Hardin 1982), according to which it is beneficial for each party not to co-operate if the other one does so, even though the non-co-operation of both parties is less beneficial for either than if both parties co-operate. One party within the household just has to sit and wait for the free ride (playing 'chicken') which will be had when the other party 'cracks' and produces the shared good. In this case, the free rider is typically the husband because of the bias created by the norm of female domestic responsibility. Other writers have also noticed this phenomenon and have described it as an example of 'moral hazard': 'The whole sexual division of labour appears to function as a vast empire of moral hazard, in which perverse incentives encourage one sex to refuse to participate in a major division of the totality of social labour' (Taylor-Gooby 1991: 202).

In the context of the household as an institution (Treas 1991) the norm of reciprocity corresponds to the ritual interaction of Carling's Exchange Model. There is a prevailing norm of equity in the division of responsibility between husband and wife and in the distribution of costs and benefits. This explains why it is felt to be fair that if the wife assumes part of the husband's responsibility in taking up paid employment, the husband in return should take on part of the wife's responsibility for household work. The fact that this does not happen actually lends support to rational choice theory because it shows that the rational decision to play chicken overrides any adherence to norms of fair play – Carling (1992: 116) refers to 'a male attitude of contrived insensitivity to domestic chaos'.

Perhaps the most commonly mentioned problem for rational choice theory is that the increased participation of wives in the labour market does *not* lead to their husbands' increased participation in household work (Geerken and Gove 1983; Pleck 1985; Berk 1985; Walker and Woods 1976; Hochschild 1990; Bagihole 1994; Bryson *et al.* 1994). Even if the 'lagged adaptation' thesis is correct, this does not explain why the adaptation does not happen more quickly. The problem lies with the Exchange Model which assumes a given total amount of work for the couple household within which the work of one party can substitute for that of the other. In reality, however, just because the wife's overall work time increases due to taking up waged work, it does not follow that the husband will reciprocate by doing some of the wife's domestic work. Instead, as predicted by the Chicken Model, the wife reduces her household work and leisure time, and her husband takes a free ride by enjoying at least some of the benefits that follow from the increased income for the household as a whole without contributing any more in terms of domestic (or paid) work. The evidence can therefore be satisfactorily explained on the basis of a combination of the Exchange Model (as applied separately to the wife, with the substitution of waged work for domestic work) and the Chicken Model, in the context of a dominant societal norm of female domestic responsibility. Only the Chicken Model can explain why over half of wives in full-time paid employment do most or all of the housework (Martin and Roberts 1984), why wives do nearly all care work for children under 5 years old (Piachaud 1984), and only half of husbands help with such work (Osborn *et al.* 1984).

Gershuny (1998: 44) proposes a different explanation of lagged adaptation, in terms of the time taken to negotiate new routines when a wife becomes employed on a full-time basis. By focusing only on the growing equality in the division of domestic work in such circumstances, however, Gershuny misses two important points. One is that the husband typically increases his domestic work by far less than the wife reduces hers, so the overall quantity of domestic work decreases. The other is that no matter how long the wife remains in full-time employment, her contribution to domestic work always greatly exceeds that of the husband. These points cannot be explained in terms of the learning of new routines, but are explicable by reference to the Exchange and Chicken Models of rational choice: the wife exchanges waged work for domestic work while the husband continues to hold out for a free ride on the domestic chores.

The norm of utilitarianism is what explains why it is typically the wife who loses the chicken game. The norms of male breadwinner and female homemaker are classic utilitarian norms because each party is responsible regardless of what the other party does, and their respective productions are both major contributions to the collective good. Acceptance of such responsibilities may not seem rational because it generates action based on estimates of constraints on time and capacity rather than on calculations of costs and benefits (Bengtsson 1998b: 12). However, action is still determined by a rational appraisal of the costs of non-co-operation (for example sanctions from the other party) as against the benefits derived from the common resource pool. A decision to free-ride brings costs for the individual which are initially incalculable, but which may become clearer as time goes on. This (rather than an explanation in terms of the acquisition of new habits and routines) could help to explain why some adaptation by the husband occurs, however small, and why it is only gradual – lagged adaptation (or should that be 'nagged' adaptation?).

Gregson and Lowe (1994) have identified another reason why wives' labour market participation does not necessarily lead to husbands increasing their share of domestic work. This relates to the capacity that households with two earners have to pay for domestic work such as cleaning and childcare. Gregson and Lowe (1994: 65) argue that such waged domestic labour is actually what enables the reproduction of the dual-career family pattern. The increasing employment of such labour has had two important effects: first, it has freed many middle-class women from the burden of carrying out the work themselves; and second, it has led to new forms of class division among women as the employers of domestic labour enjoy the ability to hire, supervise and fire working-class women. These effects in turn have meant that the cross-class norm of female domestic responsibility is beginning to have two different class versions: a middle-class one where the woman identifies more with her labour market role and sees her domestic role as primarily a managerial one (a manager of domestic labour and domestic workers) and a working-class version where domesticity and homemaking assume even greater prominence in their gender identities (Gregson and Lowe 1994: 235). Admittedly, in the latter case, the increased access to paid work can help to improve the status and self-esteem of some working-class women, but this is unlikely to apply in most situations where the labour is employed on a casual and part-time basis.

Whilst accepting that the growth of waged domestic labour is important for understanding changes in class relations and gender divisions, it is not clear that it represents a challenge to the norm of female domestic responsibility. As Gregson and Lowe (1994: 240–1) themselves recognise: 'it is the refusal of men to play an equal part in *all* forms of domestic labour which is one of the key means through which gender inequalities are reproduced'; for example: 'it is men's refusal to clean (or their inability to "see" household dirt) which all too frequently lies behind the move to employ a cleaner'. In other words, men in these situations are still quite capable of winning the chicken game: the woman remains primarily responsible for domestic labour even if she does not actually do the work herself. Gregson and Lowe rightly conclude:

Fundamentally, these two forms of waged domestic labour [cleaning and nannying] represent no more than a restructuring of the traditional form of the gender division of labour. For sure, they are a means of resolving the crisis in social reproduction within individual middle-class households, but the means of resolution is one which all too clearly continues to let men 'off the hook' with respect to domestic labour.

(Gregson and Lowe 1994: 241)

An important question to raise in connection with waged domestic labour is who is responsible for paying for it. If the woman is responsible for paying out of her own income, then this is clearly a major victory for the man. This question was not explicitly considered by Gregson and Lowe (1994), but their research appears to suggest that joint management of finances occurred in these households. If so, then nannying and cleaning in these families were regarded as to some extent a joint responsibility, although this does not necessarily signify any substantial change in the traditional gender norms (see pp. 25–30 on domestic financial management). The main point to draw from Gregson and Lowe's research is that the employment of waged domestic labour is a rational choice made by middle-class couples in order to gain greater benefits both from labour market participation and from the freeing up of 'quality time'. On the other hand, it is made possible only by the availability of labour supply from working-class women who have far fewer choices in the economic and social context of late capitalism.

A second major problem for rational choice theory is that husbands' reduced participation in the labour market does not lead to their increased participation in household work (Gershuny 1982; Pahl 1984; Marsden 1982; Berk 1985; Bell and McKee 1985; Morris 1985; Wheelock 1986; Laite and Halfpenny 1987). Here again it is assumed, on grounds of reciprocity, that a reduction in one type of work should be compensated for by an increase in the other. This is, however, simply another example of where the Exchange Model fails to hold, while the Chicken Model appears more applicable. Even on grounds of reciprocity, however, we would expect little change to occur in the household division of labour, because the unemployed husband will typically still see himself as the breadwinner, and will be actively seeking work and receiving benefits related to his past employment, while the wife's domestic responsibilities remain substantially the same, and may even increase due to the husband's (unwanted) presence in the home (Bell and McKee 1985; Leonard and Speakman 1986).

A third problem for rational choice theory is that the division of responsibilities between husband and wife is only apparently based on the norm of reciprocity. The division is not *really* equal because the breadwinning role has primacy, even in households where decision-making is shared (Blood and Wolfe 1960; Rubin 1976). The wife therefore chooses to enter a relationship in which the division of responsibility puts her at a disadvantage, and this appears irrational. The explanation for this lies in the Exchange Model in which the lower-earning wife gains advantage from the relationship (through sharing the husband's income and through payments in kind) even though it results in her exploitation. According to this model, the unequal division of responsibility is simply a consequence of the greater power deriving from the breadwinner role compared with the homemaker role. Of course this argument would apply equally where it is the wife who is the main breadwinner.

A fourth problem for rational choice theory is that where the wife earns more than her husband it does not follow that the husband is not more powerful than his wife (Stamp 1985; Hertz 1986). Komendi (1990), for example, found that in such situations wives were still doing most of the housework. This has been regarded as a crucial test of the Exchange Model which predicts that in such situations role reversal ought to occur when in reality this hardly ever happens (Carling 1992: 117–18). The solution, however, lies in recognising that resources are necessary but not sufficient to achieve a change in power relations and, in particular, to bring about a more equal sharing of domestic responsibilities. In the light of the Chicken Model the nature of power and responsibility within the home needs to be rethought. Even where the wife earns more than her husband or, as we have seen above, where the household employs paid domestic labour (for example, female cleaners, nannies, etc.), it is possible for him to win the chicken game unless she is prepared to give up her primary domestic responsibility (Gregson and Lowe 1994). McRae (1986) suggests that the latter may be very unusual, with the more likely response being the adoption of a 'super-woman' role in which the wife attempts to maintain a conventional self-image as wife and mother as a counterbalance to the counter-conventional character of her paid employment (Newell 1993). This shows the power of the norm of female domestic responsibility but it may also be in part a rational response to the more insecure and discontinuous nature of women's paid employment. If so, we would expect role reversal to be more likely to occur where, on a long-term basis, the wife is in secure highly paid employment and her husband has access only to insecure low-paid employment. Evidence suggests, however, that even here role reversal is rare because such marriages are much more likely to end in divorce (Cherlin 1978; Booth *et al.* 1984; Voydanoff and Kelly 1984). The wife exercises her rational choice and terminates a relationship from which she is deriving too little benefit in comparison with the cost.

A fifth criticism of rational choice theory is that wives do not necessarily seek paid employment in order to increase the household's income. They may do so to gain independence from their husbands (Rainwater 1984; Martin and Roberts 1984). There is other evidence, however, to suggest that it is economic pressures which are paramount (Rimmer 1981; Martin and Roberts 1984). The reality seems to be that economic factors have more weight in lower income households, and 'political' and other factors in higher income households (Morris 1990: 137). The distinction between economic need and desire for independence, however, is unclear (Cragg and

Dawson 1984) because both parties, and particularly the wife, identify their personal needs with those of the household as a whole (Hunt 1989: 72; Mason 1989). Achievement of independence for the wife could be a stepping-stone towards her leaving the marital home altogether (or alternatively asking her husband to leave).

A sixth problem for rational choice theory is evidence indicating husbands' opposition to their wives going out to work at all (Cragg and Dawson 1984; Rosen 1987). This seems irrational because it has the effect of reducing the household's total resources. It has usually been attributed to the existence of a form of traditional patriarchal authority (Oakley 1974). From a rational choice point of view, however, it could be the result of strong adherence to a norm of reciprocity of primary responsibilities (breadwinner and homemaker) – that is, from the husband's point of view, exclusive ownership of the breadwinner role is seen as a rational instrument for ensuring the fulfilment of his desires. For him, the material benefits which his wife's employment would bring to him personally are outweighed by the costs in terms of his loss of authority over her. The rational choice explanation therefore does not contradict the feminist one but attempts to make sense of how the household is (rationally) structured rather than simply labelling that structure as one of 'patriarchy'. It may also be worth noting that the observed decline in husband opposition to wives working could be an example of lagged adaptation (Gershuny et al. 1994) because husbands begin to see that the costs of their diminished authority are less than they imagined them to be.

Another interesting finding which presents a problem for rational choice theory is that in larger families the husband undertakes more paid work not in order to support his family, as the theory would predict, but in order to opt out of domestic work (Shimin 1962). This makes no sense in an Exchange Model but could perhaps be explained within a new variant of the Chicken Model, in which the husband justifies his free-ride by reference to his increased breadwinning burden. A similar pattern of 'justified' free riding may occur in smaller families where the children are very young and in which the burden of child care is at its greatest as a consequence.

Household financial management

The management and control of household finance is a key area of investigation for understanding the dynamics of gender relations within households. The task of explaining this dynamics, however, gives rise to a number of problems for rational choice theory. For example, dual earning does not necessarily produce a joint management system (Blumstein and Schwartz 1983; Morris 1990: 114), and other variations in the management of household finance seem difficult to explain on the basis of a rational model. These problems are discussed further in the remainder of this section.

After the basic division of labour within the household, one of the most significant sets of domestic relations investigated by researchers has been the

Table 2.1 Distribution of household financial management systems

Household financial management system	%
Male-managed systems	
Male whole wage	10
Housekeeping allowance	12
Male pool	15
Female-managed systems	
Female whole wage	25
Female pool	15
Joint management	20
Independent management	2

Source: Adapted from Vogler 1994.

management and control of household finances. The most sophisticated position on this issue has been expounded by Vogler (1994), who describes seven systems (Table 2.1).

This classification represents an advance on earlier typologies which included male and female pools within a broader system of joint management (Pahl 1989). Basically, the wider social base used for the Social Change and Economic Life Initiative (SCELI), involving interviews with 1,211 couples, found that it was important to break down this broad category into three:

1. the joint pool, where both husband and wife agreed that they were equally responsible for financial management;
2. the male pool, where one or both of them claimed that the husband was responsible; and
3. the female pool, where one or both of them claimed that the wife was responsible.

Only the first of these sub-categories could be genuinely regarded as a system of joint management. Having done this, the researchers found that households could be distinguished into three main types: those using joint pooling; those using one of the three male-managed systems; and those using one of the two female-managed systems (Vogler 1994: 240).

Pahl (1989) has used a resource theory of power to explain the observed variations in household financial management. Essentially, pooling systems are associated with wives in full-time employment, and segregated systems with wives in part-time employment or non-employed (independent management systems are discounted because they occur so rarely) (Laurie and Rose 1994: 234). As Vogler has put it, 'the key factor predicting whether or not couples called their system a pool was not whether wives participated in the labour market or not, but whether they were in *full-time* employment'

(Vogler 1994: 246). The resource theory of power states that only full-time participation in the labour market by the wife can provide her with sufficient resources to challenge the traditional pattern of male dominance. From a rational choice perspective, however, the situation is not particularly straightforward. For example, it might be questioned why more wives do not participate full-time in the labour market if it is rational for them to do so. It is therefore necessary to look more closely at the different household management systems in order to see if they can be understood on the basis of rational choice theory.

It might be expected that in female whole wage and female pool systems the wife would be better off because she has full power, or at least equal power, with her husband to dispose of income within the household. In reality, however, it has been found that in these households the wife generally experiences more financial deprivation, and has less personal spending money, than her husband (Vogler 1994: 240–1), a situation which has been described by Homer *et al.* (1985) as 'the burden of dependency'. As Vogler (1994: 241) has pointed out: 'This raises questions about the real meaning of equal or indeed independent female control in these households, suggesting it may be more nominal than real, heavily circumscribed by the husband's needs for personal spending money and by labour market constraints.'

In male whole wage and male pool systems, wives were predictably found to be worse off than in female whole wage and female pool systems respectively (Vogler 1994: 240). Also, where husbands managed the finances they were likely to control them too, in terms of a final say in major expenditure decisions or having the most say in important decisions (Vogler 1994: 233). In both male whole wage and male pool systems, however, the wife's access to financial resources was found to be more equal than in housekeeping allowance systems, where the husband hands over a fixed sum of money to his wife to cover day-to-day household expenditure (Vogler 1994: 240). The evidence, however, is complicated by the fact that the incidence of the different systems varies according to the level of household income (Land, 1969; Rubin 1976; Morris 1990: 113, 121; Vogler 1994: 245).

Whole wage systems generally are found only in low-income households. This can be explained on the basis that unitary control, with its minimisation of transaction costs, is more efficient in such households where there is little room for household choice, an absence of high-cost expenditure decisions, and close surveillance of day-to-day spending is required (Blood and Wolfe 1960; Land 1969). As income levels rise, however, in order to allow 'substantial discretionary spending' (Rubin 1976), there is a shift from female to male management and also to jointly managed systems. Vogler (1994: 246) found that the female whole wage system was most common where the husband was unemployed and male management systems more likely where the husband was in full-time paid employment. In general she found that wives were most likely to manage the household finances single-handedly where financial management was likely to be a burden rather than a source of power, whereas husbands were more likely to manage the money in higher income households (Vogler 1994: 243).

Evidence suggests that the management of household finance is more likely to be shared where both husband and wife are in paid employment (Gray 1979; Hiller and Philliker 1986) and, in particular, full-time employment (Vogler 1994: 245). This makes sense in terms of marriage as a partnership contract (Posner 1977) in which each party contributes to a common pool and thus avoids the costs of separate budgeting. However, as Morris (1990: 113) has pointed out, increased sharing can mean increased male involvement in spending decisions and therefore arguably increased male power. This can be explained by rational choice theory on the basis that male earnings also tend to be higher in systems of joint household management, so male power is already greater for this reason. The point is that, as household resources increase, enabling more high-cost expenditure decisions to be made, there is more that husband and wife need to discuss, which makes it more likely that the wife will exert some influence in negotiation, making systems of joint management more likely than other systems. Dual earning does not necessarily lead to a joint management system (Blumstein and Schwartz 1983) but more recent research suggests that this is the typical arrangement, especially where the high-cost expenditure decisions include the decision to employ waged domestic labour (Gregson and Lowe 1994).

The pattern suggested by the evidence, therefore, is that in the poorest households a rational approach dictates the unitary control of household finances by the wife as an integral part of her domestic responsibilities, and this leads to female-managed systems. As the income of the household grows, however, there is room for greater choice in expenditure decisions. This leads to greater involvement by the husband and results in male-managed systems because of the greater financial power of the husband where the wife is non-employed or only in part-time paid employment. Where the wife is in full-time paid employment, however, a shift to joint management occurs although, even here, it is not clear that full equality in decision-making has been achieved.

The failure to achieve full equality can be represented as a problem for rational choice theory, but the argument is much the same as that discussed above in relation to the performance of domestic work where the wife earns more than her husband; that is, the husband tends to continue to exercise more power because of the widespread social assumption of his primary breadwinning responsibility. Indeed, Vogler (1994: 253) found that patterns of financial allocation were more strongly related to the responsibility for breadwinning than to the responsibility for housework, so given the norms of male breadwinner and female homemaker (supported by the vast majority of respondents in Vogler's (1994) research), it is to be expected that inequality in financial control will continue. Even so, most couples using a system of joint management agreed that responsibilities for breadwinning and housework should be and were shared equally by the two parties (Vogler 1994: 253).

The other point which rational choice theory needs to explain is the distinctiveness of the housekeeping allowance system. Evidence indicates that this system is at the opposite extreme from joint management so far as the distribution of financial resources is concerned (Vogler 1994: 245). Laurie and Rose (1994: 235) found that the housekeeping allowance system was most common where the wife was non-employed. The system was in decline because the wife had an incentive to seek paid employment in order to supplement an inadequate allowance (Morris 1990: 121), and this tended to shift the management system towards pooling arrangements (Vogler 1994: 260). Under the housekeeping allowance system the husband's breadwinner role remained unchallenged (as in whole wage systems), and the earnings of wives did not increase their power within the household (Jephcott *et al.* 1962; Morris 1984). Where the wife's earnings were substantial, however, covering clearly visible items of collective expenditure (for example mortgage repayments or the regular payment of large bills), a shift to joint management was likely (Morris 1990: 121–2); by extension this argument is likely to hold for households employing waged domestic labour. Vogler (1994: 260) concluded that, apart from this decline of the housekeeping allowance system, there was not a lot of change to greater equality in household financial arrangements.

The evidence therefore tends to support the rational choice expectation that allowance systems (and, by the same token, male whole wage systems) will be more prevalent where: (1) the husband has an income above the level which makes a female whole wage system necessary, and (2) the wife has little or no income of her own. Essentially, these systems correspond to a 'male assumption of responsibility for some aspects of collective expenditure' (Morris 1990: 112). In this context, Komarovsky (1967) has made a useful distinction between patriarchal and egalitarian marriages. In the latter, the tendency is for the husband's retentions to be used for collective expenditure (benefiting the household as a whole), while in the former he tends to use them for his own personal benefit. The difference can perhaps be explained in terms of the individual actor's choice whether and to what extent to devote his earnings to the common good. The capacity to exercise such a choice is a clear indicator of the husband's power. This suggestion is supported by Vogler (1994: 257) who found that husbands' normative attitudes (to wives' participation in the labour market and to the domestic division of labour) were the factors most significantly associated with a housekeeping allowance system. It is also worth pointing out that because of the nature of the marriage contract, a husband operating a housekeeping allowance system will be under pressure from his wife to give priority to the needs of the household, and it is to be expected that marital conflict will be more common and more serious within such households (Pahl 1985). Rational choice theory, therefore, helps to explain the exercise of male power and female resistance in domestic relationships.

Another way of interpreting the operation of a housekeeping allowance system is in terms of the Chicken Model. The husband may set the level of the allowance and then wait to see if the wife increases it by getting paid employment. If she does not, the household as a whole may suffer because items of collective expenditure may go unpurchased. If she does, however, the husband will be able to free-ride on her earnings because a large part of these earnings will go into the common pool.

As with the housekeeping allowance system, Vogler (1994: 255) found that the factors most significantly related to the joint pool system were norms internalised in childhood (parental operation of joint pooling) and through the educational system (in particular the husband's level of educational attainment). Again, this underlines the importance of the husband's choice as influenced by early upbringing and training. In contrast, Vogler (1994: 257) found that the wife's normative attitudes were insignificant, not just for joint management but for all financial allocatory systems.

Vogler's evidence (and similarly that of Pahl 1989 1991, and Burgoyne 1990) suggests a long-standing conflict between two normative conceptions of responsibility in the household. The older conception of dual responsibility (male breadwinner and female homemaker) corresponds to a general situation of resource inequality between men and women. Over the years, however, women's economic position has improved relatively to men's and in some households (though still a minority) this makes it rational for both husband and wife to have a norm of shared responsibility. Even here it is not to be expected that shared responsibility will extend to areas of domestic activity such as child care, which typically remains the wife's primary responsibility.

This discussion raises the question of how much is changing with regard to gender relations in the household, and how such relations might change in the future. Using the British Household Panel Survey data from 1990 to 1992, Laurie and Rose (1994) found that, even over a period of twelve months, the management system changed in a surprisingly large proportion of individual households but, nevertheless, overall patterns of household financial distribution remained fairly constant (for example, the most likely changes were from a whole wage system to a shared management system and from a shared management system to a whole wage system, leaving the overall distribution of systems more or less the same). Laurie and Rose concluded that much of the volatility was due to the considerable length of time which it took for many couples to arrive at a relatively stable money management system (Laurie and Rose 1994: 239). This suggests the existence of a complex process of negotiation between husband and wife, a process of mutual learning of responsibilities, whose details have not so far been revealed by research. The only change which Laurie and Rose felt was predictable over a twelve-month period was the shift from a whole wage system to a shared management system where the wife moved into full-time paid employment (Laurie and Rose 1994: 240). This confirmed what was expected on the basis of rational choice theory, as discussed earlier. However, the shift was by no means automatic and this could perhaps be regarded as providing further support for the thesis of lagged adaptation.

With regard to possible future change in the household division of labour and power, at the level of individual actors a way forward would be to reduce the emphasis on utilitarian norms and to rely more on the norm of reciprocity; that is, to adopt a more rigorously rational approach to domestic affairs. Since most resources in the household are held in common (although some important ones, such as the family car, are appropriated by the man for use in relation to his paid work), it makes sense for the responsibility for those resources to be shared as well, and this should include responsibility for the production, distribution and consumption of those resources. Without the acceptance of commonly held responsibility, free-riding of some kind is inevitable. In order to achieve this, however, the exploitation of wives by their husbands must be abolished, and steps must be taken by government to ensure that women have full equality of opportunity with men to participate in the labour market. This means in particular tackling sex discrimination at work and ensuring that the burdens of child care do not prevent women (or men) from taking up full-time paid employment. Available evidence suggests that the provision of affordable child care would be the most important factor in bringing about such changes (Hardhill and Green 1990; Crehan 1986; Cohen and Fraser 1991; Y.Smith 1997). In a male-dominated society, however, the prospect of achieving such changes looks unrealistic, at least in the short term. From a rational choice point of view, much depends on whether the men in power see women as being part of their elite group or not, and this is by no means a foregone conclusion (see Chapter 5).

Rational choice theory, therefore, is able to explain a good deal concerning the division of labour and the control and management of finance within households. This does not mean, however, that the theory as it stands is capable of explaining everything about domestic life. For example, the formation of heterosexual ties, on which so many households are based, clearly involves more than a consideration of the economic costs and benefits of entering into such partnerships. It could be argued that the decisions of individuals in these circumstances are also based on an assessment of the emotional and wider social costs and benefits involved. This is, therefore, an example of the social construction of utility or value referred to in Chapter 1. Within the context of the household as an institution, value is constructed not only in economic terms (namely, what is produced, distributed and consumed by household members) but in terms of categories of privacy, identity and familiarity (Somerville 1997), whose currency is intimacy and lifelong obligation. Households are not only 'associations' (*Gesellschaft*), they are also 'communities' (*Gemeinschaft*).

Berger and Kellner (1964: 5) suggested a phenomenological interpretation of marriage as a dramatic coming together of 'strangers' who, through the construction of a joint biography, give meaning to their lives and to the social world. The key to understanding the force of the marital tie (and the same argument would apply to cohabitation partnerships more generally, homosexual as well as heterosexual) is therefore the construction of a common life experience in which intimacy plays a central role. Intimacy is defined by Cancian (1993: 205), following Rubin (1983: 90), as 'reciprocal expression of feeling and thought, not out of fear or dependent need, but out of a wish to know another's inner life and be able to share one's own'. The strength and durability of the sexual tie, therefore, is related to the partners' success in achieving intimacy and this itself is the product of specific forms of reciprocal action. Given the desire for intimacy, the creation of a sexual tie follows as a matter of rational choice according to the norm of reciprocity. By such means, mutual attraction is capable of giving rise to mutual attachment.

Where, however, does the search for intimacy come from? This question does not seem capable of an answer in terms of rational choice, but phenomenological theory (for example) suggests that it has to do with the fundamental need of all human beings to make sense of the world in which they live, an idea which itself perhaps follows from the basic assumptions of Enlightenment thinking. Attachment theory, for example, holds that people construct mental representations of the world, and then become attached to certain objects in that world insofar as they tend to identify themselves with those objects and attempt to preserve this sense of identity in their everyday lives (Bretherton 1985). When the object is another person, we have the presence of a private desire of a kind which, if reciprocated, can lead to intimacy and the formation of a group identity (partnership). It should not be forgotten, however, that this aspiration for a companionate form of marriage/family is a relatively recent historical phenomenon (Fletcher 1966) and in other cultures such private desires may not be recognised or may not be allowed to develop into intimacy. This in turn suggests that attachment is culturally specific and that even the assumption that people need meaning is questionable (Beckford 1989).

The creation of intimacy in itself leads to the formation of an exclusive group, with a degree of physical and emotional sharing which is not found in any other type of human group. The degree of intimacy therefore defines the privacy of the group as well as its identity based on deep mutuality and attachment. Finally, through repeated actions and the sharing of interpretations, people who were once strangers become familiar to each other, part of a single 'family', and thus the closure of the group is reinforced. The maintenance of common boundaries, the cultivation of shared 'secret' knowledge and the rituals of mutual recognition and pooled narratives all act upon one another to produce a group with uniquely strong ties and mutual commitments.

Lest this sound like an over-romanticised account of family life, it is important to note that violence is unfortunately associated with a significant proportion of such intimate relationships. The reasons for this continue to be strongly debated (Smith 1989; Dobash and Dobash 1992), but it has been observed that so-called 'domestic violence' often occurs after, or as part of, controlling behaviours by a male partner (Hoyle and Sanders, 2000). These controlling behaviours commonly involve isolating the victim from her networks and threatening retaliation if arrested or prosecuted. Such actions seem readily intelligible on the basis of the Chicken Model described in this chapter. What happens is that in certain circumstances a male actor decides to raise the stakes in order to win the chicken game more quickly or more decisively. There is an increased risk involved for him because his female partner may wish to abandon the game altogether – hence the development of the 'controlling behaviours' which are designed primarily to prevent her escape. If the female is willing to continue to play the chicken game, however, the male benefits not only in terms of free-riding but through the closer intimacy that comes from reconciliation and maybe from the shared secret of the violence itself. The woman, on the other hand, may be humiliated and demoralised by the violence, and further intimidated by the man's controlling behaviours. As a victim, she may be prevented from exercising her own rational choice. A strategy of victim empowerment (Hoyle and Sanders, 2000) is, therefore, the first requirement. This involves a range of informal and formal support so that the victim can reach a position where she can decide for herself on the most appropriate course of action to take in her particular circumstances. In a situation where her right to self-determination has been placed in serious jeopardy, the immediate priority is to affirm that right decisively. She may then choose either to stay with the man or not, on the basis of her own assessment of the benefits and risks involved.

One important implication of the existence of family commitments is that they can give rise to activities of caring which are not reciprocated. The example of child care is discussed in the next section, the argument perhaps being that the enjoyment of intimacy itself produces a desire on the part of the couple for further joint creation and joint responsibility (for example, to enrich their shared experience and embody a new shared narrative). Here the classic case is that of care by one partner for the other in the event of long-term sickness or frailty. From a rational choice perspective, it would be expected that lack of reciprocation would give rise to gradually increasing resentment on the part of the care-giver and guilt and depression on the part of the care-recipient (another case of lagged adaptation, perhaps?). The result would be that a long-term process of substantial unreciprocated spousal care should be highly unusual. In fact, however, it is relatively common (Crow and Allan 1994: 167). Evidence suggests that although some spouses resent the caring role (despite its being implicit in the marriage contract and non-negotiable) (Connidis 1989), the vast majority do it as a way of preserving the autonomy of the household (Arber and Ginn 1992: 90) along with its identity and rights of privacy (Teeland 1998). The maintenance of the domestic group identity and privacy, the need to 'keep up appearances', determines the fulfilment of such caring obligations in the longer term when the stock of loving kindness may have completely eroded away. This cannot be explained on the basis of rational choice in a narrow sense, but only in terms of a context of sociality which has been developed over many years through the shared life-course 'project' in which the two partners have been engaged. What appears to be irrational behaviour, such as continuing to look after a husband or wife when the work of doing so is damaging the health of the care-giver, can after all be explained by reference to the institutionalisation of past rational choices by the couple concerned in creating and defending their own intimate primary grouping.

Generational relations

Relations between parents and children present a number of serious problems for rational choice theory. Most anthropological and sociological literature attributes the formation and maintenance of such relations to a variety of cultural and political factors as well as economic ones. For example, Fox and Luxton concluded:

> families are products of ideologies (especially of gender differences, normative heterosexuality, romantic love, motherhood and familism itself), legal practice (especially marriage laws), and economic organisation (namely the gender inequality characteristic of the labour market). These forces recruit people to produce children, share their resources, raise their children, and care for each other. Most importantly, they give children a claim on social resources, and ensure social reproduction.
> (Fox and Luxton 1993: 23)

This is another illustration of a structural explanation which portrays human beings as the puppets of impersonal social forces. An alternative explanation is necessary, which specifically allows for the possibility of conscious social change.

First of all, at the risk of stating the obvious, parents do choose to have children (although a third of couples in Britain experience unexpected pregnancy – Anderson et al. 1994). They are not forced to have them. They may be subject to social pressures to have children, but such pressures can be resisted, and in contemporary society the economic pressures are in the other direction, against having children. The fact that people continue to have children, therefore, constitutes a problem for all types of explanation, especially explanation in terms of rational choice.

From a rational choice point of view, it can be argued that since parents are not obliged to have children, the fact that they do so means that they are likely to have expectations of those children in return for the investment they have made in them. Such expectations may vary considerably, but they will generally be governed by the norm of reciprocity; that is, in return for the care which parents provide for their children they will expect some form of co-operation from those children. This co-operation could be productive labour, as in most societies before the twentieth century, it could be obedience in carrying out the parents' wishes, or it could simply be the joy which children bring as a consequence of their own spontaneous activity and natural and social development. Whatever the expected form of co-operation, however, the undertaking of parenthood is an extremely risky endeavour, because the likelihood of non-reciprocation is very high; for example, the child may not be capable of productive labour, or in other ways may fail to follow the expected course of development. Still, from the child's point of view, obedience to parents is generally reasonable because of their dependence on them: they find that being 'good' not only pleases their parents which is beneficial to them as children, but also helps them to acquire the skills they need for adult life. A process of negotiation of reciprocal obligations between parent and child therefore begins very early on in a child's life, and thereafter the process is one of continuous adaptation to changing circumstances (Anderson et al. 1994). This process, incidentally, is not generally ad hoc but involves the articulation of plans and strategies 'within which people can make sense of events and which express a desire to control the life course in an uncertain world' (McCrone 1994: 99).

Notwithstanding the above, there are powerful arguments for concluding that the relationship between parent and child cannot be based on reciprocity. This is because, particularly in the modern world where the economic costs of having children outweigh the benefits, children simply lack the resources to reciprocate in full, while on the other hand it does not seem correct to suppose that parental obligations are in any way conditional upon a child's reciprocal performance. These constitute major problems for a rational choice approach. In reality, the norm of parental responsibility is a utilitarian norm, not a norm of reciprocity, and the collective good which co-operation serves is that of a particular ordered set of generational relations (a 'family').

Another way of approaching this issue is to think of child care primarily as a 'labour of love' (Finch and Groves 1983). In most cultures, children are thought of as 'gifts from God' (Collier et al. 1993) and the care which parents provide is then given in return. This is reciprocity of a sort, and has the advantage of viewing children as inherently valuable, but it does not seem applicable in a context where families are planned. Perhaps it is more appropriate to think of the process of having children and raising them as one of free creative activity which is done for its own sake and without any thought for what might be done in return. The free creative activity of the children (for example in their play) then provides a form of reciprocal action which is capable of giving great satisfaction to their parents, although again this cannot realistically be anticipated by the parents before the child is born. Whatever way one looks at it, the decision to have a child does not appear to be a rational one. The explanation lies deeper in the human psyche.

In order to deal with these issues, a rational choice approach would have to explain the origins and institutionalisation of the norm of parental responsibility, such that, in the words of Fox and Luxton (1993) it continues to 'recruit people' to parenthood. Parental responsibility, however, appears to be a cultural universal. What anthropologists call a 'nurturance relationship' exists in all known societies and involves affection, co-operation and enduring ties. It is not contingent on performance and is governed by feeling and morality more than by law and contract (Collier *et al.* 1993: 15). The question, therefore, is whether there is a rational order to emotional life which can explain both why people want to have children and why their commitment to them is typically lifelong and unconditional.

Cancian (1993: 205) has defined love as a 'relatively enduring bond where a small number of people are affectionate and emotionally committed to each other, define their collective well-being as a major goal, and feel obliged to provide care and practical assistance for each other'. It is love, therefore, which is the emotional source of unconditional obligation. But what is it that leads parents to love their children and how can this explain why they choose to have them in the first place? It seems that we need a theory of emotional choice, to complement the theory of rational choice.

The two reasons mentioned above for having children, namely creative production for its own sake (which includes shaping the child's development and maturation), and the enrichment of one's own life through the love and joy which children can bring to it, are not entirely convincing from a rational choice perspective. There are other ways to be creative, which are less costly and less risky, and similarly parents are taking a considerable gamble in expecting children to enhance their emotional lives rather than detract from them, although, on the whole, as Caldwell (1982: 338) points out, 'one's own children provide a unique form of pleasure which is not substitutable'. In both cases, too, it is difficult to see how such motivations can give rise to the unconditional character of the commitment which parents typically make to their children and which children in return (though in fewer cases) feel towards their parents. The exercise of creativity does not imply permanent responsibility for whatever is created and, if children do not come up to parental expectations, this is not generally regarded as a good reason for abandoning one's duty of care towards them.

An alternative explanation, more consistent with rational choice theory, is that people have children in order to ensure the continuity of their primary social group (note that this is a similar reason to that given in the previous section for spouses providing long-term care for their partners). This is more in line with the evolutionary principle that individual organisms tend to act in such a way as to promote the viability of their particular biological lineage. Betzig (1988: 9) has expressed this position most starkly by saying that we have children in order 'to get genes into future generations'. This biological determinism, however, needs to be qualified to allow for care by adoptive parents as well as biological parents (this occurs in non-human species, too). The basic point is that people want not only to maximise their resources but to transmit those resources to their 'own' people through gifts, caring work and inheritance. In this way, value is maximised on a much longer-term basis, going beyond the lifetime of one particular individual. There are still risks involved because of the trust being placed in children to accept the responsibilities expected of them but, by sharing their goods with their children in the most inclusive way, parents are hoping to buy into a more permanent source of value. This would then help to explain why the commitment of parents to their children has to be of a permanent kind, although in practice it will be socially constructed in a great variety of forms. It may happen that it evokes a complementary, though not exactly equivalent, commitment in return, but such reciprocation cannot be reasonably expected.

Once the choice has been made to accept responsibility for one's children, the responsibility typically continues for the rest of the parent's life. Evidence suggests the persistence of relations of love, affection, trust and obligation for the duration of the life course (Hockey and James 1993). Other things being equal, a parent will choose to assist their child to the extent commensurate with their perceived degree of responsibility, and this will vary from one individual to another, according to the circumstances of the unique relationship which has developed between parent and child. Even where the relationship has broken down for one reason or another, the parent may still offer assistance to a child in order to maintain their own sense of self-worth as a parent. While the child is dependent upon their parent, the parent has responsibility to develop them to the stage where they can act independently. Once a child has gained the capacity for self-determination, the parent's responsibility reduces to one of providing support on a more residual basis. When it comes to the issue of inheritance, the parent has a free choice over how much of it to spend in their own lifetime and how much to pass on to their children, provided only that their children are seen to be left in a reasonably comfortable and secure position. The rational choice is the one that most accurately reflects the parent's own private desires. Their decision depends upon how short-term or long-term a view they take with regard to the maximisation of their resources (limited only to their own life-time or extended to include future generations) and upon the degree of their attachment to their children as developed over the course of their lives. In the case of inheritance, 'jam tomorrow' may not seem like a rational choice because tomorrow never comes but, for the parent who sees their children as an extension of themselves and who already feels comfortably well off, it is arguably perfectly reasonable for them to forego further expenditure and bequeath significant assets to their children on (and even before) their death.

Having established the plausibility of rational choice theory as an approach to explaining the origins, maintenance and reproduction of generational relations, it remains to be shown how well the theory deals with the evidence in this area. One important example of such a theory is that of 'wealth flows' which explains the link between fertility rates and the balance of economic advantage/disadvantage in having children (Caldwell 1981 1982). The basic thesis is that, in societies with a stable high rate of fertility, children are a lifetime net economic advantage to their parents; that is, there is a net flow of resources from children to parents. When children cease to be of economic advantage, however, the theory predicts that fertility rates will fall (Caldwell 1982: 337). This has of course happened in modern industrial societies, and there is considerable evidence to support the claim that the fall has been associated with the increased costs and reduced benefits of having children, for example as the result of the abolition of child labour and the introduction of compulsory schooling (Caldwell 1982: 347). The reversal of the traditional economic balance was therefore due to forms of state intervention which (partially) replaced parental investment with state regulation (Paterson 1988), a replacement which has continued to grow and deepen right up to the present day (Dale *et al.* 1981). It is notable that even today, in areas of the world where families are supported by their children, most of the families are large and the level of educational attainment is very low (Mamdani 1972 1981).

This analysis helps to throw new light on the nature of economic and social change. The implication is that the most significant historical transition may not have been that from feudalism to capitalism but from forms of 'familial production . . . characterised by intergenerational exploitative economic relations which favour the older generation' (Caldwell 1982: 350) to forms of state-sponsored and increasingly state-regulated familial production which effectively reverse the traditional direction of intergenerational exploitation (Somerville 1994). In this sense, modern capitalism is inherently state-formed, because an essential element of its existence, namely human capital formation, is substantially determined by the state, through the education system.

One objection that might be made against the wealth flows theory is that it does not explain why people choose to have children at all if it is economically disadvantageous for them to do so. It is possible, perhaps, that the continuation of child-bearing in such circumstances is merely a consequence of lagged adaptation and, in the course of time, the incidence of childlessness, which is already on the increase, will grow substantially further. Caldwell (1982: 338), however, answers the objection by pointing out that people will still choose to have children, for the reasons already given above, provided that they can afford to do so. This implies that in modern societies the choice to have children has become conditional upon affluence and upon a belief that this affluence will continue. This in turn suggests that fertility rates will be sensitive to changes in household costs, especially housing costs, as well as to changes in the economic situation more generally. There is some evidence to support this conclusion, for example in Sweden Malmberg (1998) found a close correlation, over a very long historical period, between fertility rates and changes in housing costs.

Meillasoux (1981) has made a suggestion which can be used to develop this argument a little further. He found that the value of a child in traditional familial production, where neither money nor markets exist, was measured in terms of its use in consuming the surplus the family or household produced. This value could be interpreted as the marginal utility of having a child. In such societies, relations of exchange develop around the production of human beings rather than the production of food, with offspring being moved around to put 'wasted' food or labour to the most efficient productive use, typically within a wider network of kinship relations. Similarly, in modern societies, the value of a child to its parents could be measured in terms of the amount of money they can afford to set aside for its upbringing. This value is likely to be more variable than in traditional societies because the ratio of discretionary to mandatory costs will be much higher, reflecting the generally higher levels of opportunity for individual choice in modern societies. However, the decision whether or not to support a child will be similarly determined by the amount of 'surplus' available to the parents, and this will be similarly sensitive to fluctuations in mandatory costs such as those of food, clothing and housing.

These arguments can be extended to the situation where a parent is called upon to support an adult offspring in need. It could be argued that in general the parent will tend to do this where they can afford to do so, and the decision to support, and how much support to give, will be determined by the amount of 'surplus' available to them. The same arguments will presumably apply to the issue of inheritance discussed above. The parent will pass on to their children as much as they can afford to do so and the extent of this inheritance will depend upon the quantity of the parental surplus.

Unfortunately, the literature on generational relations contains misunderstandings about reciprocity. For example, Meillasoux (1981) has developed a thesis of inter-generational reciprocity according to which an individual parent pays for what he or she received as a child, and again for what he or she might receive in old age. Such a thesis, however, is not supported by the evidence. In general, child-bearing decisions are based on their more immediate costs and benefits rather than on more distant streams such as long-term security and insurance in old age (Cain 1985). Anderson *et al.* (1994: 41) found little in the way of developed demographic life plans except in relation to the number of births and the intervals between them. Following childbirth, relationships of reciprocal caring and support between generations are then negotiated and developed over time, not superimposed on the child's life course in the formalistic manner implied by the thesis (Finch and Mason 1993; Finch 1985). It is therefore not surprising to find, first, that parents do not relate the care which they give their children to that which they received from their own parents when they were children (Jones 1992) and, second, older people do not generally expect their children to reciprocate for the care which they gave them when they were younger (Arber and Ginn 1992). The view expounded by Young and Lemos (1997) according to which there is a 'lagged reciprocity' from one generation to the next is, therefore, completely without foundation. Indeed, it amounts to a form of moral blackmail in which parents unreasonably expect their children to perform services for them without receiving anything in return.

The true nature of reciprocity between parents and children has been described in detail by Finch (1987 1989). In general, although the obligations are nominally 'unconditional' (in the sense of not expecting reciprocation) and lifelong, the sense of responsibility develops only over time, through mutual interaction (Finch and Mason 1993), just as it takes time to develop the responsibilities required for a stable household financial management system, as discussed earlier. Reciprocity is therefore very important, and only the provision of care and support and of certain gifts from parents to children is non-reciprocal. Care and support are provided when needed, in accordance with a utilitarian norm of co-operation, and gifts (other than the usual ritual and reciprocated gifts) are made as part of the process of inter-generational transmission of assets (inheritance). All other activities are expected to be reciprocated in order for the relationship to remain in balance.

It is important also to note that the non-reciprocal obligations of parents to children do not go into reverse when the parents become in need of care themselves. Older people generally do not want to become dependent upon their children (Wenger 1984; Crystal 1982; West 1984; Sixsmith 1986; Qureshi and Walker 1989) and find it difficult to accept the situation when it arises (Arber and Ginn 1992: 91), feeling that they are a burden on the care-giver (Finch 1989; Qureshi and Walker 1989). By the same token, the care-giver (typically the daughter) is indeed likely to see the care-recipient (typically the mother) as a burden (Nissel and Bonnerjea 1982; Marsden and Abrams 1987). This is especially likely where the care-recipient has moved into the care-giver's own household because, in this situation, the latter's filial duties are competing with her obligations to her husband and her own children (Arber and Gilbert 1989a 1989b). The most serious problem in this case is that the care-recipient is unable to reciprocate, except perhaps in financial terms through gifts or loans or the promise of inheritance (Arber and Ginn 1992: 91). The result is that the relationship is seen as out of balance and more liable to break down (Braithwaite 1990), leaving the care-recipient in some cases a prisoner in the home (Le Play 1855; Anderson 1977). Even in such extremes, the care-giver may be fulfilling her obligations in some residual sense, but the quality of care given may leave a lot to be desired.

As with gender relations, therefore, norms of reciprocity governing day-to-day interactions and norms of utilitarianism governing long-term responsibilities and commitments are both essential in defining the character of generational relations. As we have seen, reciprocity is effectively a product of rational action and the utilitarian norm of parental responsibility can be explained in rational choice terms (though perhaps not entirely convincingly!) as a down-payment on immortality, in the sense of an indefinitely continued inheritance that is biological or quasi-biological in character.

Rational choice theory can also be applied to generational relations where the child is expected to make a contribution to household work and to the household finances. Allatt and Yeandle (1986), Wallace (1987) and Hutson and Jenkins (1989) have found that such contributions are negotiated according to a norm of reciprocity which is entirely consistent with Finch's findings, namely day-to-day reciprocal exchanges within a context of long-term unconditional commitments. In poorer households, young people contribute more of their income to the family budget (Jones 1991) and in some cases all of their earnings go into a common pool (McKee 1987). Payment of board money by young people to their parents is a frequent occurrence (Jones 1992) but such payment rarely compensates for the actual cost of a child's keep (Finch 1989) except in the case of poor families where the young person may be the main breadwinner. Similarly, young people, especially young women, may increase their contribution to domestic work but, typically, this contribution is small in comparison with that of their mothers unless the mother is ill or absent altogether, in which case the daughter substitutes for her (Leonard 1980; Hutson and Jenkins 1986).

Short-term reciprocity in generational relations is, therefore, a reality, but it is not necessarily balanced, because the parent typically contributes more than the child. This, however, is to be expected in view of the reasons discussed above for having children in the first place. Even after the children have left the parental home, Leonard (1980) found that mothers in particular continued to attempt to achieve a balance between encouraging their independence and maintaining their dependence (keeping them within the household) through gifts and services. The latter have the effect of increasing both the sense of obligation of the receiver and the power of the giver, thus strengthening the generational tie.

Morris (1990: 148) concluded that the means adopted for handling young people's contributions to household finance corresponded closely to the whole wage and housekeeping allowance systems. The young earner either handed over their whole wage and received an amount back for spending, or paid an agreed amount to their mother or father (usually mother), with the rest being retained for their personal use. The latter corresponded to a stage of greater independence, signifying a move towards a separate budgeting arrangement (Millward 1968).

Although, from a rational choice perspective, the practice of 'spoiling and keeping close' (Leonard 1980; Hutson and Jenkins 1986) seems problematic because it is inconsistent with a strict norm of reciprocity, it can in fact be regarded as a predictable outcome of the activities of the maintenance of the household/family as a group which have become institutionalised over the course of the child's development. As we have seen, it is this desire to perpetuate the primary group which can lead to permanent commitment and non-reciprocated action on the part of parents.

It was suggested earlier that intimacy between a couple might generate a desire for expanded joint creation and joint responsibility and, therefore, give rise to 'starting a family'. The relationship between parent and child, however, is qualitatively different from that between its parents. There is, so to speak, a 'generational distance' between the two parties which is supported in nearly all societies by taboos against incest (Edholm 1993: 3). This suggests that although intimacy may be sufficient to explain the decision to have children, it may not actually be necessary: for example, it may be based on a purely cold-blooded calculation of the economic costs and benefits to the parents. Either way, it is clear that, in modern societies at least, children typically enjoy membership of the same exclusive group as at least one of their parents. It follows that phenomenological theory applies in the same way because the boundaries, identity and familiar quality of that group, which form the basis of permanent commitment, have already been established, often by both parents but in the vast majority of cases by at least one parent. The 'nest' has already been built, in which the children will live and grow.

The issue of young people leaving home is particularly important to consider because it involves a splitting of the basic household group, though not usually the ending of the parent–child relationship. There have been a number of large-scale surveys in Britain focusing on this issue (Ainley 1991; Jones 1995). Ainley, for example, distinguishes four types of young home-leavers: marriers/cohabitees (who leave the parental home in order to move in with a sexual partner), 'migrants' (who leave home for work reasons), 'pilgrims' (who leave home simply because they want to), and 'refugees' (who have fled from an unhappy home). The numbers of migrants, pilgrims and refugees are similar, but the number of marriers/cohabitees is equivalent to all the others combined. Except in the case of the refugees, in which the parent–child relation may effectively have ceased to exist, leaving home is not a one-off, and young people in all the other three groups return home, often more than once, before leaving for a final time. Typically, therefore, a marrier/cohabitee will have left the parental home on at least one previous occasion. Understanding leaving home as a complex, often long drawn out, and negotiated process comes out more strongly in the study undertaken by Jones (1995). Both studies, however, underline the continuing importance of parents and, to a lesser extent, other family members, for the vast majority of young people, extending well into their adult lives.

The findings of the studies, therefore, fit very well with the rational choice perspective. Each young person sees leaving home as a kind of stake in a process of bargaining with their parents for increased freedom and independence but how they use that stake is very much in their own hands (except possibly in the case of the 'refugees'). This process continues well into adult life, as Leonard (1980) and Hutson and Jenkins (1989) have already shown.

The other literature to consider is that concerned with lone parenthood as a transition for young women, a transition which may or may not be associated with leaving the parental home. Stack (1974) found that lone parenthood was a common pattern of coping among poor African-Americans, and similar patterns have been described in other cultures (Tanner 1974; Rogers 1980) and also in poor white communities (Young and Willmott 1957; Gans 1962). Wallace (1987) argued that motherhood offers a higher status to young women than a low-status job or unemployment, but a lower status than a 'good' job. At times and in places where 'good' jobs are scarce, therefore, the incidence of single parenthood will tend to be higher. The relationship is not straightforward, however, because a young person's status is also bound up with making a successful transition to independence and this includes the formation of a home of their own. If that person is unable to do this because of their low income or inability to access affordable housing, then lone parenthood may not be seen as a desirable option. Lone parenthood as a form of transition for young women, therefore, is most likely to occur where there is access to affordable housing for low-income groups but a shortage of well-paid jobs. It is therefore to be expected, purely on the basis of young people's rational choices, that lone parenthood will be more prevalent on isolated council and housing association estates, and this expectation is borne out by empirical research (Power 1997). Needless to say, this argument is less likely to apply to lone parenthood which arises from other circumstances such as divorce, and of course does not apply at all to lone parenthood caused by the death of one parent.

One issue not fully considered in this chapter with regard to parent–child relations is that of exploitation. Essentially, the existence and character of exploitation within households depends upon the (domestic) relations of production. Where household members produce more than they consume, and the surplus (or at least part of it) is appropriated by other household members, there exists exploitation, unless the productive activity is reciprocated by those other members, leading to reciprocal appropriation. In traditional domestic economies, children are typically exploited because the product of their labour is appropriated by their parents and other adult relatives, and reciprocation is limited, with minimal child care or investment of time and expenditure in the children's welfare. In modern industrial economies, however, whether capitalist or socialist, the labour of parents on behalf of their children greatly exceeds the very limited labour of children on behalf of their parents. Strictly speaking, therefore, it is now children who are exploiting their parents. This strange situation is made possible only because of compulsion from the state which dictates children's exclusion from the labour market and their compulsory attendance at educational institutions. Since the state is responsible for causing this exploitation, it could be argued that it has a responsibility for remedying it, for example by a reciprocating recompense to parents for the losses they have incurred due to state intervention.

A possible counter-argument to this is that the state itself is investing large sums of money in children, particularly through the education system, and is therefore acting to reduce parents' educational and child-minding costs. This counter-argument would be convincing were it not for the fact that the issue is one of compulsion, not of voluntary action. If child labour were not illegal and if school attendance were left to the judgment of parents, then it would indeed be correct to argue that parents can have no right of redress from the state. It is right that parents should be free to make sacrifices for their children if they wish, but it is not right that they should be *made* to suffer for the good of their children (assuming that it *is* for their good!) without receiving suitable consideration in return. In order to achieve full reciprocity, such consideration needs to be financed out of general taxation. It might be argued that it should be paid for from a tax on childless people who currently could be said to be free-riding on the products of parental effort, insofar as the new generation adds to the value of society in general from which childless people benefit as much as those with children. Such a hypothecated tax, however, would be divisive and undesirable for a number of reasons (see Chapter 5). It is also not necessarily the case that such free-riding implies an obligation to reciprocate from a rational choice point of view. For example, Nozick (1974) argued that X may benefit from acts of Y, without being obliged to reciprocate, if the benefits are only incidental to Y's activities. This seems applicable to this case because the benefits received by childless people from the activities of other people's children when the latter grow up are likely to be only incidental to the activities of the childless people themselves.

The position of lone parents also deserves more attention than it has been given in this chapter. Obviously, neither the Exchange Model nor the Chicken Model can apply in the same way to the conduct of social relations within these households. One rare attempt to apply rational choice theory in this context, however, was that of Georgellis and Popapanagos (1995). They tried to explain the likelihood of lone mothers' participation in the labour market in terms of the costs and benefits of such participation relative to those incurred by staying at home. According to Edwards and Duncan (1997), however, this approach reached a cul-de-sac when the influence of 'cultural factors' became apparent. What Duncan and Edwards (1998) found in their own research was that the most important determinant of labour market participation by lone mothers was the 'gendered rationality' to which the mother subscribed. This concept of gendered rationality refers to the extent to which an individual accepts the dominant utilitarian gendered norm of male breadwinner/female homemaker discussed earlier in this chapter. The rationality of this norm for two-parent families has now been thoroughly investigated, but for lone parents the situation is entirely different because in their households the opportunity for a gendered division of labour may not exist. Lone parents have to act against a context that is historically and emphatically shaped by utilitarian norms of motherhood and fatherhood. They have to adapt their lives to this context and may have little influence over it. Commonly, they have recourse to local neighbourhood and social support networks outside of the family in order to ensure their own survival and that of their children (Edwards and Duncan 1997: 37). In spite of apparently overwhelming constraints, lone parents still have choices but these choices are made on the basis not so much of a rational calculation of costs and benefits as of their perceptions of what is the 'right' course of action for a mother (or in some cases a father) to follow. This means that decisions are taken primarily in order to maintain the individual's reputation for responsibility (as a homemaker or breadwinner) and this is a phenomenon that is explicable in terms of rational choice theory (Laver 1997). So, for example, African-Caribbean lone mothers, who are far more likely to support themselves from full-time paid employment, are also far less likely to subscribe to the dominant patriarchal white British norm of motherhood. In contrast, lone mothers who are most likely to rely wholly on state benefits are overwhelmingly white and believe strongly in this traditional norm (Edwards and Duncan 1997; Duncan and Edwards 1998). The rationality of different lone mothers is, therefore, bounded by the cultural context of patriarchy and ethnicity, and the choices made within this context are determined largely by the individual's perception of the benefit or harm that paid work or parental work will do to their sense of self-esteem. As McKay (1998: 123) has concluded in relation to lone parenthood: 'the relative future opportunities available to men and women could be part of the best overall explanation of changes in family patterns. The life chances that people anticipate – earnings, quality of employment and so on – affect decisions about family formation.'

Smith (1999) makes a very interesting point about lone parents when she argues that they do not usually choose to be lone parents but, having become such, they choose to continue to perform a parental role – that is, to act as *responsible* parents. This argument is used to campaign for increased state benefits to lone parents on the grounds that they deserve them in return for their contribution to reproductive labour and social stability. This is an important argument which can be used to justify an increase in state benefits for *all* parents, and an increase in child benefit in particular. After all, many pregnancies are unplanned but women choose to continue with them and to take responsibility for the resulting offspring. This assumption of responsibility should be appropriately recognised and supported by the state.

According to the argument developed in this chapter, women are doubly exploited, not only as wives but also as mothers, and this issue too needs to be more directly tackled by government policy. In fact, when wage-labour is included in the argument, it becomes possible to talk of triple and even quadruple exploitation. This is because the value of labour power generally is reduced since the cost of producing that labour power is much lower through the household economy. A wife and mother, therefore, who undertakes waged labour is doubly exploited through the domestic economy, and doubly exploited through the market economy. In the latter case, not only is she paid less than the cost of what she produces (that is, the usual form of capitalist exploitation) but her labour power itself is devalued as a consequence of the previous exploitation of her parents when she was a child. In this way, it can be argued that capitalism tends to undermine and destroy family life.

On a related point, it could be claimed that in some respects the politics of the household/family reflect those of society more generally. For example, the change in gender relations within the household economy from traditional forms of authoritarian patriarchy to modern male laissez-faire echoes the change in the global economy from hierarchical forms of direct control to neo-liberal forms of market rule. It would not be stretching the point too far to say that within the household husbands generally enjoy a form of hegemony, which is maintained through a series of unstable equilibria (Gramsci 1971; Laurie and Rose 1994; Morris 1990; Vogler 1994; Horrell 1994). The politics of generational relations, however, is rather different from this because the state is directly involved in the process of child development (Land 1978; David 1980; Lewis 1980; Reiger 1985). The situation is more akin to an unequal 'partnership' between state and parents which reduces parental freedom and autonomy while attempting to maintain their traditional authority over children. The inevitable effect is that traditional forms of parental authority are undermined, but it is not yet clear what is taking their place (Jamieson and Toynbee 1990). As with gender relations, the change may well be one from authoritarian control to permissive laissez-faire.

Conclusion

This chapter has explored the potential of rational choice theory for explaining a range of gender and generational relations, focusing on households and families. The domestic division of labour has been explained in terms of a combination of two rational choice models (the Exchange Model and the Chicken Model) operating within the normative context of a primary division of domestic responsibilities (breadwinner and homemaker). The normative context itself derives from the structuring of the labour process into two separate spheres ('home' and 'work'), which gives rise to two separate areas of responsibility. The distribution of resources within the household has similarly been explained on the basis of the assumption that the parties concerned tend to adopt rational courses of action. This does not mean, however, that gender relations can be completely explained by rational choice theory – sexual ties have been particularly singled out as requiring explanation of a different kind, for example by means of attachment theory and explanations in terms of group identity formation.

At first sight, generational relations seemed more problematic for a rational choice perspective, as the decision to have children in a so-called 'developed' country does not appear to be rational. Adoption of this perspective, however, had the advantage of drawing attention to the precise expectations of parents in having children, to see in what sense their decisions could be held to be rational or not. It was concluded that, although children are now clearly an economic burden to their parents rather than a benefit as in former times, they do provide compensation to their parents in other ways, for example through their affection and trust, and through the function which they perform for parents as a 'passport to eternity'. Also, economic factors, especially housing costs, still appeared to be highly significant in influencing changes in fertility rates, and this is just what one would expect if prospective parents are behaving rationally. The situation is complicated, however, by the fact that the state is heavily involved in the shaping of generational relations, especially through the institution of compulsory education, and the implications of this involvement are poorly understood. The picture is also obscured by a widely held myth of long-term reciprocity between parents and children, when the reality is one of short-term reciprocity only: non-reciprocal long-term obligations are confused with conditional short-term voluntary acts. Rational choice theory explains the significance of this distinction, which has itself been identified by feminist research and analysis.

The arguments in this chapter have certain radical policy implications. Perhaps the most important of these is that the tax and social security systems need to be reformed so as to redress the balance between those with and those without parental responsibilities. At present the only state subsidy specifically for parents is child benefit. This subsidy is not available to parents on income support, and for other parents it represents only a small fraction of the actual cost of bringing up a child (Piachaud 1979). The remainder of the costs is borne entirely by the parents, but the beneficial outputs from raising the child are as likely to be enjoyed by childless people as by parents generally – for example, in terms of the child's later contributions as an adult to the economy, the exchequer and public life. There is a case, therefore, for a greater element of redistribution from the childless to those with dependent children. This would have to be carefully handled to ensure that it did not discriminate against poorer households, but in principle it would be possible for the amount of child benefit to be set at a level which would be sufficient to pay for child care where this was desired, and to be payable irrespective of the parents' economic circumstances.

In general, the arguments of rational choice theory suggest that the relationship between parents and the state needs to be rethought. For example, at present the state expects parents to take full responsibility for their children but at the same time it requires them to have their children educated to a standard prescribed by the state itself. But what does the state provide in return? There is a lack of reciprocity here, which can be argued to be oppressive. This point is taken up further in Chapter 5.

3 Communities and community development

Introduction

This chapter is broadly concerned with affective and effective collective action beyond the family/household. Its focus is on the social structuring of human relationships beyond the primary group. It begins with an articulation of rational choice theory at this level and poses the question of what determines the extension of conditional cooperation and how this can be promoted. A distinction is made between patterns of co-operation at a more informal level ('communities'), and the institutionalisation of that co-operation in formal social organisations ('associations'). The chapter first explores briefly the ways in which co-operation becomes institutionalised, in markets, bureaucracies and political arenas, and indicates how these different institutional forms arise on the basis of characteristic conditions of reciprocity and rational choice, as also on the basis of characteristic types of power relations and affective ties. The social relations of community are then examined in detail, and explained on the basis of rational choice theory. The chapter concludes with an evaluation of community development, in the light of the findings concerning the nature of communities.

According to rational choice theory, people will co-operate with others initially if there are clear reciprocal benefits for them. Neighbourliness, for example, according to which generally small-scale acts of assistance are performed in the expectation of possible reciprocal acts in the future, is a classic case of such balanced reciprocity (Procter 1990; Devine 1992). Even in this case, however, there is no guarantee that any given act of neighbourliness will be reciprocated – for example, the demand for it may never arise. In contrast, market exchange always involves a direct relationship between two reciprocal acts, namely purchase and sale. Contractual relationships, of which market exchange is perhaps the prime example, are also the only ones which assume a necessary relationship between rights and duties, for example a vendor's right of ownership is inseparable from a purchaser's duty to pay. The outcome of the act of exchange is then that the purchaser acquires rights over property, and the vendor receives payment which can be used to make possible further acquisitions. One way of moving beyond domestic relationships, therefore, is through participation in a network of contractual relationships, in which money or some equivalent of it is the medium of exchange, leading to an ever-expanding web of ordered relationships.

From a rational choice perspective, this might appear to be the ideal situation, because it portrays social reality as a free and fair association of autonomous rational individuals. However, such contractarianism presupposes that everyone must produce as well as consume, and in practice only certain kinds of production are governed by contractual relations, for example paid employment. Adoption of a contractarian route to rational social organisation, therefore, would lead to the exclusion of non-contractual forms of production such as women's labour in the home. It would also have the effect of bracketing off the production system, which can be exploitative, thus giving rise to further structured inequalities of ownership.

Even where the reciprocity is immediately balanced, as in market exchange, the extension of co-operation by individuals which it involves depends upon trust, and upon the keeping of trust. The importance of such trust has long been emphasised, going back at least to de Tocqueville (1966), and the implication is that contractual relations are not fundamental but dependent upon the prior existence of norms, skills, and cultures of trust and mutuality, which de Tocqueville called 'social capital'. The argument is that social capital is developed within the primary group, and then 'spills over' (Olson 1965) into all other instances of social interaction. Reciprocity, both generalised and complementary (see Chapter 2), then 'forms a kind of global culture of humanity that applies in every interaction, imposing certain obligations and constraints on all exchanges' (Jordan 1996: 23).

By making contractual relations possible, social capital also makes private capital possible. As Marx (1968: 81) said, private capital is the expansion of value (through cycles of investment, production and exchange), and this itself creates further social capital, but only for an exclusive group, namely the owners and controllers of private capital. Rational choice theory can be interpreted as saying that individuals have a propensity to maximise value in terms of both private and social capital. This helps to explain why reciprocity spills over from kinship relations to a wider society.

Extension of reciprocity involves giving up some individual freedom in return for benefits. In the family/household, we have seen that this involves benefits in terms of care and support, intimacy, and so on, in return for sexual fidelity (perhaps) and the assumption of basic responsibilities (for breadwinning or homemaking). In relation to children, it could mean parental sacrifices in return for what could be fancifully represented as a stake in immortality. Beyond the household, benefits may often be 'family-like' in their informality, for example the rights to access common resources which exist in some communities (Ostrom 1990; Crow 1997b: 11). Over the course of time, however, networks of reciprocity tend to become formalised and institutionalised. Contractual relations have perhaps been the most successful of these more formal relations because they involve a direct and legally explicit relation between rights and duties.

Beyond the family/household, individuals interact within a social context which is to some extent already given. This social context, as we have seen in previous chapters, is one in which, just as within families, it may be rational for an individual to make choices which actually reinforce his or her disadvantaged position. Such an individual may give up some freedom in return for certain benefits, for example taking up paid employment, which involves a market exchange of labour for wages, and also commits that individual to participation in a bureaucratic organisation. This participation in turn could entitle the individual to a range of benefits from that organisation in return for loyalty or action aimed to benefit the organisation as a whole. Labour market participation therefore appears to be perfectly rational as a means to maximise individual resources, but at the same time it consigns individual workers to relations of exploitation, and also of alienation because of their lack of control over what they produce and how they produce it. There is therefore a tension between market relations, which presuppose equality among individuals, and bureaucratic relations, which involve hierarchy and inequality.

Within bureaucracies, whether private or public, the costs and benefits of group activities are not shared equally among the members, so the extent of reciprocity is very limited (the nearest equivalent within families would be the housekeeping allowance system, where the domestic worker is 'paid' only for her costs in maintaining the household). Another way of expressing this is to say that the domain of the commons within bureaucracies is narrow, or at least that access to common resources is restricted; for example, for a private company, profit is a resource common to the organisation as a whole, but access to that resource is limited to the company owners. The dominance of private capital therefore produces an exclusive group which tends to limit the social capital of workers, who may then in some cases form their own groups in order to resist this imposed limitation. Similarly, in public, non-profit bureaucracies, control of common organisational resources is typically monopolised by a small elite, through systems of hierarchical authority (so-called 'line management'), and workers generally have access to resources only in a privatised form, namely through wages and individualised benefits, not through collective power and influence over resource distribution.

Apart from domestic relations, social capital, contractual relations and bureaucratic relations, state action typically introduces a new type of relationship, namely that between bureaucratic structures and citizens. This is not the same as a contractual relationship between bureaucracies and individual users/consumers/customers, which is typical in the private sector. Rather, the relationship is non-contractual, in the sense that there is no direct relation between the taxes due from a citizen and the benefits to which that citizen is entitled, or between the services provided to that citizen by the state bureaucracy and the services required in return. This situation cannot be represented as a rational pooling of resources as in Rousseau's 'social contract' (Rousseau 1968), or as a generalised version of neighbourliness, for the simple reason that the contributions made to the common pool are compulsory, not voluntary. There is therefore a genuine problem of lack of reciprocity in this relationship, and this perhaps helps to explain the antipathy to state action which is common among rational choice theorists (for example, Olson 1965). Recognising this problem, the state does try to establish at least a semblance of reciprocity, for example through social insurance policies, but these attempts are inevitably unbalanced because the relationship between state bureaucracy and individual citizen is fundamentally unequal. The state therefore has to derive legitimacy for its actions from other sources, for example through forms of representative democracy, but these are generally very crude means of ensuring effective accountability to the public (see Chapter 5). Rational choice theorists are therefore on strong ground in arguing that state action should be kept to the minimum required to promote conditional co-operation among individuals and to redress serious inequalities of power. This is not to say, however, that relationships of trust between state and citizens cannot develop over the course of time within historic 'settlements' such as the post-war welfare state which allow for a more interventionist state role (Clarke and Newman 1997).

The types of social relations discussed so far are listed in Table 3.1. Domestic relations were covered in Chapter 2. Informal group relations will first be considered in this chapter. The other types of social relation will be examined in Chapters 4 and 5. It should be noted that although not all state–citizen relations are characterised by forced participation and domination–subordination (otherwise democracy would be a sham by definition), such characteristics lie at the core of the state's identity as a source of authority that can command obedience from those over whom it has jurisdiction.

Communities

There are possibly three main ways of beginning to think about non-domestic informal group relationships, and these have been described by Lee and Newby (1983) and Willmott (1986) as relationships based on locality of residence, networks of common interest, and possession of a shared identity. The first type of relationship involves neighbourly co-operation, the second involves associations which may or may not be based on the neighbourhood,

Table 3.1 Types of social relations

Social relations	Participation	Basis of interaction
Domestic	Voluntary	Reciprocity
Informal group	Voluntary	Reciprocity
Contractual	Voluntary	Reciprocity
Bureaucratic	Forced	Domination
State–citizen	Forced	Domination

and the third involves forms of culture such as shared history, language and lifestyles. This chapter is concerned mainly with the first type of relationship.

The current position with regard to neighbourliness has been well stated by Crow:

> while we may know a considerable amount about neighbours, this remains an area where speculation abounds. Much of our knowledge is open to competing interpretations based on contrasting assumptions about issues such as rationality, choice and social change. Without theoretically informed research it will not be possible to come to a view over whether neighbouring is better understood as rational or emotional, material or symbolic, chosen or forced, short term or long term, declining or persistent.
>
> (Crow 1997a: 29–30)

The purpose of this chapter is primarily to make some sense of existing research from a rational choice perspective, to indicate the ways in which rational choice theory can throw light on the dynamics of co-operation within neighbourhoods or local communities. It will be shown that neighbouring is better understood as rational, material, chosen, long term and persistent.

First of all, there is no compelling reason for supposing that individuals will approach their relationships with their neighbours in a radically different way from how they approach their other relationships, for example within their families. If rational choice theory is therefore capable of explaining key features of domestic relations, as we have seen in the previous chapter, it is to be expected that the theory will be also applicable to neighbourly relations. In co-operating with other individuals, local residents will typically act so as to maximise the benefits to themselves and minimise their costs, accepting certain obligations to one another in return for the advantages of community membership, governed by the norm of reciprocity, and drawing a clear line of demarcation between group 'insiders' and 'outsiders'. The context of co-operation is of course different for members of a local community from what it is for a household, being a residential locality rather than a single dwelling-place. One striking difference here is that the extent of the common resource in the case of local communities is typically not very well defined in comparison with households, with the result that the boundary of the community is much more strongly contended, and disputes over that boundary figure far more prominently. For this reason alone, we would expect to see more emphasis on issues of symbolic meaning and identity than we found in the context of domestic relations, although here too they were seen to be of not inconsiderable importance.

The literature on community and neighbouring is truly vast (see Crow and Allan 1994, and Davies and Herbert 1993, for comprehensive reviews from sociologists and geographers, respectively). Much of the evidence is apparently conflicting, but there are several important common and recurring themes. A general distinction can perhaps be made, for example, between effective and affective notions of community (Gyford 1991), with the former being the space within which individuals interact and the latter being the individuals' perceived or conceptualised sense of what the community is. A community in an effective sense is therefore identified with an arena of interaction, a network of relationships, a geographically circumscribed neighbourhood. A community in an affective sense, in contrast, signifies an identification of individuals with an idea of a community, a shared attachment to a particular area, and a sense of enjoying common cultural practices and traditions. Because effective and affective aspects are always found in combination, it seems reasonable that a theoretical approach to communities should attempt to explain both aspects within a single theory. This is therefore the approach that is adopted in this chapter, which will show that rational choice theory on its own is sufficient to explain community relations that are not based on kinship ties. This explanation is possible because relations with neighbours other than kin are largely premised on norms of reciprocity and utilitarianism.

Another general distinction found in the literature is that between traditional and modern communities (Abrams 1980). Traditional communities are characterised as closed, densely networked, enduring structures, commonly based on so-called 'occupational communities' centred on mines, factories, ports and other workplaces. In contrast, modern communities are portrayed as 'communities of limited liability', where more restricted patterns of sociability indicate that individuals have more control over and are more selective about their involvement in local social networks (Crow and Allan 1994: 2). It is not surprising, therefore, that this distinction has been likened to one between 'coercive communities' and 'communities of choice' (Douglas 1987), although it is perhaps better represented as one between communities which are dominated by kinship relations and those which are not. The unconditional obligations of kinship relations, as we have seen, can be viewed as coercive, in contrast with the conditional character of other forms of obligation, which presuppose that the individual concerned is a free agent.

Finch and Mason (1993) found a hierarchy of obligation and responsibility within families, namely spouse, relative in lifelong household, daughter, daughter-in-law, son, other relative, non-relative. This hierarchy can be explained in the terms developed in the previous chapter, specifically through the differential construction of exclusive groups incorporating different degrees and qualities of intimacy, within a system which assigns primary domestic responsibilities to women. Non-relatives appear at the bottom of the hierarchy, meaning that they have the least onerous obligations, and are therefore more free to choose whether, and to what extent, to participate. It follows, therefore, that a community in which close relatives are more predominant in social interactions will appear more 'coercive' than one in which relatives are more or less absent.

The distinction between traditional and modern communities has been criticised on the grounds that family and kinship relations continue to be central in community formation and interaction (Fischer et al. 1977), particularly in working-class neighbourhoods, for example in providing support for unemployed people in finding jobs (Coffield et al. 1986; Allatt and Yeandle 1992; Morris and Irwin 1992; Jordan et al. 1992). As Crow and Allan (1994: 54) point out, it is also likely that the socially cohesive and harmonious character of the past has been exaggerated. It is therefore possible that, although there has been some movement over the years in the direction of looser, more instrumental structures at the neighbourhood level (for example, compare Holme 1985, with Young and Willmott 1957 or Firth 1956), the differences between traditional and modern communities are not as great as people have supposed.

Hojnacki (1979) suggested a different way of representing the alleged historical change in the nature of communities or neighbourhoods, in terms of a distinction between traditional and 'emergent' communities. Traditional communities were conceived as small, homogeneous, clearly defined, with many neighbourhood organisations and organised sub-group interaction, whereas emergent communities were thought of as very large, heterogeneous, with no agreed boundaries, few or no neighbourhood organisations, and limited sub-group interaction. This typology, however, did not take account of the nature or significance of social interaction within the neighbourhood – for example, were kinship networks and obligations and specific occupations more predominant in traditional communities, and friendship and acquaintance networks more prevalent in emergent communities?

Warren and Warren (1977) developed a more sophisticated analysis which was perhaps the first to move away from the traditional/modern dichotomy and attempted to explain observed differences in neighbourhoods in terms of three variables: interaction, identity and linkage. Interaction refers to the effective notion of community, identity to the affective notion, and linkage to the degree to which neighbourhood residents are in close contact with people outside the area. On the basis of these three criteria, Warren and Warren (1977: 96–7) were able to identify six neighbourhood types. Within this typology, traditional communities can be identified as those which have a high degree of interaction and a strong sense of identity, but lack contacts with the outside world. In contrast, there is no such thing as a modern community, but rather a variety of possible structures, depending upon different combinations of values of the three key variables.

Warren and Warren's typology is perhaps a little contrived, and does not deal with the dynamics of change within communities, but it has the merit of drawing attention to the importance of a community being linked to the world around it. In contrast, Weenig et al. (1990) have developed a two-dimensional typology which accounts to some extent for processes of community change, but which does not incorporate information concerning contacts with the outside world. Essentially, Weenig *et al.* explain the effectiveness of communications within a neighbourhood in terms of the strength/weakness of the sense of community and the frequency/rarity of neighbouring activities. Neighbourhoods with a strong sense of community and many neighbouring activities tend to have more efficient information diffusion and stronger influence on resident behaviour. Features of community are therefore explained in terms of the key effective characteristic of neighbourhood social interaction and affective characteristic of community identity/attachment.

One technique which has been widely used to understand the nature of (effective) communities is that of social network analysis. This technique focuses on the totality of informal relationships in which an individual is involved. Use of this technique has revealed that there are four key variables for making sense of networks: size, or the number of potential and actual contacts (by a 'focal person'); composition, for example what proportion of the contacts are relatives; structure, for example the density of interconnections within the network; and contents, for example the levels of supportiveness in the network (Davies and Herbert 1993: 68). A clear advantage of the network approach is that it is rigorous and concrete: 'Instead of referring loosely to community relations or degrees of community solidarity, it provides a means of mapping out the full set of informal relations to which any individual is party and then linking the connections between these others' (Crow and Allan 1994: 180). Research employing this technique has shown the 'fuzzy reality' (Harper 1992; Crow and Allan 1994: 181) of the boundaries of most people's personal networks; that is, most people are uncertain about who exactly is included in their network and what geographical area is covered by the network. Wellman *et al.* (1988), in studies of East York, Toronto, found that informal ties occurred over such a wide area that geographical conceptions of community were unable to explain people's incorporation into the social realm. Crow and Allan (1994: 182) suggest that this is because the focus of the technique is on personal networks rather than local communities: in the former, kinship relations will tend to predominate, and it is likely that these relations will be spread over a wider area, not located exclusively within an immediate or bounded neighbourhood. The network approach can therefore be misleading because it abstracts informal interaction from the larger set of relationships: 'analyses of interpersonal ties do not define fully the dimensions that characterize the content of *local* community life' (Davies and Herbert 1993: 73).

Notwithstanding the problems with the network approach, other studies within this paradigm have confirmed the findings of Wellman *et al.* that social support networks, perhaps largely based on kin, have become more spatially extended and more varied over the course of time (Fischer *et al.* 1977; Connerly 1985; Fischer 1982; Deng and Bonacich 1991). This in itself suggests that there has indeed been some shift away from traditional communities whose members had little contact with those outside their local area, and towards communities where people have an increasing quantity and depth of links over a wider territory. The research is inconclusive, however, because it is based largely on white, middle-aged North Americans of British-Canadian descent.

Looking at the nature of effective and affective communities in greater depth, Davies and Herbert (1993) have identified seven major types of social interaction and eleven dimensions of attachment and symbolic meaning. The types of social interaction are: the use of community facilities; informal interaction, on a scale of increasing intimacy, from neighbours to workmates to friends to kin; mutual co-operation, involving exchange of goods or services, or the giving and receiving of information; formal organisations, for example for religion, leisure or sport, or to defend, promote and advance the community itself; political participation, connecting local residents to wider sources of political power at an urban, regional or national level; a supportive environment, in terms of productive relations with external organisations; and economic or capital flows, in terms of investment or disinvestment in the area (Davies and Herbert 1993: 64–6).

Considering these types of interaction in the light of rational choice theory, it can be seen that community facilities represent common resources which, as was stated in Chapter 1, are what provide the material basis for a community. Such resources can be extremely variable, including schools, shops, parks, even roads – they could include less tangible goods such as the general amenity of the area. The character of informal interaction, as already explained, depends largely upon social distance from kin, varying from unconditional obligation to one's closest relatives to strictly conditional obligation to neighbours, with friends and workmates coming somewhere between. Mutual co-operation is ambiguous: this could refer to a contractual relationship, for example between a shopkeeper and a customer in the area, or it could refer to the services provided by voluntary groups and knowledgeable individuals, or it could refer to a state–citizen type of relationship between teachers and students in a local school. Strictly speaking, only the voluntary type of relationship is characteristic of a community. The other types of relationship could be described as being *in* but not *of* the community.

From a rational choice perspective, there can be only one overriding reason for going beyond everyday rituals of neighbourly recognition to offering more substantive forms of co-operation and assistance, and that is the prospect of receiving benefits in return, either immediately in terms of enhanced status and influence, or in the future, should the giver herself come to be in need. Formal organisations then typically arise in order to maximise the benefits for co-operating individuals in terms of their enjoyment of leisure pursuits or in terms of their overall power and influence within the community and beyond. Once formal organisations are set up, utilitarian calculations come into play, and the now established means of maximising value then lead on logically to wider forms of political participation, involvement with powerful outside organisations, and action to secure increased investment in the area generally.

Turning to the notion of affective community, Davies and Herbert's eleven dimensions encompass a variety of features such as attachment to the area, satisfaction with the area, community control over the area, area status and general appearance, expectations of mutual aid, common standards of behaviour, and sense of belonging (Davies and Herbert 1993: 102–4). To some extent, these affective dimensions can be interpreted as predictable corollaries of (effective) community interaction. The quality of informal interactions among neighbours, for example, will be strongly correlated with expectations of mutual aid and with agreed standards of behaviour (on child care, noise and so on). Individuals will tend to accept and follow certain norms of conduct if conformity to such norms can be seen to produce a more congenial environment for all. This in turn results in greater satisfaction with the area generally, improved appearance and status of the area, and stronger attachment and sense of belonging to it. The process of affective development is therefore engendered by attention to the level of everyday informal interaction, and this development is assisted by the formation of formal organisations which promote increasing community control and serve to sustain and enhance the community's achievements at the informal level. Although presented in a static way, therefore, Davies and Herbert's typology can be understood in terms of dynamic processes of community growth (and conversely of community decline).

As mentioned earlier, the issue of boundary definition is a crucial one for local communities. The theme of 'insiders' versus 'outsiders' has been a recurrent one within the literature (Rees 1951; Vidich and Bensman 1960; Elias and Scotson 1965; Morris and Mogey 1965; Rainwater 1971; Suttles 1972; Elias 1974; Pahl 1975; Connell 1978; Strathearn 1981; Moore 1982; Giarchi 1984; Cohen 1985; Phillips 1986; Gilligan 1987; Pearson 1993; Spain 1993; Day and Murdoch 1993). Within traditional communities, some studies have suggested that gossip and mutual surveillance have been the primary means by which community boundaries are policed (Elias and Scotson 1994; Roberts 1995; Tebbutt 1995). Other studies point to the importance which communities attach to newcomers' 'fitting in' and participating in community activities (Phillips 1986).

The basic functions of boundary maintenance can be summarised as those of keeping insiders in and keeping outsiders out (Crow and Allan 1994: 10). Essentially, communities exert constraints and impose obligations on their members in return for providing social support. In traditional communities, the dense social networks make 'chains of interdependencies' (Elias 1974) which are strong enough to discourage individual action that goes against local traditions (Anwar 1985; Robinson 1986). From a rational choice perspective, we would expect such constraints and interdependencies to work in the interests of the community as a whole, because if they did not, the tendency would be for individual members to flout the rules and reject the traditions concerned. This also suggests that the idea of a coercive community is something of a contradiction in terms, and that where coercion does appear to exist it is likely to be a product of domestic relationships (for example, domination of children by their parents), or of bureaucratic or state–citizen relationships which are more typically based on coercive interaction.

The evidence on community boundary maintenance indicates a wide variety of dynamic possibilities. At one extreme of exclusivity, an individual is treated as a 'stranger' until their family has lived in the community for at least two generations (Rees 1951; Day and Murdoch 1993). In Padstow, for example, in order to be an insider an individual needed to be Padstonian by birth and by lineage (Gilligan 1987). In these communities, dominated by traditional occupations such as agriculture and fishing, it appears that only a pattern of settlement continuing over more than one generation is sufficient to secure community membership, and this has the effect of making the criteria for community membership very similar to those for family membership – one is born or adopted into such communities in much the same way as children are born/adopted into families. From a rational choice perspective, this has the advantage of creating strong mutual obligations among community members, which help to ensure a 'well-defended neighbourhood' (Suttles 1972). The disadvantage of such communities, however, is that they are vulnerable to global economic changes which bring about the decline of their dominant occupations. This is an inevitable effect of what Warren and Warren (1977) described as their lack of linkage with the outside world.

Only slightly less extreme than these 'family communities' (Richards 1990) are those where incomers are expected to meet certain standards before being accepted, and so if they do not meet those standards they may never be accepted at all. In this case, after one or two generations, the distinction between insiders and outsiders is reproduced in a distinction between 'respectables' (representing the members of the exclusive community group) and 'roughs' (representing residents in the area who are effectively excluded from community membership) (Morris and Mogey 1965; Klein 1965; Stacey 1969) (although it should be noted that this is only one way in which the distinction between 'respectables' and 'roughs' can be generated). For example, Elias and Scotson's study in 1965 of Winston Parva showed how status distinctions between a 'civilised' established group and 'problem' families of outsiders could be reproduced in the next generation. This happened because the newcomers did not show a willingness to fit in, but remained attached to patterns of behaviour that were regarded as normal and acceptable in their communities of origin but were disapproved of by the existing residents, for example noisy enjoyment and pub-going (Crow and Allan 1994: 72). In contrast, Phillips' study of Muker in North Yorkshire shows how where newcomers are prepared to 'muck in' (Phillips 1986: 151), by joining community organisations and taking an active part in village affairs, they may become accepted into the community after a certain period of time. Such acceptance strengthens the existing community because it is acceptance on the latter's terms, but it also allows for possible change in the community through the influx of new blood. From a rational choice perspective, the extension of membership to such newcomers represents a benefit to the group which is greater than its cost: the risk of erosion of traditional community relations appears to be more than outweighed by the value of the new linkages gained with the world beyond the community's boundaries.

The studies discussed so far have been of communities dominated by established residents. In other cases, however, the newcomers are rather more powerful in comparison with the locals, and consequently the outcomes are less predictable. Spain (1993), in a study of gentrifying neighbourhoods, found that as the numbers of better-off settlers grew to a 'critical mass' community resources became redistributed in their favour and conflict over resource allocation ensued. Even in Padstow, locals found that the incoming tourism entrepreneurs were too powerful to be controlled. They resented them because they did not seek to assimilate into local community life, but the usual double mechanism of inclusion and exclusion, or incorporation and resistance, did not work (Gilligan 1987; Crow and Allan 1994: 74–5). The typical response of local communities to such powerful immigrant groups appears to be a strategy of containment and isolation of the 'foreigners' in order to preserve the integrity of long-established traditions. For example in Peterhead (Moore 1982) the growth of the oil industry in a traditional fishing community did not break down existing divisions along lines of religion and class, and similarly in Dunoon (Giarchi 1984) the impact of industrial and military development did not lead to any real integration with, or acceptance by, the local community: 'The image of an invasion of the locality by incomers who were responsible for the decline of the local way of life contrasted with the reality of their segregation from the established residents most of the time' (Crow and Allan 1994: 80). From a rational choice perspective, the strategy of the indigenous community is only to be expected in the face of a newcomer group which does not accept its standards and is not prepared to participate in existing community organisations.

Where the incomer groups are very powerful and/or numerous in comparison with established residents, there is a danger that the latters' defensive, boundary-maintaining strategies will fail, and they will become 'encapsulated' (Crow and Allan 1994: 81), forming a 'community within a community' (Newby et al. 1978). This occurs typically in the case of an influx of urban middle-class commuters into rural working-class communities. As a result, a self-contained and tightly knit group of locals becomes stuck on an isolated council estate (Newby et al. 1978), or at least there develops a clear polarisation and simmering conflict between the locals and the newcomers, in which the former look like the losers (Pahl 1975; Connell 1978; Strathearn 1981). There appears, therefore, to be a structural similarity between processes of community change which are the result of rural and those which result from urban gentrification.

The literature on community, and in particular on ethnicity, indicates that there are different degrees of encapsulation, depending on class, ethnicity, and occupational type (Anwar 1985; Robinson 1986; Werbner 1988; Sarre *et al.* 1989). The situation is complex, and a number of important distinctions have to be made in order to avoid causing confusion. First of all, encapsulation by a host community, as happens with the containment of 'roughs' within a designated area (for example through local authority housing allocation), or with the creation of 'ethnic villages' on inner-city 'reservations' through effective exclusion as a result of non-conformity with 'English' standards and ways of life (Sarre *et al.* 1989), is something rather different from encapsulation caused by in-migration and effective invasion from more powerful groups. The processes of community change seem radically distinct, being highly conservative and stabilising in the first case, and destabilising in the second. Nevertheless, the effects on the encapsulated population are much the same in both cases, namely isolation and exclusion from the good things in life enjoyed by the dominant majority.

A second important distinction is between encapsulation and assimilation. Whether encapsulation occurs within an indigenous community or an arriviste community, there always exists the possibility of assimilation. This can come about through the minority community's adapting its standards of public behaviour to those of the majority and becoming accepted within the majority community's organisations. Attempts at assimilation, however, can be just as problematic for excluded groups as encapsulation:

> To strive for assimilation is to risk rejection by white society and consequent marginalisation and resentment, while the opposite strategy of minimising contacts with white society through the creation of an encapsulated community carries with it a different set of drawbacks, not least the danger of reproducing the conditions of social and economic disadvantage to which most ethnic minorities are subject.
> (Crow and Allan 1994: 106)

These remarks in relation to ethnic groups can equally well be applied to groups excluded on grounds of class or status, such as Elias and Scotson's 'cockney colony'. The general dilemma for excluded groups here can be summarised as one of 'heads you win, tails I lose', and this in itself shows the effectiveness of the majority community's exclusionary practices. A third important distinction is that between cultural homogeneity and heterogeneity. In general, it can be argued that the greater the degree of cultural difference between locals and newcomers, the greater the likelihood of not fitting in, and therefore the greater the likelihood of conflict and/or encapsulation (either of newcomers by the established community, or of locals by the new community). This helps to explain why ethnic groups are apparently more vulnerable to encapsulation than, say, groups of 'roughs'. On the other hand, however, the greater the degree of cultural difference *within* a community, the greater the likelihood of newcomers being able to fit in, not merely because it is more likely that they will find people of like mind to themselves but also because such a community is likely to be more tolerant of cultural difference generally. Evidence to support this comes from Wallman's study of Battersea (see also Dhooge 1982: 120). Interestingly, she found that neither skin colour nor language were central or even persistent issues in this mixed area (Wallman 1984: 8). Similarly, Scherer's study of Harlem suggests that it is not so much a shared culture which is the foundation of community but rather a shared experience of living in a particular locality, with open access to community resources, reinforced by regular mutual recognition. More recently, Sampson (1991) has claimed that what he calls 'acquaintance networks' are responsible for mediating residential stability and social cohesion, irrespective of socio-demographic characteristics such as age and life-cycle stage, and ecological contexts such as urbanisation and heterogeneity. All this suggests that there is an important distinction to be made, not so much between traditional and modern communities, but between communities based on ties of kinship and those based on ties of acquaintanceship and friendship. The former are relatively homogeneous, while the latter may be (though not necessarily) more heterogeneous.

Evidence certainly confirms that what may be called multicultural communities are very common, for example in American suburbs (Thorns 1976: 57). Many writers, however, in Britain as well as America, have described what can perhaps best be termed a 'tendency towards homogeneity'. The 25 per cent per year residency turnover rates found in some US suburbs, for example (Thorns 1976: 56), would appear to be sustainable only on the basis of cultural similarities (social class, income and lifestyle) between leavers and newcomers. Gans (1967), among others, has detailed the processes by which community organisations in new neighbourhoods work to re-establish traditional social patterns by finding 'like-minded people' beyond immediate neighbourhood contacts. Similarly, in Britain studies of new towns such as Crawley have shown the progressive development of greater homogeneity in different neighbourhoods along lines of social class (Heraud 1968). Again, studies of commuter villages and suburban fringe estates in Britain have found that neighbourliness develops on the basis of geographical proximity and demographic similarity, that is among young families, older couples, and so on, living generally within a few doors of each other (Carey and Mapes 1972).

Rational choice theory helps to make sense of much of the foregoing evidence. From this perspective, a community will admit as members only those who are seen as likely to contribute more to the community than they will take out. The perception of who is a suitable member, however, will vary according to the dominant conception of the nature of the community in question. Where 'community' is identified with strict codes of behaviour, for example including attendance at Sunday services, non-Christian or non-religious people will be excluded. Where 'community' is interpreted in a wider sense, however, for example to include anyone living in the area who is prepared to engage in reciprocal interaction, the prospects for social inclusion are obviously much greater. We would therefore expect culturally homogeneous communities to be more exclusive than heterogeneous ones, and this is indeed what we find in the literature. More heterogeneous communities, however, are more complex, and make for more difficult self-regulation. It could be argued that greater heterogeneity increases the risk to a community (for example, because of possibly greater difficulty in developing mutual aid and conditional obligations), but it also increases the potential benefits in terms of linkages with the outside world.

One important point here is that social exclusion by a community does not necessarily involve residential segregation. For example, Harris (1972) found that in Ballybeg in Ulster, Catholics and Protestants living in the same area could be simultaneously 'neighbours' and 'strangers'. Similarly, Rex and Moore (1967) specifically problematised the concept of segregation, finding that although there was considerable segregation within Sparkbrook as a whole, individual houses and streets were often markedly unsegregated. In this respect, Britain differs greatly from America, where most black people live in areas where the majority of the residents are also black (Peach 1996). It is likely, however, that over the course of time the 'tendency towards homogeneity' will result in greater residential segregation. This has already happened in Northern Ireland (Jenkins 1984), and there is also evidence to indicate the increasing concentration of minority ethnic groups in particular urban areas of Britain (Robinson 1993).

The tendency towards homogeneity is not inevitable. Clearly, as in the case of Northern Ireland, it will be accelerated where there is a perception of greatly increased risk, for example from sectarian violence or from racial harassment, leading in extreme cases to the phenomenon of 'ethnic cleansing'. Where the risk presented by heterogeneity appears low, however, as in Battersea, and/or the advantages of such cultural diversity seem important, for example for increasing the community's resources (new investment in the area, new opportunities for access to employment, and so on), then homogenisation may never take place. In each case, the outcome is decided on the basis of the balance of costs and benefits to the community (or communities) as a whole.

The dynamics of social exclusion by communities therefore take the same form, whether the excluded are minority ethnic groups, 'foreigners', 'roughs', or other groups held to be 'deviant' by the standards of the community. Particularly when a community feels itself to be under threat, it 'can make virtually anything grist to the symbolic mill of cultural distance, whether it be the effects upon it of some centrally formulated government policy, or a matter of dialect, dress, drinking or dying' (Cohen 1985: 117). Strangers are assimilated only on the community's terms, and to suit the community's own interests. The rational choice of its members may involve certain constraints on their part, for example in 'keeping up appearances' (compare the maintenance of the household as a unit described in Chapter 2), but in return they enjoy the benefits of belonging to an exclusive group with rights to access important communal resources.

From a rational choice perspective, the main disadvantage of a more homogeneous traditional community is its social inertia. It is more difficult for such a community to respond productively to wider economic and social changes. For example, dissenting members of the community, who are the most likely internal agents of change, are also the most likely to move away because they are least integrated into that community. This leads to an increasing cultural homogeneity and social cohesiveness of those that remain (Bulmer 1978), which reinforces the community's inertia. In the long run, the accumulating loss of more active community members can make it difficult to sustain community traditions, as has apparently happened in areas such as the West of Ireland (Brody 1973) and Teesside (Allen 1990). In extreme cases, where the community also suffers serious economic decline, the result can be the winding down and death of the community (Porteous 1989).

The East End of London has attracted considerable attention from researchers into community over the years. This is perhaps because the area has been subject to successive waves of immigration over several hundred years, involving an extraordinary variety of ethnic groups. According to Cohen (1984), the pattern of settlement has been one where a new incoming group becomes established by dissociating itself from an even more conspicuous set of 'outsiders'. In such a situation, integration, let alone assimilation, is really out of the question, but this reality is typically not recognised by those who have been established for the longest period of time, namely white working-class households. Unlike in Battersea, ethnicity is a major issue, and hostility to those who wish to maintain a separate non-white cultural identity is common (Cornwell 1984). The culture of East Enders is therefore not unlike that of traditional occupational communities (in this case, based on dock working and the 'rag trade'), when threatened by competition from in-migrating groups. Given the lack of alternative sources of employment and the shortage of affordable housing for unskilled workers, white racism in this area can be understood as a rational means of restricting access to such scarce resources so that they can be enjoyed only by long-established members of the community.

The variety of relationships between locals and newcomers can perhaps best be represented in terms of a continuum, with highly powerful established groups at one end and highly powerful in-migrant groups at the other (Table 3.2). In some cases, in-migrant groups have travelled long distances in order to settle in a local area. Typically this occurs for economic reasons, to raise the migrants' standard of living. The usual pattern here is one of what has

Table 3.2 The relative power of locals and newcomers

Community	Degrees of power		
Already existing	More powerful	Equal	Less powerful
Newly arrived	Less powerful	Equal	More powerful
Result	Assimilation or encapsulation of newcomers (assimilation more likely)	Continuing conflict and/or segregation	Assimilation or encapsulation of existing residents (encapsulation more likely)

been called 'chain migration' (Anwar 1979; Williams 1983), according to which 'pioneer' settlers are followed by members of their immediate family, and then by other relatives and acquaintances from their community of origin. Kinship relations are crucial to the success of such migration. As Crow and Allan (1994: 85) point out: 'kinship networks operate to promote chain migration by channelling information about job vacancies and by providing residential aid to new migrants.' Evidence confirms that chain migration can produce effective re-establishment of dense, close-knit networks of kinship and friendship in new localities (Anwar 1985; Shaw 1988; Werbner 1984; Grieco 1987; Clark and Taylor 1988; Devine 1992), although encapsulation may well result (Crow and Allan 1994: 102–5). One paradoxical consequence of such migration is that its success tends to reinforce the traditional norms and practices of the migrating community, and this can lead to an exaggerated emphasis on their 'difference' from those of the community in whose area they settle. In such circumstances, perhaps encapsulation is a not altogether surprising result (Anwar 1985).

Finally, there have been numerous studies of communities which have suffered from mass unemployment and from redevelopment. On unemployment, studies have indicated that it does not appear to have had much effect on community structure (Harris 1987; Bostyn and Wight 1987; Howe 1990; Jenkins 1983; Evason 1985; Gillespie *et al.* 1992; Coffield *et al.* 1986; Allatt and Yeandle 1992; Morris and Irwin 1992). As Crow and Allan put it:

> One of the more surprising findings thrown up by recent research into economic restructuring is the discovery that the rapid decline of employment in traditional industries has not been accompanied by wholesale change in the communities which grew up around the mines, factories and other workplaces of Britain's industrial areas.
> (Crow and Allan 1994: 47–8)

There appear to be two main reasons for this. One is that these are largely traditional occupational communities, dominated by kinship ties, and unemployment tends to reinforce dependence on these ties for day-to-day survival (Allatt and Yeandle 1992; Morris and Irwin 1992). The second is that access to paid employment depends mainly on networks connecting the individual to labour market forces, and these networks may well be prevalent in some local communities, making community ties more important for the individual concerned (Harris 1987; Coffield *et al.* 1986).

The problem which community poses for unemployed people is that they are less likely to be connected into such networks and therefore more vulnerable to social isolation (Pahl 1984; Harris 1987). Bostyn and Wight's research on Cauldmoss, for example, found that in spite of the presence of support from relatives, 'in the long run unemployment pushed individuals into a marginal, isolated and excluded position peripheral to mainstream community life' (Crow and Allan 1994: 49; see also Wight 1993). Communities are therefore relatively powerless in the face of major changes in the economic system. Also, the community's maintenance of conformist patterns of breadwinning and job search, even in areas of the highest unemployment (over 50 per cent), can have the effect of exacerbating the social isolation of unemployed people (Howe 1990). This can lead to the apparently irrational situation, as in parts of West Belfast, where fewer than one in five young people are finding jobs within two years of leaving school, yet traditional divisions continue between the sexes, between respectables and roughs, and between conformists and non-conformists (Gillespie *et al.* 1992). This is not really irrational, however, because, as we have seen in Chapter 2, unemployment does not diminish women's traditional domestic responsibilities, and therefore neither does it reduce men's basic breadwinning responsibility. Family and community norms therefore effectively conspire to lock young people into traditional roles, irrespective of the current state of the labour market. If they cannot gain access to paid employment or full-time education or training, they must remain dependent upon their parents or else end up on the streets. This in itself may help to explain the hostility to local community expressed by young people, and particularly by young men, in certain areas (Campbell 1993).

It has been suggested that the one impact which mass unemployment does have on local community structure is to introduce a new division between the employed and the unemployed, or between the securely employed and the not securely employed/unemployed (Pahl 1984; Warwick and Littlejohn 1992). Because the latter are not able to undertake reciprocal action or to participate to the same extent in community affairs, they may become 'grimly "home-centred"' (Binns and Mars 1984: 674) and increasingly disconnected from the usual patterns of communal sociability. Effectively, however, this does not represent a change in community structure but rather a loss of a proportion of its membership, who have simply dropped out of community life. As we have already seen, continuity of community relations is quite compatible with such processes of social exclusion.

So, in order to explain the functioning of communities, it is sufficient to invoke only the postulates of rational choice theory, and it is not necessary to have recourse to a separate theory of social ties beyond the ties of kinship. Communities can be seen either as dominated by family connections, giving rise to virtually unconditional obligations among their members, or as involving primarily conditional obligations, arising out of neighbourly interaction and voluntary co-operation. In the latter case, communal interaction is more clearly based on rational norms of reciprocity and utilitarianism. In the former case, communities can be explained in terms of a rational extension or spill-over of domestic and familial processes into the home area and the parochial realm. This is why 'women are amongst the foremost members of community and voluntary organisations' (Deem 1986: 58), because it is seen as an extension of their domestic responsibilities. This does not necessarily mean, however, that their status is thereby enhanced, because 'work women undertake in the community, on behalf of the community, is largely invisible, making women seem part of the community, whilst being excluded from it' (Dominelli 1990: iii).

In both cases, whether family-based or neighbour-based, communities are typically divided between locals and newcomers, between middle-class and working-class, between rich and poor, between 'respectables' and 'roughs', between white and black, between men and women, and between old and young. The character of these divisions varies enormously from one community to another, but the variation exhibits a common pattern related to the degree of power exercised by the different groups within a community in their struggle for control over the community resource pool. Essentially, whatever their detailed characteristics, groups which are more powerful than their competitors will tend to assimilate or encapsulate them. However, the exact process of change is not inevitable, because the degree of power held by any particular group is subject to considerable fluctuation, depending, for example, upon the state of its organisational development, the amount of its social capital and the capacities of its individual members. The task of community development, therefore, is basically one of empowering the less powerful groups. This is obviously extremely difficult, and there is little evidence of any great success, but it is not impossible.

Community development

Davies and Herbert (1993: 110) define community development as: 'the purposeful, locality-based attempt of people – either from inside or outside an area – to initiate some action to improve their local environment, associations, services and other attributes in their area.' This definition accords with the assumptions of rational choice theory, namely that people are capable of rational co-operation within groups in order to achieve benefits for the group as a whole. In order to overcome the 'free rider' problem, however, there have to be selective incentives and sanctions for the group members

(Bengtsson 1998a). This suggests that it should be possible to explain the nature and extent of community development in terms of specific innovations within the community, specific interventions from outside the community, or specific interactions between the community and the outside world which produce new incentives/sanctions for collective action.

Interestingly, Davies and Herbert (1993: 112) identify three approaches to community development which correspond to these three types of causal factor: technical assistance, self-help, and critical or conflict approaches. Technical assistance represents a form of intervention from outside the community, whereby 'experts' define and control the development programme. Essentially, middle-class professionals and bureaucrats diagnose the community's problems of lack of capacity, lack of private or social capital, and lack of effective organisation, and then devise what they see as appropriate solutions to those problems. The approach has been aptly described as development *in* the community, not development *of* the community (Littrel and Hobbs 1989), because in practice it has increased divisions within the community (between those with access to technical assistance and those without), imposed alien values on the community, and marginalised the weaker and more vulnerable community members. In relation to slum clearance and redevelopment in particular, the effect of the technical assistance approach has often been negative and destructive:

> The historic network of local social integration in many older areas of the cities, where the residents were close to local shops, entertainment and relatives, was replaced by an often isolated, crime-ridden life on the windswept margins of the city.
>
> (Davies and Herbert 1993: 116)

A good example of the problems with the technical assistance approach is to be found in McCulloch (1997), where an all-male professional team was 'parachuted' into the area, and then proceeded to co-opt a small group of local people which then dominated the whole process (p. 59). Such problems are typical of area-based policies in which community development is imposed from outside and the involvement of the community itself is negligible – for example, City Challenge in England (Hart *et al.* 1997: 188) or local authority dominated regeneration in Scotland (Collins 1997) or the on-going saga of redevelopment in London's Docklands (Colenutt 1991; Church and Hall 1989; Brownill 1990).

Notwithstanding these criticisms of the technical assistance approach, researchers have long ago identified the elements required for the approach to be successful, and these have been summarised in the acronym 'A VICTORY' (Davis and Salasin 1975): Ability, Values, Information, Circumstances, Timing, Obligation, Resistance, and Yield. These elements centre on the relationship between the community and the assisting group. The two parties must understand each other well, in terms of their different knowledges, values, needs, aspirations for the community, and so on. If they can then agree on the needs, there is a good chance of success (Davies and Herbert 1993: 117). The likelihood of such understanding and subsequent agreement is increased by resident participation in the planning process, use by community groups of advocacy professionals (for example 'tenants' friends'), intermediaries employed by the intervening outside organisations (for example tenant participation officers), and more effective formal organisation of residents (through more inclusive tenants' and residents' associations). The model for successful community development by the technical assistance approach is therefore one of a genuine partnership between the assisting group and the community (Somerville and Steele 1995).

From a rational choice perspective, it makes perfect sense that, in order to succeed, an assisting group must above all ensure that it 'fits in' with the established group, which is the community. Otherwise, it will be seen as an 'outsider' group, which will be resisted, resulting in possible encapsulation of the assisting group or disintegration of the established group. The elements of 'A VICTORY' are simply those which are essential to the process of 'fitting in' to an already existing community. This process can therefore be compared directly with that by which newcomers are assimilated into any community as discussed earlier in this chapter. If the newcomers are seen as being a net benefit to the community rather than a net cost, then it is to be expected that the technical intervention will be successful – members of the assisting group will be accepted as members of the community for so long as they bring a net benefit to that community.

In contrast to the technical assistance approach, the self-help approach 'is based on the principle that people should and can collaborate in an area to provide the needs and services they require' (Davies and Herbert 1993: 119). This approach goes back to de Tocqueville (1966), and has been continually renewed over the centuries through frontier communities in the New World and through co-operative and anarchistic movements in the Old World. 'It is seen as a return to the fundamental principles upon which the New England communities of the seventeenth century were based, keeping alive the concept that the spirit of "the people" should be the primary source of power' (Davies and Herbert 1993: 120; see also Perlman 1979; Fisher and Kling 1989). In recent years, it has revived as a reaction against insensitive technical assistance and as a reflection of the practice of neighbourhood organisations (Birklen 1983; Bender 1986; Hallman 1984; Marshall and Mayer 1983). Currently, it appears to form the inspiration for communitarianism (Etzioni 1995).

In spite of the strength of its ideological support, there are serious problems in practice with the self-help approach. These relate mainly to three possible situations: lack of linkage with the outside world as discussed earlier in this chapter in connection with traditional communities; 'free-riding' by some community members on the efforts of others; and the occurrence of dependency in any case because of the community's reliance on outside experts for their initial stimulus and on governments for facilities and educational programmes (even Neighbourhood Watch programmes rely on police guidance and monitoring). For example, if a community does not have great capacity of its own, then self-help will only serve to ensure that it remains disadvantaged. In practice, even the most deprived communities appear to have substantial social capital of their own, in terms of local interaction and identity (Littrel and Hobbs 1989; Summers 1986), which can be used as the basis for far-reaching community development (Kotler 1969; Williams 1985). Some problems, however, are simply not solvable by a self-help approach, for example poverty and urban decay.

Rational choice theory predicts that only a small minority of community members is likely to be active in a self-help movement. These will be the 'fiery spirits' (Elster 1989) and their fellow-travellers, who like to be at the forefront of communal activity and who may be driven by traditional communitarian ideology. Unless there are clear incentives or sanctions to the contrary, most community members will choose to 'free-ride' on the work of these activists. This can give rise to problems of the emergence of a more or less exclusive elite or else the 'burn-out' of the activists, depending upon the scale of benefits to be gained from active participation.

In spite of the problems with the self-help approach, there is evidence to indicate that it can succeed, under certain conditions. These conditions include links with outside sources of support, skills in communication and in human resource and financial management, high levels of social capital (including density of community organisation and high levels of community participation and support), self-sustaining enterprises, tangible benefits to the community, and community initiation and continued control of the self-help programme (Perlman 1979; Marshall and Mayer 1983). Clearly, a disempowered community, or a disempowered group within a community, is unlikely to meet such conditions without a significant degree of technical assistance.

The third approach to community development, namely the critical or conflict approach, focuses on the deliberate use and even creation of confrontation by professional organisers, to remove injustice and imbalance in the social distribution of values (Davies and Herbert 1993: 123). Its origins lie in the work of Alinsky (1969 1972) in Chicago in the 1930s. According to this approach, the impetus for development has to come from the community itself, which formally invites the professional organisers into the area to work with them. These outsiders then need to conduct research in order to gain an understanding of the area and identify its existing power structure. After this comes a period of community organisation and mobilisation. This stage involves a number of types of activity, deploying a range of techniques, concerned mainly with: identifying issues and priorities for the community as a whole; building community consensus through increased rates of interaction, for example through door-stepping and meetings; increasing the number, membership and linkage of formal organisations within the community; focusing on a single winnable issue that represents the heart of a problem in an area, preferably visible and non-divisive, in order to have the widest appeal – for example, community clean-ups; identifying an adversary, that is a visible entity to fight against and on which to concentrate problem issues, though through indirect pressure not direct confrontation which would fail; and building links to support groups and agencies outside the community. The next stage involves planning and mounting campaigns to achieve community goals. This requires activities such as: continuous pressure on the adversaries, for example through use of the media, through forms of direct action, and through strikes and boycotts; building an independent basis of knowledge and skills; using tactics in which it proves enjoyable for community members to be involved; and selecting targets where victory appears to be reasonable and realistic. Such activities give rise to the next stage, which is that of resistance from the adversary and its allies. According to Alinsky, this resistance can occur in four ways: fragmenting the issue or stalling for time, resulting in the movement running out of steam; neutralising the effectiveness of community leaders by co-opting them into the existing power structure or by threatening them; punitive tactics, for example using police force to close down opposition – this can succeed, but can sow the seeds of greater conflict in the future; and mediation tactics, for example using mediators or arbitrators, or offering incentives to come to an agreement such as increased funding for the area. The final stage is then that of sustaining community organisation after the initial euphoria of mobilisation or success. The main problems here are: becoming generally worn down by the outside opposition, the burn-out of key organisers and voluntary staff, the loss of 'fiery spirits' to pastures new, and the drying up of funding. The literature shows, however, that there are ways of preventing or overcoming most of these problems, for example by creating appropriate monitoring organisations within the community which act as early warning systems, by appropriate training programmes for community activists, and by democratic procedures which ensure the incorporation of as many community members as possible into the main community organisation. Only the problem of loss of funding is more intractable: Davies and Herbert (1993: 129) affirm that this 'can only be conclusively resolved if a local area has the authority to levy taxes or legitimate access to part of the tax revenue'. A way has to be found to ensure that communities are more viable in economic terms, for example through the creation of community corporations (Hallman 1984) and the support of micro-economies at the community level (West and McCormick 1998).

The conflict approach shares some of the problems of the self-help approach, namely free-riding by some community members and possible dependence on outside experts. It secures linkage with outside support, and this increases its chances of success in comparison with self-help, but at the same time this increases the risk of losing the most capable and effective members of the community to alternative pursuits and careers. Success for the conflict approach also depends crucially on reaching consensus within the community, and this is not possible in many areas which are socially divided, as described earlier in this chapter. Nevertheless, it is arguable that for a relatively disadvantaged community the conflict approach represents the best option, because such a community would tend to be overwhelmed or undermined by technical assistance, and left still disadvantaged by a self-help approach. The task of community development can therefore be restated as one in which a community builds its own capacity through struggle, selecting the forms of technical assistance it needs as it develops. One problem with this, however, is that the community has to have already reached a certain level of development in order to know what forms of technical assistance it needs and to issue invitations to the appropriate professionals or consultants. Where this is not the case, technical assistance may be the only possible positive option.

Rational choice theory again explains both why the conflict approach is more likely to work and why such an approach is inherently risky. Using outside professionals under one's own control is a rational strategy for a body which wants to increase its human and social capital: it is demonstrably more effective than relying on self-help (not using outsiders), or being dependent on professionals not under the community's control (technical assistance). The techniques of community mobilisation also make sense in terms of maximising value for each individual community member. In general, unity brings strength, whereas division is always a source of weakness. However, techniques which depend upon active informal and formal participation always come up against the free-rider problem, hence the need to make such participation attractive and rewarding. The conflict approach achieves this in a variety of ways, so as to accommodate a wide range of tastes, attitudes and aspirations: for excitement, comradeship, the development of personal and organisational skills, the sweet scent of victory, and the satisfaction of a job well done. By means of such incentives, high levels of communal solidarity can be achieved, although generally there must be some basis for this in terms of common allegiances and shared ideology in order for collective action to be effective (Cornwell 1984; Parry *et al.* 1987; Marris 1987). Formal organisations of an appropriate kind can then be developed to deal with the remaining problems of external opposition and internal sustainability, designed to maximise the influence of individual community members through building both their human and their social capital (both within and across the community's boundaries). Ideally, from a rational choice perspective, this in turn should bring about the community's economic development and regeneration.

In practice, the drive towards unity can itself create a number of problems for community development, as explained by Brent (1997). Brent makes the point that 'community formation is intrinsically about creating difference' (Brent 1997: 75). This is because, as we have seen earlier in this chapter, the existence of community involves the creation of boundaries between insiders and outsiders. Community development involves the growth of both individuals and groups as complex identities, and this process of growth tends to make them increasingly different from one another. This does not in itself mean that it is more difficult for them to work together, but the need to create a sense of unity 'inside' the community inevitably leads to the exclusion of some residents – for example Asian women who do not participate in local social events. Brent (1997: 76) therefore argues that 'community cannot, because of that boundary which is a necessary constituent of its existence, create an all-inclusive unity'. As Ambrose (1986) has pointed out, communities are typically divided. A further important point that Brent (1997: 78) makes is that: 'The greater the pressure for unity, the more pronounced the external divisions, so there is an increased prevalence of internal splits, as different sections are anathematised in the search for an ultimately unrealisable uniform and pure community.' For example, younger residents can become alienated as the community becomes defined as an exclusive group of middle-aged and older residents, and community practices develop which are oppressive of young people. In extreme cases, this can result in young men acting as the destroyers of what is supposed to be their own community (Campbell 1993). The final point which Brent makes is that, on the basis of the above arguments, what is required for community development is what he calls 'unicity' (Brent 1997: 81) rather than unity, that is an arrangement which acknowledges and indeed values multiplicity and diversity – a community which, while not actually welcoming or embracing internal conflict, at least recognises that it is inevitable and can be healthy, bringing positive benefits for the community as a whole.

Gilchrist (1992 1995) and Gilchrist and Taylor (1997) have shown how the problems of initial lack of development and lack of unity (or unicity) can both be overcome by the adoption of rational strategies on the part of the change agents brought in to serve the community's interests. The general issue of what works in community development has also been discussed in depth, in different ways, by Taylor (1995), Hastings et al. (1996), Skelcher et al. (1996) and J. Smith (1997). A considerable amount of research has been conducted in this area, from a variety of perspectives, but a number of common findings can be identified. These relate to the following issues: the inclusion of minorities; the development of social capital; the prevention of oligarchy; the role of community organisations; the linkage of the community to outside sources of power and influence; the sustainability of community development; and the feasibility of community empowerment generally.

On the basis of thirty-three studies of over a hundred housing estates in Britain which had experienced community development, Taylor (1995) reached the following conclusions: even the most deprived communities contain substantial human and social capital which can be harnessed given the right approach; providing technical assistance to communities is essential; the ways in which mainstream services are delivered to these areas need to change; community development needs to create long-term job opportunities and community-owned assets; and long time-scales are required for effective resident involvement. These conclusions are broadly consistent with those from American research and with what one would expect on the basis of rational choice theory – for example the need to create lasting economic value through paid employment and capital ownership. However, they raise a number of further questions, such as: what is 'the right approach'? what forms of technical assistance are essential? how exactly do mainstream services need to change? and how are long-term job opportunities and community-owned assets to be created? These questions are addressed to some extent by Hastings *et al.* (1996) and Gilchrist and Taylor (1997), and less directly by Skelcher *et al.* (1996).

Hastings *et al.* (1996) consider the issue, which was raised in the above discussion of the conflict approach, concerning how a community can acquire the original capacity to know when to call in appropriate technical assistance. They suggest that outside organisations can act as catalysts in such a process, by contacting existing local groups and community bodies and explaining what can be done for them. Ranges of options for development can then be explored with the community, and eventually written up in the form, for example, of a 'Residents' Expectations Document'. All this suggests that at this stage the 'right approach' is one of technical assistance, but it is a special form of such assistance in which the outside professionals provide information to the community and begin to learn about the nature of the community, its problems and its priorities for action. When the community members feel they have been sufficiently informed (and this could involve a certain amount of training and education), they can then decide whether to continue working with these particular professionals and whether to seek other forms of technical assistance.

What prompts an outside organisation to act as a catalyst in this way? There appear to be three possibilities: first, the organisation may be politically motivated, acting on the basis of a wider agenda of social reform or revolution, as described by Alinsky (1969 1972). Historically, however, such action has been unusual and generally ineffective. Secondly, the organisation may be a charity, such as many of those working in community development in developing countries today. In spite of criticisms of charities over the years, especially from marxists, there is evidence to show that charities can be effective (albeit limited in comparison with the power of governments and large corporations) in both stimulating and sustaining community development in certain areas (Craig and Mayo 1995). Thirdly, and arguably most importantly, the organisation may be directed or financed by government, so that the assisting professionals are paid out of public funds and may be pursuing state objectives, for example of urban regeneration, economic improvement and crime reduction.

Jerry Smith (1997: 174) comments further on the role of professionals in promoting community development. He suggests that: 'Community empowerment is more likely to result from professionals sharing problems, ideas, decisions and responsibilities with communities than from simply providing services and resources, no matter how sensitively delivered.' The point being made here is that community development is more likely to succeed where the relationship between outside professionals and community members is one of reciprocal interaction rather than a one-way process of distribution. In the words of the slogan, this means that 'hand-ups' are better than 'hand-outs'. From a rational choice perspective, this is only to be expected, because non-reciprocated gifts, however desirable, tend to create dependency, whereas arrangements based on reciprocity, as we have seen, lead to the extension of individual autonomy and an increase in social capital. Rational choice theory therefore clearly explains why 'top-down' forms of technical assistance tend on the whole to be less empowering of communities than so-called 'partnership' approaches. Hyatt (1995) found that in fact the value to a community of employing outside specialists depended, among other things, on the extent to which the community itself had sought such intervention and had been involved in their selection and signed their contract.

Gilchrist and Taylor (1997) and Skelcher *et al.* (1996) have more to say about how exactly to build up social capital so that the community can reach the position of being in control of its own means of technical assistance. Gilchrist and Taylor affirm that the task of community work is to develop capacity within the whole community. Following Milofsky and Hunter (1994), they first suggest that within any residential area there exist so-called 'background communities' which are loose informal alliances that throw up formally organised coalitions when informal associational processes are unable to get a task done. Through numerous 'junction points' and 'organisational intelligence', these networks store individual and organisational capacity which can be drawn on when necessary. 'Every foray into a more formally organised activity brings more experience into the background community' (Gilchrist and Taylor 1997: 176), which also offers feedback on the foray and therefore provides a degree of accountability. Developing this community capacity can then be achieved by the following means: building overlapping networks, based on thick and varied links between people and offering a variety of access points; encouraging the organisation of events which make networks visible, reinforce links and give people a sense of common identity; switching neighbourhood-based networks into more influential and better-resourced circuits, allowing power to flow into marginalised communities; ensuring the expertise gained through specific actions flows back into the community at large and is translated into capacity to respond to further needs and opportunities; and ensuring that information flows in and out of networks and that more formal activities exercise responsive accountability to 'background communities' (Gilchrist and Taylor 1997: 177). Interestingly, the explanation of these findings about how community capacity is developed involves not only rational choice theory (for example, maximising value through the extension of reciprocity and the increase of net inward capital flows, and the application of sanctions to ensure a wide distribution within the community of the benefits from formal activities), but also phenomenological theory to underpin the pattern of reciprocal interaction within the community and show how it is based on and in turn reinforces a common attachment to the area.

Skelcher et al. (1996) looked specifically at the issue of social capital in terms of the development of community-based networks and partnerships. They made an important distinction between the opportunity to network (for example through social events, conferences and seminars) and the capacity to engage (in terms of time, organisational support and resources) (Skelcher et al. 1996: 16). Community development involves both the provision of opportunities for people to interact in ways which will lead to the expanding and strengthening of their networks, and the introduction of measures which will help to increase the resources available to community members so that they can take advantage of such opportunities. According to Skelcher et al. (1996: 23), strengthening the opportunity and capacity to network is achieved through: the development of skills; the creation of an ethical stance – recognising the values of good governance, such as openness, pluralism, democracy and altruism, as against exclusion, discrimination, elitism and self-interest; support for network roles, such as those of leaders, link-persons, supporters and managers, by means of training and material assistance; the creation of an 'awareness' resource in the locality, to sustain the network through individual comings and goings; and the use of information systems to overcome constraints of travel and to make links to national and international levels.

From a rational choice perspective, some of these measures appear quite logical, for example developing skills, providing assistance, and creating common resources and information systems in order to sustain community interaction and community linkage with the outside world. Others, however, require further comment. For example, we have seen earlier in this chapter that openness and pluralism in relation to 'outsiders' may not always be appropriate, because if the outsider group is more powerful it may only serve to hasten the community's encapsulation. A clear distinction therefore has to be made between the values which members of the community practise among themselves and those which they follow in relation to the rest of the world. As we saw in Chapter 1, maximal inclusion of group members goes hand in hand with strongly defended group boundaries which clearly exclude non-members. The 'altruism' of each group member is simply the other side of the coin from the 'self-interest' of the group as a whole.

Skelcher et al. (1996)'s concept of network roles is an original one. Arguably, what they are saying is that there are certain roles which have to be carried out in order for a 'background community' to give rise to successful formal organisation leading to genuine community development. Although their evidence for this is based on research into urban regeneration projects, there appears to be no good reason why their claim should be restricted to such situations. The role of the leader, then, is to draw and hold together network members, bringing together previously unconnected individuals, for mutual support or for project and policy development (Skelcher et al. 1996: 18). This is not a role which is necessarily performed by one person, but certain individuals, as we have seen, do act as 'fiery spirits'. Skelcher et al. (1996: 18) call these community 'champions', but they suggest that the ability of such individuals to by-pass the bureaucracy and make things happen may not always be a good thing. This could be because the 'champions' have not followed Alinsky's 'rules for radicals' – for example, they may not have devoted sufficient effort to carrying the rest of the community with them, or they may not have focused on a clearly winnable issue, or they may have created unnecessary or increased hostility from the bureaucracy in response to what the latter perceive as a failure to go through the proper channels. Community leaders do not have to be such colourful or charismatic individuals, but they have to be highly motivated, hard-working and doggedly persistent in order to play their roles successfully.

Many other writers have commented on the importance of leadership, and indeed this appears to be a key theme in the socio-psychological and managerial literature on group dynamics and group development (Homans 1961; Shaw 1976; Adair 1986). Wiewel and Gills, for example, suggest that:

> The most important problems facing community development forces are the qualitative ones, involving the quality of leadership and the tension between leadership and its connection to constituents. Without well-trained, committed leadership with organic, democratic linkages to constituents who, in turn, sanction the community organisation, the community development movement loses any progressive character.
>
> (Wiewel and Gills 1995: 137)

A second role which Skelcher et al. (1996: 18) identify as necessary for community development is that of the 'link-person', who ensures that, as far as possible, community members remain up to date and in touch with each other. This role is best filled by someone who has links with outside bodies which can be valuable for channelling assistance – for example, a resident who has relevant professional connections, especially for access to sources of funding. The role of link-person is often confused with that of a community leader – for example, Shaw (1988: 144) has described most Asian community leaders in Britain as 'in many ways on the periphery of the community', acting as negotiators in 'the competition for scarce public resources that *community leaders* vie for on behalf of each *community*' (Baumann 1996: 197). There would appear to be two different roles which are being discussed here, although these may be played by the same person: strictly speaking, a community leader cannot be on the periphery of the community, but must be at the heart of it, so some of these Asian 'community leaders' must be link-persons rather than leaders. On the other hand, a community member who is not a leader will not have sufficient authority within the community to negotiate on its behalf in crucial debates over funding, so in this case it must be leaders who are involved.

A third role is that of the 'supporter', who makes individual community members feel valued and assists their contribution to community activity, and a fourth role is that of the 'manager', who implements the ideas developed through community interaction.

All these roles would appear to be essential for sustaining community development in the longer term. From a rational choice perspective, the different individuals can be seen as having slightly different values whose maximisation is complementary and mutually reinforcing. The community leader, for example, enjoys the exercise of personal power and influence, and values the respect in which she or he is held by the community. The link-person gains satisfaction from achieving something which is highly valued by the community, and may also simply enjoy the variety of networking involved in performing their role. The supporter then follows a social norm of co-operation (Elster 1989) which can be defended on rational grounds (see the next paragraph), and finally the manager can be seen as representing a formal organisation produced by community development, holding a position of achieved status, possibly with financial remuneration (for example, a paid job, or a right to office space and reasonable expenses, or specific decision-making powers).

The values and practices of community leaders and link-persons make participation seem more attractive to other community members, for example through ideological motivation or through improved access to valued resources. These individuals are therefore crucial to the initiation and consolidation of community development, but the institutionalisation of such development, which is essential for its long term sustainability, is left mainly to the supporters and managers. What may be happening, for example in the situations described by Skelcher *et al.* (1996), is that the initiative of the small minority of 'social entrepreneurs' (Leadbeater 1997) creates opportunities and incentives among the majority to take on the role of supporters, and this leads directly to the creation of formal community organisations which require managers to make them work. Supporters may be motivated by a norm of reciprocity, but Bengtsson's research (1998b: 12) on housing estates suggests that this is less common than one would expect on the basis of rational choice theory. The more likely motivation is one governed by the norm of utilitarianism, according to which community members make their contribution when they are asked to do so by other members. The core of activists, consisting of the community leaders and their networks of friends and relatives, will then be joined by a much larger group, whose decision to co-operate will be based on a rational judgment of the following: the net collective benefits of the proposed action to the community, the need for the individual's contribution at the point s/he is asked, and the time and capacity the individual has to make a contribution (Bengtsson 1998b: 13). This suggests that success in community development depends very much upon convincing most members that what is proposed is in the interests of the community as a whole and that their contribution towards such development is vital, as well as upon ensuring that community members have the necessary resources of time and skills.

Skelcher et al. (1996: 31) suggest five strategies which could maximise the degree of support for community development among residents: taking positive steps to widen access to the development process – for example, considering the timing and location of events, making it easier for those who would otherwise be excluded, and identifying link-people who are able to connect the core of activists to other groupings; providing opportunities for everyone to discuss and shape the overall process; developing group-work skills, to facilitate a process in which all can be heard with respect and decisions can be reached through consensus-seeking; being open to the outcomes of the development process which have been stimulated; and developing the capacity to link networks and to develop forums and 'clearing houses' for community members' experience. They conclude that for effective community development, there is a need to develop a specific culture, involving a common language (for example a common understanding of such terms as 'consultation'), an ability to understand and act within different organisational cultures, and a common set of ground rules of operation, including negotiating questions of decision processes, confidentiality and openness, the nature of agreements between members, and the methods of resolving conflicts and disagreements (Skelcher et al. 1996: 39).

Similarly, Hastings et al. (1996: 22) suggest a number of steps which can be taken to improve the prospects of 'meaningful community input' into the process of urban regeneration. These steps include: encouraging community activists to develop their own agenda and priorities, and getting these recognised and shared by other community members; getting away from 'men in suits on parachutes' by locating assisting professionals in the local area; chairing meetings in a style which includes community members in discussion, welcomes their contribution, and creates an atmosphere indicating that things will not move ahead without the community's agreement; training representatives of agencies working in the community to work closely with local residents; funding community organisations to recruit their own support staff and providing independent budgets for training and developing community members; and finding ways for community representatives (community leaders and link-persons) to cope with or limit their range of activities in order to avoid being swamped by the extent of work involved in community development. All these measures could be described as examples of positive measures of technical assistance, and the last one in particular reflects Alinsky's tactical rule that community activists should concentrate on what they can handle.

The above discussion implies that the formation of community organisations is an essential ingredient of community development. It is not sufficient to rely on informal relations of kinship and neighbourliness if communal resources and assets achieved through community action are to be conserved and enhanced for the future. As Gilchrist and Taylor (1997: 176) have put it, informal networks are not appropriate for sustained formal activity or service delivery – more formal structures are required. Keyes (1987) summarised the different roles played by community organisations: area or turf-based defence of areas under threat; increasing local control over area-impacting decisions; providing a form of resident participation; as a means to increase external funding to the community; and increasing the degree of communication and networking between the community and the outside world. All of these roles can be interpreted as formalisations of what already occurs within communities on an informal basis, as crystallisations of the patterns of interaction within 'background communities'. This can be shown by comparing them with the evidence concerning the functioning of communities discussed earlier in this chapter, where it was noted that all communities tend to define boundaries between insiders and outsiders (hence 'area-based defence' and emphasis on local control) and to involve forms of reciprocal interaction. It is also in the rational self-interest of communities to maximise their access to external resources (under their own control) and to develop productive linkages with outside organisations.

One of the risks of increasing formalisation is that a community may come to be dominated by an unrepresentative elite (Tarrow 1994). After all, formal structures in general are typically dominated by elites and have strict codes of behaviour (Whyte 1966). Community leaders have pre-set roles which are resistant to change (Cohen 1985: 32), and leaders maintain their positions through the regular exercise of specific skills (Whyte 1955). However, Cohen (1985: 34) has suggested that this can also happen with informal structures, where informal 'leaders' may have more influence within the community than formal ones. On the basis of social network analysis, Davies and Herbert (1993: 68) have pointed out that the formation of rigid cliques, with fellow-travellers and dissidents, is actually typical of many voluntary groups which have no hierarchy or authority structure linked to outsiders. The way forward, therefore, does not lie with eschewing formal organisation, but with ensuring both the inclusiveness of informal interactions and the accountability, responsiveness and representativeness of formal structures. Hastings *et al.* (1996: 18), for example, have made a number of recommendations in relation to accountability: adopting a membership structure which facilitates involvement from a wide range of local groups and interests; producing a regular newsletter or community magazine; undertaking community development work in parts of the area where community activity is limited; finding decent premises that are accessible and attractive, where residents can meet together and with other groups; checking that community representatives are accurately reflecting the needs and views of the wider local community (for example, through local surveys); and training and preparing new activists, and finding the resources to pay for this.

The issue of elitism is similar, though not quite the same, as the issue of the optimum size for a network of community activists. It can be safely assumed, on the basis of overwhelming research, that the group of activists will always constitute no more than a minority of the total of community members (although it should be remembered that the definition of 'activist' is inherently vague), and therefore measures to ensure their relatedness to the rest of the community will always be relevant. A smaller group, however, is likely to be more at risk of becoming a self-perpetuating elite, and less likely to be connected to the outside world, than a larger group. On the other hand, in a larger group communication and decision-making are likely to be more complex and more difficult, and there is a greater risk of fragmentation due to value conflicts, although this is balanced by a lower risk that loss of members will affect the group's viability (Skelcher *et al.* 1996: 19). What actually happens, of course, depends upon the values and practices of the individuals concerned, particularly those playing the role of 'supporters'.

With regard to inclusiveness generally, Crow and Allan (1994: xvi) have reminded us that although geographical presence may be necessary it is not usually a sufficient condition for an individual's inclusion in a community. This point has been amply reinforced by the literature on encapsulation and on community conflict discussed earlier in this chapter. More specifically, the literature on 'race' and ethnicity has pointed to the need for new forms of representation specific to black and minority ethnic communities, such as through religious and cultural organisations (Gilroy 1987; Harrison *et al.* 1995), even though this can serve to highlight differences and therefore increase racial tensions within an area (Jeffers *et al.* 1996). Gilchrist (1992) identified the stages followed in one successful attempt to overcome white racism and include black people in a community development process, namely: prioritising contact with black members of the community; bringing the issues and grievances raised by such contact back into the formal arena of the community association; confronting attitudes and practices directly through 'evaluating' the association's success in representing the whole community, by pointing out the discrepancies and presenting possible explanations for those discrepancies; setting up a training programme for all association members to raise their awareness of racism and examine ways of developing anti-racist strategies; and marginalising those who opted out of the training and development programme. With hindsight, however, this could be regarded as a high-risk approach which depended heavily for its success on the good will of the majority of the white population in the community.

Jerry Smith makes an important point about the meaning of representativeness which is relevant here:

> Elected councillors are representative in a narrow, political sense. In a broader, sociological sense, they are often anything but, being over-

whelmingly male, white and middle-aged. A community group with an imperfect constitution, but which draws its membership and its agenda from the residents for whom it speaks, is arguably more 'representative' than one which is scrupulously constitutional but elected at a poorly attended AGM and whose active members are disproportionately of one gender, ethnic or age group.

(J. Smith 1997: 177–8)

The point is that a community organisation is to be assessed not in terms of how representative of the community it is in a formal democratic sense but in terms of how well it reflects the views of that community in which it is based – that is, responsiveness and accountability to the community are just as important as formal representation, if not more so.

The issue of inclusiveness is similar to that of representativeness. Community organisations which are lacking in representativeness in Smith's sense, or lacking in responsiveness or accountability to their communities, are very likely to be exclusionary groups, in the sense that certain sections of the community will tend to be ignored by such groups. If community development is in the hands of such groups, then it is clear that it will tend to be one-sided and biased. Inclusiveness, however, refers to processes of informal interaction as well as those of formal organisations, and this is where the prescriptions of Hastings *et al.* (1996), Taylor (1995) and Skelcher *et al.* (1996) come into play, as well as the positive aspects of the self-help and conflict approaches. Indeed, it may not be stretching the point too far to suggest that the positive measures in all three approaches are all concerned with making both the community and its organisations as inclusive as possible. Community development is therefore to be identified with the development of the community as a whole, and development which is confined to one section of the community, such as white people, or working people, or non-disabled people, or established residents, or which omits one section such as a particular age group or ethnic group or newcomer group, cannot be regarded as community development. This is because such 'development' can only exacerbate internal tensions and divisions, and can therefore be damaging in the medium to long term.

What, then, counts as success in community development? The answer to this question remains disputed. Jerry Smith suggests that in Britain community-led initiatives such as Miles Platting Community Assembly (Manchester), Belle Isle Estate (Leeds), Pembroke Street (Plymouth) and Meadowell (North Tyneside) all succeeded because they were characterised by 'a strong, committed local leadership with a "vision" which enables it to link capital investment to jobs and training, and to use physical refurbishment to "lever" funds from non-housing sources to provide for other community needs' (J. Smith 1997: 173). Even some of these 'flagships', however, can be criticised for not being sufficiently inclusive, and they have not all stood the test of time (Belle Isle and Pembroke Street are perhaps notable exceptions). Understandably, therefore, other commentators, such as Power and Tunstall (1995), are less optimistic about the prospects for lasting community development in the absence of more radical social change. Without the latter, even the most (apparently) successful community development initiatives could be argued to be no more than 'spurious islands of social cohesion amongst the mass of the poor' (Watt 1999 – personal communication).

Nevertheless, J. Smith (1997: 179–80) has argued that community development can indeed be sustained, provided that three conditions are fulfilled: first, collective ownership, for example in the form of a tenant-run local housing company, with control over community assets such as community centres, youth and sports facilities, and with a Community Development Trust managing these assets and acting as a holding company for service-based community enterprises in security, environmental maintenance, community care, child care, catering, and property maintenance and management; second, 'community spirit', in the sense of 'psychological ownership' of an estate, involving a commitment to the future of the area; and third, community management, meaning localisation of service delivery under the control or strong influence of the community, for example Tenant Management Organisations.

Community ownership and management, as defined by J. Smith (1997), if sufficiently inclusive, would appear to be exactly what are required in order for a community to maximise the utility of its members. Such a policy therefore seems to be the logical conclusion to be drawn from a rational choice perspective. The third condition, community spirit, would probably follow from the satisfaction of the other two conditions (so again, perhaps, there is no need to invoke any theory of attachment). In practice, however, the vast majority of communities needing development are very far from owning and controlling their common resources. J. Smith (1997: 181) suggests three reasons why this should be: financial, because short-termism and uncertainty militate against the time-scales required for effective community involvement; organisational, because community development is dogged by competition among agencies for resources and power; and psychological, because those in authority are reluctant to hand over real power and resources to communities or to change traditional ways of delivering services. Arguably, however, these three reasons boil down to one, which is that there exist powerful exclusionary groups at national and local levels, and poor and deprived communities carry little political clout.

Successful community development may therefore require an element of action from outside the community to counter the damaging effects of these exclusionary groups. This argument brings us back to the question of the possibility of progressive technical assistance. This possibility is again debatable. Hastings *et al.* (1996: 36) list a number of factors associated with organisational weakness in a community, such as an absence of a history of community activism, a low level of community activity, network poverty, an absence of a representative body, lack of unity (or unicity) and a general lack of participation in voluntary organisations. Where all these gaps are filled, however, and where a level of consensus has been reached among the main participants about their roles and expectations, Hastings *et al.* (1996: 37) believe that 'top-down' initiatives (that is, technical assistance) can work. This belief, however, contrasts with their own finding from ten case studies to the effect that there was no substantial evidence that outside agencies were prepared to consider the need to change the way in which they conducted their business in order better to facilitate the community role (Hastings *et al.* 1996: 40). 'Success' therefore seems to be understood in a strictly limited sense, in terms of such 'positive impacts' as: raising local organisational capacity; raising local individual capacity; providing positive role models for other residents; creating optimism and a sense of pride in the area; and improving the image of the area held by outsiders (Hastings *et al.* 1996: 43). They conclude (p. 44) that many outside agencies 'are happy to ask the local community about their aspirations and preferences, but they are not willing to transfer the power to these communities to act on the basis of these preferences'. The result is that, as Hart *et al.* declare:

> Organisations are effectively creating a myth of empowerment by ignoring consumer demands; making closed decisions; not providing alternative choices; breaking promises; withholding information; not providing adequate support. Perhaps more significantly, they are paying lip-service to the notion of empowerment by engaging consumers in lesser decisions and not involving them in those considered by the community to be the significant ones.
> (Hart *et al.* 1997: 197)

Hart *et al.* (1997: 200) offer two further explanations for the lack of effective community empowerment. The first is that:

> Local service providers cannot deliver the participation that local residents demand, because they do not have the power to do so, their real accountability is elsewhere.

The second is that:

> Conversely, by demanding the empowerment of the citizen by the public sector, the government has also moved the responsibility for the success or failure of projects onto the individual. If those individuals within the community fail to get involved, there is no recourse to the government.

The first of these explanations refers to the structural characteristics of public and private bureaucracies which deny the possibility of autonomy for local service delivery units. The second points to an important aspect of government policy which denies its own responsibility for community empowerment. Both of these arguments will be considered in Chapter 4.

Skelcher *et al.* (1996: 45–6)'s comments point further to the existence of inherent weaknesses in community governance of any kind, and hence indirectly indicate the need for support from established forms of political organisation. The problem is that the strength of community networks lies to a large extent in their informality, but long-term stable governance requires the institution of formal relationships.

> However, their very informality places them outside the conventions of openness and public scrutiny to be found in other parts of the public sector. There is a dilemma here, since increasing the formalisation of the community network may undermine the very benefits it offers. It is important, therefore, that the outcomes of networks – in terms of decisions and strategies – have a point of reference or accountability somewhere within a formal governmental body. Without such accountability, the governance role of community networks is devalued.
>
> (Skelcher *et al.* 1996: 46)

Again, this introduces us to issues which will be covered more fully in Chapter 4.

Other researchers have argued that community action is essentially limited in the face of managerial, economic and class power (Mullan 1980; Saunders 1979; Cooper and Hawtin 1997 1998). The question is, however: how limited is this? Some writers, for example Loney (1983) and Crow and Allan (1994: 135), have pronounced a mixed verdict, concluding that the power of community groups to achieve their aims varies considerably from one case to another. Cooper and Hawtin (1997: 115–16), however, specifically criticise Taylor (1995)'s key ingredients for successful community development. They argue that contradictions are likely to arise between the priorities of a local community and the needs of the wider business community, that small-area-based targeted regeneration projects lead to the displacement of the problems to neighbouring areas and conflict among areas generally, and that Taylor's prescriptions assume no need for broader changes at the macro-political and economic levels:

> Existing power relationships and the structural causes of urban deprivation are not questioned and therefore remain intact. . . . In this context the long-term aim of sustainable regeneration through community development is unlikely to be achieved because the structural causes of neighbourhood decline – economic downturn, de-skilling, political and social exclusion and so forth – are not being addressed.
>
> (Cooper and Hawtin 1997: 115–16)

Cooper and Hawtin (1997)'s criticisms appear to imply that technical assistance approaches to community development are, on their own, inevitably doomed to failure. This is because such technical assistance is given according to the rules of an economic and political system that is repeatedly destructive of communities. However, this argument assumes that all technical assistance can be clearly identified as supporting or reinforcing the status quo. In reality, as we have seen earlier in this chapter, the situation is not usually clear-cut enough to allow for such definitive judgments. There is typically some room for manoeuvre, and the possibility of progressive technical assistance cannot be ruled out a priori. Communities are certainly linked into the wider society in order to survive, but the linkages are generally loose and fluid, and this presents opportunities for progress. Success in community development is therefore not an all-or-nothing scenario but rather a process of continually increasing community capacity and community control. It is not a matter of distinguishing once and for all between situations where 'people have gained genuine control over their lives' (Cooper and Hawtin 1997: 278) and those where they have not, but of identifying those processes which tend to move people in the direction of increasing control over their communities and those which do not. Community development is inherently fragile, because each community on its own has little power in relation to the global economy or national governments. Even the smallest investment in a local area, however, can make a significant difference to existing power relationships. The needs of the wider business community do not necessarily or always override the priorities of the local community, the development of one community does not have to be at the expense of another, and the development of a sufficiently large number of communities would almost certainly entail broader economic and political changes. In order to safeguard and enhance the achievements of community development, therefore, and to produce truly sustainable regeneration, the task is to apply the lessons described in this chapter on a wider basis, making appropriate use of forms of technical assistance, self-help and conflict strategy and tactics.

The real significance of Cooper and Hawtin's arguments is that they take us beyond the arena of community interaction to consider the relationships between community action and wider social forces. Hastings *et al.* (1996: 32) point out that community organisations usually have minimal input to some of the most important stages in community development, for example in analysing the problems of an estate within a wider framework and devising the overall approach. At a strategic level, community organisations have influenced the content of some initiatives, but generally their influence is confined to arguing for certain issues to be taken on board, for example housing issues and social and community concerns, but not employment, training or economic development. Most community involvement takes place in the implementation phase, after key decisions have all been taken. Cooper and Hawtin (1997) are stressing that this needs to be explained, and it cannot be done in terms of the rational choices made by community members. Rather:

> What is needed is a model which allows an examination of the *way* in which power is exerted over disadvantaged communities to exclude them. By developing a coherent understanding of the processes of social exclusion, it will be possible to design appropriate strategies for genuine community empowerment.
>
> (Cooper and Hawtin 1997: 106)

This will be discussed further in Chapter 4.

Returning to the issues discussed earlier in this chapter, it could be argued that the literature on community development has perhaps not paid sufficient attention to the importance of the social divisions which arise in real communities. For example, it might be that the conflict approach is more likely to succeed when the community concerned is more homogeneous, because, other things being equal, it is easier to mobilise such a community around a single issue. Such mobilisation, however, might further disadvantage a less powerful minority within the community who do not give this particular issue such a high priority. In general, a community which is dominated by a group of established residents is likely to become even more dominant after a process of community development unless specific steps are taken which have the effect of changing the balance of power within the community. Such steps are unlikely to be taken, however, without appropriate technical assistance, and the professionals who provide such assistance must be fully committed to the empowerment of the community as a whole (Popple 1995). The problem then is that the outside professionals will need to confront the established group with the evidence of its exclusionary character and, as in the example described by Gilchrist (1992), this can be a risky process. There is a case, therefore, not only for ensuring that technical assistance does indeed conform to certain standards of social justice, but also for making access to that assistance conditional upon the community's meeting certain standards of inclusionary practice. All of this requires a degree of state regulation, which will be discussed further in Chapter 5.

A final issue to consider in this chapter is that of whether community development needs to adopt a different approach in relation to communities based on kinship compared with those which are based on weaker ties of neighbourliness and shared identity with the area. As mentioned earlier, communities based on kinship will appear to be more coercive because of the unconditional obligations involved, but even in the most voluntary of communities individuals will be subject to a certain amount of constraint. For example, they may be unable to leave the area because of their poverty, or they may be newcomers to the area and not yet accepted by the community. It seems likely that poorer communities which are more kinship-based will need more technical assistance in the form of access to paid employment, while poorer communities which are more anonymous will require more community work in bringing people together and building up organisational capacity in the area. It is dangerous to generalise on this, however, and in each case preliminary work with the community will be indispensable in deciding what is the most appropriate approach to take. It may be the case, for instance, that kinship has become less important in the construction of community than it was in the past, but it is not clear that anything in particular follows from this with regard to how one should approach the issue of community development. Rational choice theory suggests that an open-minded empirical approach is most advisable in this area.

4 Contractual relations and social divisions

In the previous chapter, a distinction was made between different types of social relations on the basis of the ways in which they institutionalise co-operative human action. For example, domestic relations institutionalise co-operation through a labour process which has characteristic forms of exploitation and assignations of moral obligation. Similarly, neighbourly relations institutionalise co-operation through reciprocity of a specific type, and since these relations are non-exploitative they could be regarded as a model to be followed and promoted. Both domestic and neighbourly or informal group relations, however, can and do develop into more formal arrangements where reciprocal interaction is direct and/or guaranteed. Arrangements of this kind are called contractual arrangements. For example, within domestic relations, the marriage contract has developed historically, originally as a way of securing a man's 'ownership' of his wife (or wives) (Pateman 1988). Within community relations, contractual arrangements develop typically in order to secure the effective delivery of community services, and to establish a degree of community 'ownership' over communal facilities and assets. The whole point of contracts is that they are legally binding on the contracting parties: entry into the contractual relationship is voluntary, but once entered into the parties accept certain obligations to each other. It is this 'rule of law' which makes possible substantive and non-ritualistic social relations that go beyond the purely personal relations of home and community.

Contractual relations have important advantages over domestic and informal group relations. They are better able to secure specific performance and therefore more efficient economically. They are potentially fairer than domestic relations because they are based on formal equality (equal exchange), and fairer than informal group relations because within the latter reciprocity is not always forthcoming or equal. For these and other reasons, many thinkers, from Adam Smith to Friedrich von Hayek, have argued that societies are best organised through a system of contractual relations, although many of these thinkers have balked at extending this system into the domestic sphere. From a rational choice perspective, such contractarianism seems logical, because it allows maximum freedom for individuals to enter into the social relations that they judge to be most beneficial for them. There is a continuing dynamic, however, between contractualisation and informality, which Adam Smith himself recognised. As mentioned earlier, contractual relations are dependent upon the existence of social capital, but social capital itself has developed unevenly in a historical and geographical sense, resulting in differential advantages for contracting parties. Crudely speaking, where social capital has developed most, contractual relations have been able to flourish most successfully (Putnam 1993). Although contractual relations assume formal equality between the parties, therefore, these same parties may be highly unequal in terms of their ownership of both social and private capital. In such circumstances, the extension of contractual relations can be oppressive for those whose capital is meagre or non-existent. This in turn gives rise to demands that contractual relations should be limited or regulated.

The inherent advantages of contractual relations from a rational choice point of view suggest that they should be promoted wherever practicable, while their contextual disadvantages should be mitigated as far as possible so as to achieve substantive equality among the contracting parties. In the absence of such equality, contractual relations are likely to have the effect of institutionalising forms of exploitation. This is in fact what has happened with the development of capitalism and bureaucratised labour. Because private capital accumulated under the ownership of minority elites, new social class divisions were created between those who owned such capital and those who did not. Further capital accumulation then resulted in the formation of bureaucracies, in which voluntary and formally equal interaction became replaced by hierarchical domination. Yet these new relations were still contractual, being based on a contract between an employer and an employee. Such contracts have little in common with the classic market contract between a seller and a buyer: rather than being designed as a fair and equal exchange, the employment contract is intended as a means of control over the employee. The latter is paid a wage or salary, but in return she or he does not simply produce a certain output, but also submits to the employer's particular regime. From a rational choice perspective, this is problematic because it means a denial of the individual's free choice, although it has been argued that this is compensated to some extent by the wages received (for example, see Beynon 1975). The rational expectation is then for individuals to become self-employed or run their own businesses wherever possible. The main factor which prevents this from happening is the capacity of corporations (businesses owned by groups of people, for example a family or a collection of shareholders) to dominate markets, to operate increasingly on a global scale, and to undercut and crowd out their smaller and less powerful competitors. Again, this suggests a need for specific regulation and constraints.

In the history of political thought, there has been a long debate about whether interaction between free individuals (in a so-called 'state of nature') is likely to prove constructive or destructive (originally, Locke versus Hobbes, and later liberalism versus conservatism). Such a state of nature, however, is a myth, as is the natural law that goes with it. The reality is, as we have seen in previous chapters, that social interaction always takes place within already existing institutional contexts, and the rules of co-operation and conflict are also developed within those contexts, such as the family and community. The attraction of contractual relations is that they offer the promise of being able to break free from domestic and communal obligations and to engage directly with strangers for the purpose of mutual advantage. A rational choice perspective suggests that since individuals act so as to maximise their utility, the general effect of extending the scope of contractual relations should be productive rather than harmful. However, the reality again is that individuals continue to remain embedded within familial and informal group structures, enabling some of them to gain greater advantage from contractual relations than others. In this situation, contractualisation is typically both constructive (e.g. for owners) and destructive (e.g. for non-owners).

There remains a problem for rational choice theory in explaining how free contractual relations become transformed into oppressive bureaucratic relations. Historically, as mentioned above, this has happened because of the way in which private capital accumulates, enabling an exclusive group of capital owners to seize and retain control over the production of goods. Non-owners then freely contract their labour-power to such owners, but their labour is alienated from them and they are subject to what Foucault (1977) has called 'techniques of domination'. With the institutionalisation of this employer–employee relationship throughout society, the associated techniques of domination come to be applied in areas of work that appear far removed from that of capitalist production.

As Weber (1968) recognised, the growth of bureaucracy can itself be interpreted as a rational process, because it is designed to achieve clear goals with maximum efficiency. This argument, however, applies only to the rationality of the organisation in serving the interests of an exclusive elite, not to that of the individuals working within that organisation. The problem with Weber's approach is that it appears to subsume the autonomy of the individual within a wider collective 'spirit', and this tends to play down the significance of alienated labour and social control. From a rational choice perspective, it is the collective which must justify itself to the individual, not the other way round.

A crucial question to be posed of contemporary contractual relations, then, is the extent to which they are constructive or destructive of individual and collective empowerment. This question can be interpreted at a number of different levels: family, community, and wider economy and society. At a family level, a major contractual relation is that of marriage, and this can be constructive in the sense of promoting permanency and stability, but destructive in reinforcing female subordination. At a community level, contractual relations can be associated with any of the three major types of approach in community development: they can be used either to establish bureaucratic authority over individuals (for example, in the disempowering forms of technical assistance) or to free individuals from such authority (for example, in the setting up of resident-controlled companies). At the level of the formal economy, they can be constructive in opening up new opportunities for mutual benefit (for example through 'free trade'), and they can be destructive in undermining informal systems of mutual aid and replacing them with formal systems of supervision and control.

The key issue of contractual relations, therefore, can perhaps be framed in terms of how they can be made to be more constructive and less destructive, more empowering and less disempowering. The resolution of this issue itself depends upon the extent to which contractual relations have become institutionalised within 'structures of dominance', resulting in systematic oppression and social exclusion. This question can only be fully answered when we come to consider systems of governance (Chapter 5), because in contemporary society the state is intimately involved in the construction of such structures. Here, it is appropriate to look at how intractable class divisions in particular are, because there is clearly a connection between the degree of openness of a class structure and the opportunities for individuals to maximise their utility. From a rational choice perspective, a society with greater internal social mobility should be less exclusionary of social groups (compare the discussion of communities in Chapter 3), although this does not necessarily mean that it will be less exploitative of individual members (consider Young 1961 – a meritocracy can be even more oppressive than a society in which those at the top do not 'deserve' to be there).

Classes form largely on the basis of shared positions in the formal contractual economy, that is based on standard types of employment contract (Marshall *et al.* 1989). There is a sense, therefore, in which modern class divisions are crystallisations of relatively inchoate sets of contractual relations. One problem with many studies of social mobility, however, especially in England, is that they are articulated within static programmes of 'class analysis' which have little bearing on the issue of the formation and maintenance of exclusionary groups or the dynamics of contractualisation (Goldthorpe 1987; Marshall *et al.* 1989). In these studies, social mobility is understood as a change in the class position and orientation of individuals (from 'origins' to 'destinations'), not in terms of processes of transition of social groups into and out of key social networks and institutions. Payne (1992: 231), for example, points out that 'the boundaries between the social divisions of the three classes [service class, intermediate class, and working class] have weakened', in the sense that it has become more likely for individuals to move from one class to another. This does not tell us, however, whether the class structure as a whole has become more or less open to any given social grouping. It is also far from clear why the upward 'moving column' of material mobility to which Payne refers should present a problem for a class-based perspective, because increased material prosperity for all is not incompatible with a growing gap between rich and poor. There is also no contradiction between a general increase in upward mobility (whether absolute or relative) and a reduced upward mobility for a number of specific social groups. In any case, Payne's optimism is directly contradicted by Erikson and Goldthorpe (1992)'s conclusion that the class barriers to social mobility have remained more or less unchanged over the last thirty years.

In contrast to the English approach to class analysis, three other approaches to social mobility can be distinguished. One is associated with the so-called 'sociology of consumption' (Burrows and Marsh 1992), and derives from the work of Pahl (1984 1988) and Saunders (1986). The second adopts a post-industrial international comparative perspective, and is identified with the work of Esping-Andersen and his collaborators (Esping-Andersen 1993). The third proposes a more explicitly dynamical approach, and is expounded principally by Leisering and Walker (1998).

The first approach, which I call consumptionist, holds that consumption activity forms an increasingly important source of social stratification independent of that deriving from social class. The main social classes are allegedly fusing gradually into an increasingly comfortable, culturally standardised, and privatised 'middle mass' (Saunders 1986; Pahl 1988). Consequently, divisions arising from production are said to be declining in importance, while those arising from consumption are becoming more pronounced. In practice, however, even in the USA where these processes are alleged to be most advanced, there is little evidence to suggest that the establishment of a 'mass culture' has been associated with a decline in class-based forms of social organisation (Grusky 1994: 21). It is simply not the case that, just because the 'moving column' of material mobility (to use Payne's expression) involves increasing consumption, the role of production is bound to be downgraded.

The relevance of the consumptionist approach here is that it is associated with an argument that the new 'middle mass' has become increasingly detached from a socially isolated and hopeless 'underclass' (Auletta 1982; Pahl 1988), an argument which has been considered in much more detail in Morris (1994) (see below, pp. 94–95). However, while being highly critical of the 'class analysis' approach, the consumptionist writers have not proposed any coherent alternative criteria for the identification and measurement of social mobility, whether in relation to participation in the labour market, dependence on state benefits, or 'deserving' status.

The international comparative approach looks potentially more fruitful, for three reasons. It is based on a greater breadth and depth of empirical evidence, it has a more pragmatic approach to ideological and theoretical assumptions, and it focuses on the causes of social change as well as its outcomes. The question which Esping-Andersen poses is how recent changes in advanced capitalist labour processes have affected social mobility and class formation. Evidence from six countries (Britain, Germany, Sweden, Norway,

USA and Canada) indicates some potential for class closure (a socially constructed system of barriers to upward social mobility) 'in terms of a relatively closed mobility circuit between unskilled service jobs, sales jobs, and including probably also unemployment and household work' (Esping-Andersen 1993: 231). The extent to which this has actually occurred, however, appears to vary, with major differences emerging between the American countries, the Scandinavian countries, Britain and Germany. Esping-Andersen (1993: 235) concludes that in the American and Scandinavian countries 'from the point of view of class formation, fluidity and mobility patterns are simply too strong for any significant social closure to occur'. In America, this is due primarily to the expansion of (low-paid) private sector service jobs, and in Scandinavia it is the result mainly of the growth of the public service sector. In Britain and Germany, in contrast, mobility is more restricted, but even in these countries the 'degree of class closure is highly uncertain' (Esping-Andersen 1993: 235). Esping-Andersen's general point is that although recent developments in capitalist labour processes have created the potential for the formation of a new non-mobile 'underclass', there is some doubt about whether this has actually happened, and if it does happen it is likely to take different forms in different parts of the world.

Esping-Andersen qualifies his conclusion in two ways, the first of which relates to gender and the second to education. These factors, together with the welfare state, are used to explain the international variation in mobility regimes. On gender, Esping-Andersen points to the possibility of an underprivileged 'class' of unskilled women, moving within a closed circuit between unskilled services, low-end sales and low-end clerical work (Esping-Andersen 1993: 235). This could develop in any of the six study countries. On education, he stresses that the upward mobility out of the (private or public) service jobs is increasingly related to the possession of educational qualifications, so those without such qualifications may find themselves moving only within 'a circuit of essentially similar unattractive jobs' (Esping-Andersen 1993: 235), which could turn out to be a form of class closure. Another effect of the increasing importance of educational qualifications is that mobility to the top layers of the stratification system becomes more and more difficult. Consequently, 'the role of education in the post-industrial order may be to assure openness at the lower rungs of the stratification, but solidification and class closure at the top' (Esping-Andersen 1993: 235–6). The differences in national mobility regimes can be explained by reference to the degree of citizen participation in further and higher education (high in America and Scandinavia, low in Britain and Germany), the degree of public welfare provision relative to private welfare (high in Scandinavia, low in America), and the nature and extent of female participation in the labour market (high but segregated in Scandinavia, high but less segregated in America, lower and segregated in Britain and Germany).

Empirical research therefore tends to suggest that, in attempting to understand class relations (arising mainly out of the formal contractual economy) and social change, a more holistic approach needs to be adopted, that is the labour market needs to be considered alongside systems of education, welfare, citizenship rights and the ascription of gender roles. This approach will be discussed further in Chapter 5.

In their discussions of social mobility, both consumptionist and comparative approaches highlight the question of the existence and character of an 'underclass' or 'outsider' group, which is socially distinct from (and below) the main social classes. Theories of social exclusion have therefore been framed mainly in relation to this alleged entity. For example, van Parijs (1987) has talked of an insider–outsider cleavage in terms of 'a closed labour market of (upgraded) insiders enjoying high wages and job security, and a swelling army of outsiders including youth, long-term unemployed, early retirees, and discouraged workers' (quoted in Esping-Andersen 1994: 699). These theories have been comprehensively and systematically reviewed by Morris (1994) (see also Morris and Scott 1996).

Morris (1994: 80) identifies two general theoretical or ideological positions with respect to an 'underclass'. One is broadly 'cultural', seeing the source of their social exclusion as lying in the attitudes and behaviour of the underclass itself. For example, Murray (1984) has argued that welfare dependency has encouraged both the break-up of the nuclear family household and socialisation into a counter-culture which devalues work and promotes dependency and/or criminality. The other is termed 'structural', and sees the source of social exclusion as lying in the structured inequality which disadvantages particular groups in society, for example the failure to provide sufficient secure employment to meet demand, and the consequent destabilisation of the male breadwinner role.

Some writers, notably Wilson (1987), have attempted to integrate 'structural' and 'cultural' approaches, but Morris argues that they are irreconcilable (Morris 1994: 87). She sees the 'cultural' position as incorrect and ideological, and the 'structural' position as correct and scientific. Many of her criticisms of the 'culture' theorists appear to be valid, for example, lack of evidence for a 'culture of dependency' or for a link between nuclear family break-up and decline of work ethic. It is not possible, however, to identify a clear boundary between 'structure' and 'culture', at least not without being far more explicit about the theoretical underpinnings of the 'structural' approach. A social structure is, after all, only an ordered set of social relations, and these relations could just as well be 'cultural' as 'economic'. It may not be the theoretical approach of the 'culturalists' which is at fault, but rather the particular empirical evidence they rely on and the correlations which they draw between different pieces of such 'evidence'. To be more specific, their assertions about the nature of people's attitudes (for example in relation to paid work) may be incorrect, as also their assumptions about the links between such attitudes and evidence of irresponsible or criminal behaviour. Their overall approach, however, which sees action as produced by individual choice against a background of social pressures and norms, is not to be dismissed so easily.

The structural factors which Morris regards as most important in giving rise to social exclusion are the labour market and the state. She is uncertain as to which of these has priority, and therefore suggests that they relate to two different issues (social class and social citizenship, respectively). The whole force of the concept of 'underclass', however, is precisely to make a connection between these two issues, by implying that those who do not fit into the class structure will tend to be the same people who are excluded from social citizenship. Other structural factors which Morris mentions include social isolation, racism, and traditional gender roles, but she does not make it clear how these factors relate to the (more fundamental?) structural factors of labour market and state. It is at least arguable that structures of community, white dominance and patriarchy are closely bound up with class and politics, and therefore it is reasonable to expect a more holistic approach to this question. For example, in the American context, the issue is surely not whether it is racism or unemployment which is responsible for the exclusion of the 'ghetto poor' (Wilson 1987), but how precisely capital flows and racial discrimination combine so as to produce the ghetto phenomenon. Or again, in relation to lone mothers, the issue is not so much whether they might form an underclass (Murray says yes, Morris says no), but the precise ways in which capitalist structures based on male wage-labour oppress women with responsibilities for children. In this context, it is perhaps worth noting that American research has indicated that it is not single motherhood as such which causes the social exclusion of this group, but the combination of single motherhood with social isolation and lack of exploitable skills (Jencks and Petersen 1991). Indeed, for many unskilled married women, the position may not be so very different (see Esping-Andersen's comments on women referred to earlier).

Perhaps the main problem with Morris' 'structural' approach is that it neglects the role of agency, and in particular the views and practices of the socially excluded themselves. What, after all, is a 'structural' factor but a social process which has been abstracted from human activity? One example should serve to clarify this point. Gallie (1994), who largely shares Morris' 'structural' approach, has argued that the chances of obtaining paid employment are related to the structural conditions of the labour market rather than to 'cultural' considerations such as the degree of commitment to work. All studies of the labour market have shown, however, that 'informal patterns of association can be critical in determining who is successful in the search for employment' (Morris 1995: 38; see also Coleman 1990; Daniel 1990), and such informal connections would appear, in Gallie's and Morris' terms, to be 'cultural' rather than 'structural'. The distinction between 'structural' and 'cultural' factors is therefore either not as clear-cut as these writers claim, or else the way in which they wish to draw it is theoretically flawed. Perhaps the important distinction, after all, is not one between 'structure' and 'culture' (which is in fact based on an outdated base/superstructure model of society), but one between progressive and reactionary social forces, between social processes which promote social inclusion and those which lead to social exclusion, between processes which increase and those which reduce the degree of control which people exercise over their everyday lives. It should be noted, however, that this suggestion raises many further questions about the theoretical bases on which such distinctions might be made, and some of these questions are considered in Chapters 5 and 6.

The third approach to social mobility explicitly allows for the actions of individual human beings in determining the outcomes of social processes. This dynamic approach conceptualises society as existing in a condition of continual flux, in which individuals follow trajectories that consist of sequences of states and transitions (Walker and Leisering 1998: 18). Walker and Leisering (1998: 24) argue that: 'Knowing the histories of individuals, their trajectories in appropriate domains, and the institutions and sequence of events that have impacted on their lives, should make it possible to disentangle the effects of personal and structural factors.' In other words, the solution to the problem of how to understand the deep causation of social change lies through the conduct of longitudinal studies of appropriately contextualised interactions among individuals. The proponents of this dynamic approach, however, do not explain how particular domains, contexts, institutions, etc., come to be constructed as 'appropriate'. Theirs is essentially an empirical theory of agency, and one which does not tell us how to distinguish, for example, between structurally probable and improbable trajectories. There is also a hint of positivism in the theory, in that it suggests that social change might be explicable entirely in terms of patterns of observed events.

The theory used in this book is dynamic, in that it is based on the courses of action followed by individuals in time, but it is not positivistic because it views individuals as essentially autonomous agents. The patterns it conceptualises are those produced by rational choice not behavioural routines. Rational choice theory can be construed as a normative theory of agency, and for this reason it has been supplemented by 'structural' concepts such as those of exploitation and domination. In general terms, this book has shown that individuals build up their social capital through their family connections (as explained in Chapter 2) and through their local community networks (as described in Chapter 3). Families and communities, however, are already differentiated along class lines, and this means that social capital also varies according to social class (Hall 1997). This inequality of social capital then results in a differential access to contractual relations and unequal opportunities for social mobility. Thus the combination of all the free rational choices made by individuals produces a situation in which some individuals are systematically exploited and oppressed by others. This is achieved and maintained primarily through the dominance of private capital, whose existence is itself premised on the individuated possession of utility. The assumption that individuals act so as to maximise their value is itself based on the assumption that they can 'own' this value that they are maximising. In a relationship of exploitation, however, part of this value is alienated from the exploited and accrues to the exploiter. Exploitation in the labour process then reinforces and exacerbates the inequalities in social capital which individuals already bring with them to the labour process. In this way, 'structural' patterns emerge which appear to deny the reality of human agency. However, the social forces which underpin exploitation can be resisted, so the position of the exploiters is not unassailable. This point is discussed further in Chapters 5 and 6.

The argument here is essentially that it is the nature of the exploitation in the labour process which is fundamentally responsible for social polarisation (understood in terms of a growing gap between rich and poor, and between the powerful and the powerless), and hence for social exclusion (understood in terms of the denial of access to the standard of living enjoyed by mainstream society). In advanced capitalist countries such as Britain there are two main types of labour process. The first is generalised commodity production, where labour itself is a commodity. The second is the domestic labour process, where labour is not commodified. (Other types of labour process in advanced capitalist countries include simple commodity production, and forms of voluntary work, but these are less important and therefore not discussed in this book.)

Under generalised commodity production, labour is exploited by being paid less than the value of the goods or services which it produces. Under the domestic labour process (discussed in Chapter 2), labour is exploited by not being paid at all (in money or in kind), or by being paid at a rate which bears little or no relation to the value of its product. The nature of the exploitation in the two cases is entirely different. In the former case it gives rise to the reproduction and expansion of capital, and in the latter case to the reproduction and growth of labour. It is precisely their interconnection, however, which is the key to understanding the causation of social exclusion – the key which unlocks the secret of how free people become oppressed. Basically, non-commodified domestic labour processes produce and reproduce the labour required for commodified labour processes, while commodified labour processes produce and reproduce the capital which is required to pay labour what it needs to maintain its domestic economy. This is a complex and delicate relationship, which can easily break down as a result of changes in either type of labour process. Examples of such changes include a growth in the numbers of lone mothers and a decline in the profitability of certain types of commodity production. Both of these can lead to the disconnection of domestic labour from commodified labour. In the former case, this is because of the burdens of child care, and in the latter case because of the decline in demand for commodified labour. This fragility of the link between domestic and commodified labour presents risks to the individuals affected in terms of increased exploitation and immiseration (because of the excess of labour supply over demand), but also opportunities for resistance and transformation (because of the challenge posed by women to the established pattern of double exploitation).

The above conception of a duality of interrelated labour processes can be used to make sense of research findings such as those of Esping-Andersen and his colleagues. For example, what Esping-Andersen (1993: 235) calls the 'gender-divided process of class formation' can to some extent be related to the fact that a large proportion of women are doubly exploited in the domestic economy. This double exploitation follows from the fact that they perform labour not only for their male partners, but also for their children, for which they receive no equivalent value (Somerville 1994). The existence of such double exploitation in the home is another reason why, as Morris (1994) has argued, the term 'underclass' is simply not appropriate to understanding the position of women in society. However, Morris does not follow up this argument to question the whole rationale of the orthodox approach to 'class analysis' based on people's occupations. Esping-Andersen's excluded group of unskilled women is in fact produced not by capitalist labour processes alone but by the duality of capitalist and domestic labour processes. In the face of such multiple exploitation, lone parenthood can actually be regarded as a means of defence (because of the elimination of domestic male exploitation), although not necessarily a very effective one.

Similarly, the role of education in increasing or reducing social mobility can be explained by reference to the effects of domestic labour in providing 'added value' to the next generation in relation to the opportunities provided by changes in capitalist labour processes. Again, it is the interrelationship between labour processes of the two types which defines the structural role of the processes concerned. The capacity to provide 'added value' to children, for example, will to some extent be related to the function of the parents in capitalist labour processes, and the capacity for young people to take advantage of new job opportunities will to some extent be related to the 'added value' which they have had invested in them by their parents. The picture is further complicated by the fact that it relates only to the economic dimension of social exclusion. For education in particular, the political/institutional dimension, encompassing mainly the state education system, is just as important for determining social outcomes. This dimension has its own capitalistic (or quasi-capitalistic) labour processes, and it has its own ascriptions of roles for domestic labour, for example, on homework, discipline, and moral and financial support for schools and the schooling process.

Labour process analysis therefore has considerable potential for explaining social exclusion arising from forms of capitalist and domestic exploitation. It suggests that women and unskilled people will be particularly likely to lose out, and this is confirmed by the findings of empirical research. The analysis also explains why the dimensions of gender and skill, although always co-present, are nevertheless articulated on quite different bases.

Katznelson (1986) suggests that the labour process represents the first of a number of levels at which social class can be analysed. The second level to consider would then be the level of social reproduction, which encompasses all the means by which labour is reproduced in the wider society. It has long been recognised that such social reproduction involves processes of cumulative advantage and disadvantage, and is therefore a major source of social division and exclusion (Bourdieu and Passeron 1977). The domestic labour process itself is one of the types of process contributing to social reproduction, and therefore provides a key link between the two levels. Of the other types of process, probably the most important are those associated with state regulation: legal and political institutions, national economic and financial management, education, defence and welfare in the broadest sense. All of these processes, separately or together, can either mitigate or exacerbate the forms of division and exclusion arising from the development of the (dual) labour process. The general tendency of their development, however, is to produce a 'division of welfare' (Titmuss 1958) which mirrors rather than reforms the prevailing division of labour (Mann 1992) – this in itself suggests that the labour process is in some sense more fundamental.

This tendency becomes considerably stronger when the duality of labour processes is considered, that is, domestic labour as well as wage-labour. This is because much of state regulation is concerned with reinforcing certain norms of the domestic economy, as well as increasing productivity of labour and profitability of capital. The result is that state policies and services reflect the domestic division of labour as well as the capitalist division of labour. For example, in a country where as many women as men participate in the labour market, this is likely to be reflected in greater state provision of welfare for women (and this can itself include the provision of employment, thus reinforcing the role of women in the labour market). Or again, so long as the responsibility for child care remains primarily with women, it is unlikely that their overall position in the labour market will ever be equal to that of men. This inequality will then continue to be reflected in state regulation which condones sex segregation in the workplace and 'supports' female caring in the home.

Social reproduction analysis could include a treatment of class 'strategies' of inclusion and exclusion such as those originally identified by Parkin (1979). The key argument here is that social classes at this level can be characterised in terms of the social bases on which they exclude other people from their membership. The middle classes, for example, can be identified in terms of the 'assets' which they hold relating to property, credentials and social organisation (Savage *et al.* 1992). Similarly, the working-class can be recognised as those whose main 'asset' is labour power. This serves to distinguish them from those who do not participate, or (according to the working class exclusionary strategy) do not deserve to participate, in the labour market. In Britain, traditionally such 'non-deserving' cases have been mainly women, ethnic minorities, older people and foreigners generally (Mann 1992). In such ways, it can be seen that what might be called a political-ideological dimension tends to reinforce the social exclusion which is already being generated through the labour process. This tendency, however, is by no means inevitable, and it is important to bear in mind that inclusionary political action is possible, and can be successful.

The reference to the exclusion of ethnic minorities and older people suggests that there may be social bases for exclusion other than those deriving from the labour process (which is the source of the 'assets' mentioned above). If exploitation is the key to explaining social exclusion, then discrimination on grounds of 'race' or age presents a problem, because there is no counterpart to such discrimination in either the capitalist or the domestic labour process – contrast discrimination on grounds of sex or skill. It seems, therefore, that exclusion based on 'race' or age is likely to have its source elsewhere (for example, based on exclusionary homogeneous 'communities' or 'clubs' going beyond a local level, or on patterns of labour market segmentation, or on bureaucratic constructions of formal labour market 'careers'), though this should not be taken to imply that it is less deep-rooted or less impervious to change. There are those who argue that the capitalist labour process is inherently racialised, particularly in the USA (Leiman 1993), but it is difficult to see how capitalist exploitation in a racially divided country is radically different from that in one which is racially more homogeneous.

Patterns of exploitation in capitalist labour processes are reinforced by the assumption that workers are paid fairly, according to their skills, experience and effort, that is according to the value of their individual labour. It follows that the groups most likely to be socially excluded are people burdened with domestic duties (for example, carers), lacking job skills (for example, untrained or impaired in some way), lacking relevant experience (for example, school-leavers or those made redundant in declining industries), and (of course!) the lazy, the workshy, and the criminally inclined. Other groups could be excluded on grounds of age (for example, people under 18 and over 65) or 'race' (as in the USA, apparently). The former is often justified, though unconvincingly, on grounds of skills and ability (immaturity of the young, declining faculties of the old), but the latter is more obviously a product of group exclusivity and prejudice against 'outsiders'.

Exploitation in the capitalist and domestic labour processes therefore gives rise to characteristic patterns of social division and exclusion based on class, sex and skill. Current changes in capital–labour relations in a variety of countries can be explained by reference to the articulation of such characteristic patterns. It is primarily the dual labour process which determines the tendency for the social exclusion of people who are female, unskilled, or so-called 'economically inactive'. This represents the first level of social exclusion construction.

Social division and exclusion which are originated at this first level are then largely conserved and reproduced through social institutions outside of the labour process, in particular through law, politics, education and welfare, with these institutions themselves assuming the form of capitalist and domestic labour processes. The vying for power among different groups at this second level, for example, between employers' and workers' organisations, or between middle classes and working classes, then produces two types of exclusionary effect. The first type consists of modified forms of old exclusions deriving from the exploitation of labour, for example exclusions of women and unskilled, and the second type consists of new exclusions, for example, of foreigners, immigrants and non-whites, or of young or old people, which are generated primarily at the level of politics and culture.

Finally, further exclusions are created at a moral or ideological level. Here, prevailing assumptions about appropriate roles in the domestic and capitalist labour processes, as well as in social reproduction more generally, give rise to the negative labelling, punitive treatment and possible exclusion of those whose characteristics or behaviour do not conform to the expected norms (as mediated through legal, political, cultural and communications systems). All three levels are in reality overlapping and enmeshed together, and can be distinguished from each other only for the purpose of conceptual analysis.

Combating social divisions

As a consequence of being situated in a real context of exploitative labour processes, therefore, rational choice theory develops into a theory of social division and social exclusion. Exclusionary groups form in order to maximise the utility of their members, and this results in the growth of networks based on (among other things) social class. Individuals who cannot gain membership of such networks then become 'socially excluded'. Social exclusion is thus produced by the lack of access to the contractual and other relations which form the basis for class formation. The socially excluded are those who find themselves outside of the class relations arising from contractual arrangements.

Lack of mobility into contractual relations is clearly not the same thing as lack of mobility within the class system. There is a difference between an exploited class which has difficulty in emancipating itself and groups of people who are excluded from the labour market altogether. Nevertheless, as shown above, there is a link between the two, in that it is the nature of the exploitation, not only in the capitalist labour process but also in the domestic labour process, which helps to explain the general character of excluded groups. Overcoming oppression and exploitation, therefore, necessarily requires an alliance among all oppressed groups.

The issue of collective resistance to oppression at this level can be considered in the same way as that of community development discussed in Chapter 3. There it was noted that in spite of considerable evidence showing what works in community development communities were still largely being denied the opportunities they needed. As Cooper and Hawtin (1997: 106) put it: 'What is needed is a model which allows an examination of the *way* in which power is exerted over disadvantaged communities to exclude them.' Now it can be seen that the power concerned is that of private capital (the state is considered in Chapter 5), which essentially develops communities on its own terms and therefore denies the autonomy of those communities and hence of their individual members. Autonomy therefore has to be recaptured by the community as a whole developing its own social and private capital so as to put its relationship with external powers on a more equal footing.

As for communities, so for individuals and groups more generally. The labour movement, for example, could be regarded as a community in a broader sense, arising from a common experience of exploitative labour relations, and giving rise to working class organisations such as trade unions. On the whole, however, such organisations are reactive rather than proactive, that is they seek an accommodation with private capital through 'free collective bargaining', rather than the overthrow of exploitative relations and the establishment of workers' control. Their stance is therefore analogous with that of the 'self-help' approach in community development, with which in fact they are strongly linked (through the co-operative movement). Trade unions can therefore be successful in their defence of individual members, in building social capital generally and in securing a better deal from employers for all their members, but they cannot be expected to achieve a significant increase in social mobility or a radical change in existing class relations.

So how exactly is power exerted over people so as to oppress and exploit them? Within families, it is achieved through the social construction of the domestic labour process (see Chapter 2). Within the labour market, it is achieved through the exchange of wages for labour-power, which is then expected to perform according to the employment contract. In both cases, the compliance of the individual is secured through the individual's own free choice (even in an arranged marriage, the consent of the individual is required). It is then typically but incorrectly assumed that the individual, having chosen her or his role, has acquiesced in the oppression that goes with it, and that thereafter they are individually responsible for what happens to them in playing that role. This assumption of individual responsibility is then used to absolve the oppressor from their own responsibility for the situation. Consequently, this assumption lies at the core of ideologies which support the power of capital.

Healy (1997) provides a good example of the approach of private capital in relation to the regeneration of Cruddas Park. She points out that although business people played an active and positive role, they attributed problems to individual people rather than institutional structures, and were not interested in a lasting commitment and long-term perspective of systematic institution-building aiming at enabling the community to take care of its own future problems. As was seen in Chapter 3, this is a common fault of technical assistance programmes. The point can be extended, however, to the approach of employers in dealing with their workforce: although employers may be keen to see their employees as skilled and well-developed as possible in terms of job-related criteria, they are not generally interested in reshaping the company to meet the workers' needs for individual or group autonomy, and they are certainly not aiming to enable the workforce to take control of the company itself.

The way forward in dealing with private capital is far from clear. In general terms, if we accept that it is desirable for social relations beyond family and community to be contractual relations in order to maximise value for all, then we should aim to expand non-exploitative contractual relations and eliminate exploitative ones. It is difficult to see how this can be achieved except by the breaking up of complex hierarchical organisations and the promotion of genuine self-employment. This will make it less likely that a choice to enter into a contractual agreement will commit an individual to her or his own exploitation. The socialist alternative, namely the replacement of private capital by forms of collective ownership, would have the merit of abolishing exploitative contractual relations, but also the disadvantage of overriding individual ownership of capital. Socialism would therefore result in new problems of free-riding by individuals and oppression by the collective. These arguments are considered further in Chapter 5.

The argument about the limitations of socialism is typically answered by an appeal to a principle of subsidiarity, that is that the forms of collective ownership and control should be developed at the lowest level possible that is compatible with individual freedom (for example, the system of workers' self-management in the former Yugoslavia). The idea is that socialism can be saved by abandoning its statist form and advocating a radically decentralised version. The problem with this, however, is that the lowest level of ownership compatible with individual freedom may well be individual ownership. It is true that collective ownership and control of many goods may be desirable in the interests of maximising value for all members of the collective, but this needs to be justified in every case: collectivisation needs to be shown to be an enhancement of individual freedom, not a restriction. In the case of a workers' collective, for example, so-called 'scientific management' teaches us that there may be a trade-off between reduced autonomy for individuals at work and increased wages which can increase their freedom of action outside of work. The main point, however, is that this is a trade-off which the workers themselves should be able to decide to make. In theory, workers could be emancipated through self-employment rather than through socialism.

To a great extent, workplaces can be regarded as contractualised communities. In an analogy with community development, forms of 'labour empowerment' can then be distinguished. Just as communities need provision of jobs, investment and infrastructure (Mayo *et al.* 1998), so do workplaces. Similarly, top-down forms of technical assistance (for example the introduction of management consultants) can be disempowering of the workforce, forms of self-help (such as workers' co-operatives) can be isolating, and radical approaches (such as syndicalism and nationalisation campaigns) can occasionally be successful. As with communities, the challenge is to identify which combination of elements in any given case is most likely to achieve 'labour empowerment' in the sense of the workforce as a whole being enabled to choose its own way forward.

A final analogy with communities relates to the viability of what have been called 'area-based' approaches in the case of community development and what could be termed 'workplace-based' approaches in the case of worker empowerment. The argument that Marxists have used in the past (Eyles 1979) is that approaches which are focused on specific geographical areas are doomed to fail because they do not tackle the wider social forces that are responsible for the problems of these areas. We have seen in Chapter 3, however, that approaches that concentrate on the development of social capital in such areas can be of positive value, although they need to be supplemented by measures that link the community constructively to the outside world. Currently, this linkage is increasingly understood in terms of integrating area-based programmes within regional, national and continental (for example European) strategies (Parkinson 1998) – the socialist ideal of a global strategy still looks a long way off. Even at a regional level, however, the extent of integration is negligible (Parkinson 1998), suggesting that there is continuing force in the marxist argument. On the other hand, it may just be that integration within strategies which are virtually certain to be top-down is not the best way of empowering local communities. After all, the discussion in Chapter 3 suggested that an approach which built upon the community's own developing capacity, where the community itself chose its own aims, its own forms of assistance, its own links with the outside world and its own pace of development, was likely to be most effective. Unfortunately, however, such a high degree of autonomy is unusual among more disadvantaged communities (perhaps by definition?), and where it does exist the community's development may even be at the expense of other communities in the area or region.

The foregoing discussion suggests that the practice of community development needs to be qualified by a consideration of its effects on the wider society; in other words, there needs to be due regard to the promotion of equality of opportunity, at a regional, national and international level. Constructive engagement with the outside world requires not only the internal development of a community's social capital but also some form of partnership with other communities, where a partnership is defined as: 'a long-term relationship in which two or more partners in mutual trust share responsibility for joining resources to achieve a common goal for their mutual benefit and empowerment' (Chigudu et al. 1996: 8). In view of the pronounced lack of success of disadvantaged communities in achieving their empowerment, it can be argued that such an approach is also the most rational one – the more extensive such partnership networks are, the better the chances for empowerment success.

As with communities, so with workplaces. Approaches which concentrate on developing social capital can lead to increased trust among the workforce and consequently greater employee control over the work process; that is, greater (though still very limited) freedom and autonomy for workers, both individually and collectively. This greater autonomy, however, exists against the background of a collective consensus about company aims and acceptance of fundamental relations of line management and exploitation. It also exists within the framework of a market in which the company has to compete in order to survive, and this market is increasingly global in character. Any process of labour empowerment, therefore, is always constrained by the two enduring realities of company bureaucracy and competitive markets. In order to mitigate the disempowering effects of such realities, workers have to organise themselves collectively across the company as a whole and across the industry in which their company operates. As is well known, in spite of a number of notable victories, this activity has not been entirely successful over the past hundred years or so, and capitalism has in fact gone from strength to strength. There have, however, been 'historic compromises' at a national level, and these will be referred to in Chapter 5. Workers' organisations have also been generally more successful than communities in building 'partnerships' beyond their original sites of collective action (workplaces) and across industries, and this has contributed significantly to their achievements at national level. On the whole, however, it is arguable that workers' control today looks at least as far off as community control.

Finally, social divisions of gender and 'race' are as prominent in workplaces as they are in communities. In fact, as would be expected on the basis of the argument in Chapter 2, both communities and workplaces are structured on the basis of gender relations, though this does not mean that they are patriarchal in any straightforward sense. Just as stereotypical assumptions about the woman's role help to explain why women take a predominant role in community organisations, so stereotypical assumptions about the man's role help to explain why men predominate in workplace organisation. As usual, the realities of the woman's burden of responsibility (without power) in communities and lack of responsibility (again without power) in workplaces are to be explained in terms of the rational choices available to men and women arising from the organisation of the domestic labour process described in Chapter 2. This brings us to a full vicious circle or Catch 22, because the source of the domestic division of labour itself lies in the unequal resources that men and women earn in the workplace. The gender division of labour in the home partially determines gender divisions at work, and vice versa.

In relation to 'race', the pattern of causation has more to do with the character of the exclusive groups formed through social interaction within communities and workplaces. Where these groups are culturally more homogeneous, exclusionary practices are more likely to have a racial aspect. Discrimination against 'outsiders' can arise in more or less the same way in both types of situation. At bottom, racisms are based on simplistic reductions of a group identity to a few features which are deemed to be 'essential' for membership of that group (Husband 1982). Racism is therefore fundamentally irrational, and this poses a problem for a rational choice theorist. The solution lies in distinguishing between what directly maximises utility and what is a means towards such maximisation (Nozick 1993). Racism in itself may not be rational, but racist practice and ideology could be a rational means of achieving advantage for a particular set of individuals. By forming an exclusive group, people with a common ethnic or cultural identity may be able to promote their own interests at the expense of people with a different ethnic identity. This needs to be corrected if it results in systematic discrimination, which is a form of oppression. Within a workplace, such discrimination could also be irrational if it meant that the 'best people' were not getting the jobs, because that would mean in turn that value was not being maximised for the controlling group. Further explanation of racism requires a closer examination of the politics of exclusionary groups, based on kinship, community, and so on. At a personal level, it has to do with the way in which an individual makes the transition from the world of the familiar to the world of strangers. At an institutional level, however, it has to do with the complex history of slavery, colonialism and imperialism over the centuries.

Foucault and rational choice

In order to achieve a deeper understanding of how workplace relations oppress people, it is necessary to reiterate that bureaucratic relations are inherently different from contractual relations, although paradoxically they are expressed *through* contractual relations. Whereas contractual relations are freely entered into by individuals, bureaucratic relations exercise power over individuals. Foucault's work is helpful here, in explaining the nature of this power. Essentially, Foucault extends and complements Weber's formal definition of bureaucratic rationality (O'Neill 1986). Unlike Weber (1968), who proposes a series of abstract ideal types, however, Foucault (1980) sees bureaucracy as consisting of spheres of power/knowledge centred on specific institutions (such as industrial workplaces) and discourses. Foucault calls bureaucratic power 'disciplinary power', and he contrasts this with 'monarchic power'. The difference between the two has to do with the way power is manifested and how individuals see themselves in relation to specific sites of power. With monarchic power, power rests in specific individuals who hold power and exercise it over others. In this situation, people know they are not free, because they are 'subjects' of the person who holds the power. With disciplinary power, however, power is inherent in the practices within specific institutions, and internalised in the minds and bodies of its 'subjects', so that they believe themselves to be free even when they are most oppressed. Indeed, their freedom is an effect of the power itself.

Foucault's ideas seem to accord well with the reality of modern workplaces. Employees enter into contracts voluntarily, but as a result find themselves subject to all forms of disciplinary control which ensure their willing compliance with the employing organisation's regime. There are some problems, however, with Foucault's analysis, from the point of view of a rational choice theorist. For example, the latter would argue that the freedom of individuals who sign an employment contract exists independently of the institutions to which they belong as a consequence of such signing. Admittedly, this freedom is limited by their economic and social circumstances, but it is not entirely dictated by disciplinary power.

A second problem, related to the first, is that according to Foucault's way of thinking, resistance to disciplinary power, no matter how necessary it may be, appears futile because it takes place entirely within the disciplinary regime and typically results in the further development and deepening of its 'normalisation'. The forms or techniques of power may be transformed through struggle but not the institution itself. If freedom is more than a construction of disciplinary power, however, there always exists the possibility of resistance which can transcend that disciplinary power – that is, the possibility of liberation (this is considered further in Chapter 5). Workplaces are not 'total institutions' (Goffman 1961), and therefore the undermining and overthrow of such institutions from within is possible, though obviously extremely difficult. It can be accepted that capitalist organisation and control of the labour process has developed through a dialectic of power and resistance (Clegg and Dunkerley 1980), but the outcome of such a dialectic is impossible to predict in any given case.

A third problem with Foucault's analysis is that in practice bureaucracies often, and perhaps typically, function as quasi-monarchies (Findlay and Newton 1998). The system of line management means that each worker is 'responsible' to one higher in the hierarchy, and in each case this superior worker has it in his or her gift to advantage or disadvantage their subordinates. Again, perhaps because the institution is not a total one, meaning that individuals, including managers, are not entirely disciplined by its rules, a multiplicity of sites of monarchical power can exist and even thrive: 'rules were made to be broken'. In practice, therefore, workplaces always display uneasy combinations of disciplinary and monarchic power. In such circumstances, a variety of forms of institutional discrimination (racism, sexism, disablism, ageism, heterosexism, etc) is inevitable, along with a continuing tension between the increasing discipline of individuals and the development of more sophisticated resistance by those individuals. It is difficult to see how this can be explained except in terms of a conflict between the oppressive demands of large corporations and the needs of free human beings. The trick is to achieve a form of disciplinary power, expressed in the core values and culture of the organisation, which will be actually liberating for its workers. Such liberation, however, can be achieved only by granting real autonomy to the workforce, for example within a context of worker democracy.

One way forward might be to examine more closely what is meant by the ability to do a job. In the current jargon, this is referred to as 'competence'. At present, disciplinary power in workplaces could be argued to be inherently disablist, because it systematically excludes and/or devalues those who are judged to be not 'competent'. Some employing organisations, however, take responsibility for developing competence in their employees through appropriate programmes of training, education and practical experience. If such self-development meets the needs of the employees themselves, and not just those of the organisation, it could be argued that this is a most effective way of expanding disciplinary power. At the same time, though, in what sense can such a process be regarded as oppressive? Herein, perhaps, lies the key to understanding the global success of large capitalist corporations, namely a virtually unbeatable unity of market freedom with bureaucratic power that is continually constructive and reconstitutive of its core of human capital. This does not mean, however, that capitalism is necessarily successful in meeting the needs of either its workers or its consumers. Even the most enlightened corporation is still founded on the exploitation and alienation of labour, and even the most competitive markets are inevitably biased against the poor. Taken together, we have what Foucault (1980) called a 'global unity of domination' based on the disciplinary power embodied in the normalised self-expansion of value that is the hallmark of capitalism everywhere.

Problems for rational choice theory

The argument in this chapter can be summarised as follows. In advanced capitalist societies such as Britain, all social divisions arise out of a complex structure of labour exploitation which has been established historically through the expansion of contractual relations. Key elements of this structure are the home and the workplace, whose institutionalisation and spatial separation have enabled the structure as a whole to be reproduced through the exercise of rational choice on the part of the actors concerned. We saw in Chapter 2 how the isolation of the individual household ensured that the rational choices made by its members would reproduce domestic relations of exploitation. Similarly, the isolation of individual workplaces facilitates the reproduction of capitalist exploitation. All this is well supported by historical and sociological evidence and analysis. From a rational choice theoretical perspective, however, it must still be regarded as problematic, for the following reasons.

First of all, contractual relations have been presented as rational because they serve the mutual benefit of the contracting parties. In order to work, however, the contracting parties must fulfil the terms of their agreement. The question is: why should a rational person carry out their part of the bargain if they can gain an advantage by reneging on the agreement (compare the discussion of free-riding in Chapter 2, which could take place in spite of – admittedly non-contractual – agreements between husband and wife)? This question can then be generalised into the form: why should a rational person accept the rule of law if or when it does not suit them (especially, one could add, if it involves their exploitation)? Rational choice theory provides two types of answers to these questions: one is in terms of sanctions which penalise those who break their contracts, and the other is in terms of an individual's reputation for honesty, which is essential to build in order for other people to be willing to enter into contracts with him/her, but is easily lost if the individual defaults in their contract performance.

There are problems with both of these types of answer. In the case of reputation, it is clear that this can be effective within communities where everybody knows everybody else, but where interactions among individuals are more anonymous breach of contract is likely to look more attractive to rational individuals and therefore sanctions become essential in order to neutralise such attractiveness. The problem with sanctions, however, is: who is going to enforce them? This question indicates that as soon as we go beyond family and community we hit a major problem of collective action, namely how can a large group of individuals, most of whom are strangers to one another, be rationally expected to co-operate in dealing with recalcitrant or deviant members of their group?

The standard answer to this question in rational choice theory is for the group to employ an independent 'enforcer' (Laver 1997: 68), who proves his competence in competition with other prospective enforcers. The group members cede to this individual or organisation sufficient coercive resources to deal with free-riding by individuals or small groups, but not enough to allow the enforcer to subjugate the group as a whole. This, however, gives rise to a second-order collective action problem, namely how to ensure that the enforcer does not use his power to oppress the group? This problem is again solved in terms of the enforcer's need to maintain his reputation, because if he loses it he will be replaced by one of his competitors. According to rational choice theory, therefore, compliance with contractual obligations, and the elimination of free-riding generally, is best secured through second-order contractual arrangements.

The argument of rational choice theory implies that there have to be compelling reasons why free people should accept obligations. In the case of family, we saw in Chapter 2 that obligations arose out of deep-seated attachments; in the case of community, we saw in Chapter 3 that they arose out of patterns of reciprocity, the maintenance of which can now be partly explained in terms of the advancement and protection of personal reputation; in the case of contractual relations, however, we now see that obligation arises as a by-product of the need to secure the discharge of the contract itself.

Rational choice theorists in political science have tended to see the enforcer as being a politician or political entrepreneur (Laver 1997: 68 – but compare Nozick 1993), and this will be discussed further in Chapter 5. The problem with this view, however, is that, in Foucauldian terms, it assumes that enforcement is monarchical rather than disciplinary, albeit a constitutional rather than a Hobbesian absolute monarchy. After all, just because enforcement is necessary in order to assure discharge of contractual obligations, it does not follow that there is a specific actor who is an enforcer. Essentially, what enforcement achieves is a situation where the costs of free-riding (or defection) exceed the benefits, and this can be achieved as effectively, if not more so, by disciplinary power as by monarchical power.

Another problem with rational choice theory here is that in real contractual relations of employment as opposed to states of nature, mechanisms of enforcement already exist – they are institutionalised in bureaucratic relations. The collective action problem that this presents is rather different from the one defined in the theory of rational choice. Workers who enter into these contractual relations are not thereby accepting the legitimacy of bureaucratic enforcement, and insofar as they do not accept such 'authority' they will tend to seek ways of combining and organising among themselves in order to resist it. Such collective action, however, gives rise to its own problems of free-riding, which themselves have to be solved through the personal reputation of trade union leaders and workers' representatives, and specific sanctions against so-called 'scabs'. It is the historical resolution of these collective action problems that has led to the formation and maintenance of the labour movement. Indeed, it could be argued that the numerical strength and success of working-class resistance in the face of monarchical power was one of the factors which historically paved the way for the transition to disciplinary power in capitalist workplaces.

We are left with the problem of how free individuals come to be subject to bureaucratic power, whether monarchical or disciplinary. We can conclude, however, that this is essentially a historical question. Jared Diamond has conveniently summed up the situation as involving one of two possible alternatives: a merger of smaller groups under the threat of external force, or a conquest of smaller groups by a larger or more powerful one (Diamond 1997: 189). In the former case, the result is a form of disciplinary power, in the latter case one of monarchical power. In both cases, however, the individual submits to the rule of others. In the same way, whether it is the monarchical power of executives or the disciplinary power of the labour market, individuals in the modern world are subjugated to forces over which they have little or no control.

Conclusion

In this chapter, it has been argued that the articulation and expansion of contractual relations has given rise inexorably to exploitation on a global scale, and of increasing sophistication. Two main types of social division have issued from this contractualisation: a division between exploiters and exploited, and a division between what might be called the 'contractualised' and the 'non-contractualised', that is between those who are included and those who are excluded from contractual relations. In spite of major economic and political upheavals over the years, these types of social division have become firmly entrenched in late capitalist societies, with available evidence indicating little mobility across the social divides of class, gender, and indeed 'race' and age. This chapter has attempted to explain this development and entrenchment in terms of the rational choices of individuals operating within a context of a dual labour process (domestic and contractual): choices made within the contractual labour process largely give rise to and reinforce the division between exploiters and exploited, and choices made within the domestic labour process are important for understanding and reproducing (though not causing) the division between included and excluded. The chapter criticised alternative attempts to explain social divisions and social change in terms of 'structural' or 'cultural' factors alone, on the grounds that these accounts do not make specific theoretical allowance for the autonomy of rational human beings.

Notwithstanding this rather gloomy diagnosis, rational choice theory also gives us hope that liberation is possible. For example, the problem of labour exploitation itself can be seen as one of collective action, namely how can the exploited act together on a global scale in order to force corporations to be accountable and cede their elite control to a wider constituency? What forms of enforcement are required in order to make this happen? How can we ensure that the development of new forms of enforcement does not lead to new forms of oppression and subjugation, as Foucault believed was inevitable? These questions will be considered further in Chapter 5. Here it is appropriate only to point out that corporations are themselves subject to the discipline of the market, and can therefore be tamed through the power of 'exit' (for example, consumer boycotts) as well as through the power of 'voice' (for example, strikes). The question is whether such powers are sufficient on their own to achieve the accountability of bureaucracies, or whether more radical measures are required to bring about the full emancipation of the working class and of oppressed people generally.

5 State–citizen relations and social justice

This chapter is concerned to do three things: to explain in general terms how the modern form of the state developed; to reconsider the approach of rational choice theory in explaining the relations between the state and its citizens; and to show how such an approach can be used to justify programmes of political reform. Rational choice theory is used specifically to reinterpret themes in political philosophy and to launch a radical critique of current forms of governance. The underlying purpose of the chapter as a whole is to show how rational choice theory can be used to throw light on the process of development of the relations between the state and its citizens. It will be argued that the interactions among individual citizens produce patterns which crystallise into specific institutions. These political institutions, like the institutions discussed in previous chapters, such as the family, the community, the market and bureaucracy, then function as boundaries or limits within which rational choice is exercised. As individuals then make their choices within this framework, prevailing forms of political rule become established and modified. Forms of political rule are explained in terms of the concept of hegemony, which broadly speaking represents the expression of disciplinary power through state–citizen relations.

Changing hegemony

Many writers have seen the development of capitalism as having distinct historical phases, such as competitive or liberal, Fordist and post-Fordist (Aglietta 1979; Lipietz 1985; Boyer 1986). In the liberal or competitive phase, which took place roughly from the seventeenth century in England until the late nineteenth century, capitalist firms were generally small, bureaucracy was relatively undeveloped, and the state consisted primarily of coercive apparatuses such as armed forces and means of punishment. In relation to the market, the state's role in this phase was to provide a framework of law and order, to enforce the discharge of legal contracts and to set the standards for fair and equal exchange (for example through control of the minting of coinage), and to support the expansion of capitalist relations abroad. From the later nineteenth century until towards the mid-twentieth century, a process of 'social evolution' (Hayek 1982) led to markets becoming dominated by small numbers of increasingly large firms. These firms, as we saw in Chapter 4, became bureaucratic in order to secure more effective control of their workforces and to increase the profitability of capital. Fordist methods of mass production succeeded because they not only produced greater profits but also increased labour productivity. This in turn enabled companies to pay their workers higher wages, thus attracting labour away from domestic service and crowding out competitors who paid lower wages. Although there is no simple unilinear relationship between Fordism and class politics, this development did facilitate mass forms of class organisation, as workers in large firms acted collectively to resist capitalist oppression. This resistance then arguably 'spilled over' into the political arena, leading to universal franchise and the formation of working-class political parties. Because of the numerical strength of the Fordist working class, they were able to exert increasing influence on the political process, leading to growing state intervention to advance the interests of that class, within an overall framework of capitalist discipline.

Gramsci has described the relationship between the working class and the ruling class at national level as one of 'unstable equilibrium', and the disciplinary power which operates through this relationship is termed 'hegemony' (Gramsci 1971). Over the course of time, this hegemony has become highly complex and sophisticated – so much so that writers today are unable to agree on whether it has changed fundamentally since the Fordist heyday of the immediate postwar period. It seems appropriate, therefore, to review the main characteristics of the postwar 'equilibrium' or 'hegemony' in order to establish what, if anything, has changed. Clarke and Newman (1997) have identified what could be called three dimensions of this equilibrium, each of which involves a specific kind of 'settlement': a political/economic settlement, a social settlement and an organisational settlement. The first is based on bipartisan agreement (a long but uneasy truce in the class struggle) around social reformist welfare policies and Keynesian macro-economic policies. The second is based on similar agreement concerning divisions of labour and welfare along lines of gender, age, able-bodiedness and 'race'. The third is founded on standardised modes of state co-ordination and control through bureaucratic administration and public professionalism. Equilibrium is maintained primarily through bi-partisanship of policy and neutrality of implementation. These three 'settlements', however, are not the only features of the postwar hegemony. Equally, if not more important, was the military settlement established through Allied victory in the war, and maintained through NATO in 'uneasy truce' with the Soviet bloc up to 1989. This international settlement contrasted with the primarily national form of the other three settlements.

From the end of the 1960s onwards, it has been argued that the postwar national settlements have begun to unravel and we have moved into a situation of disequilibrium (for example, Lash and Urry 1994 – from 'organised' to 'disorganised' capitalism). Social reformist welfarism and bureau-professionalism have been attacked from both the Left and the Right, and Keynesianism has been largely abandoned. Feminists, anti-racists, disability activists and others have condemned the white, patriarchal, 'normalising' bias of the 'welfare state', which has effectively excluded many social groups from the 'settlement' – for example, lone parents, black and minority ethnic groups, and disabled people. The degree of impact of the critique from such 'outsiders', however, is debatable, and it is likely that, as outsiders, their influence in changing the prevailing hegemony was marginal. The 'uneasy truce' was indeed broken in the 1970s and 1980s, but this was arguably due more to the declining power of national organised labour in the face of international competition. The emergence of long-term mass unemployment was probably crucial in the undermining of that power, leading to a new ascendancy of the power of capital on the international stage. Some writers (for example Sklair 1998) now claim that there exists a transnational capitalist class, while a transnational working class still looks a long way off. In such circumstances, elite groups are clearly able to be more assertive in their relationships with less powerful groups, leading to increased exploitation in the workplace and cuts in welfare provision. 'Free collective bargaining' has been replaced by (among other things) the manager's 'right to manage', and a collective concern to meet people's needs has been replaced by media-driven hype about 'welfare scroungers' and a more general acceptance of what is seen as the inescapable reality of globalisation.

The postwar national settlements have therefore arguably been undermined by increasing global economic interdependency. How far this process has gone, however, is a matter of fierce debate. Has there been a radical change of hegemony, for example, and is a new form of bipartisanship emerging that is substantially different from the old? Clarke and Newman (1997) claim to have identified a new form of hegemony called managerialism, which has its own discourse and practices. A key feature of this hegemony is the dispersal of state power to other agencies, which is associated with a wider shift from monarchical to disciplinary power in the organisational regime. Fordist power is essentially monarchical because it is monopolised by an elite group – managers and shareholders in the case of private corporations, bureaucrats and politicians in the case of public institutions. Under the postwar settlement, the public sector expanded to meet the demands of those excluded from power in the private sector (consisting largely of sections of the working class and their families), but key employment relations deriving from the commodification of labour power remained unchanged. When members of these excluded and powerless groups faced the public sector as consumers, therefore, they met bureaucratic structures that were essentially similar to those which were responsible for their exploitation as producers. The welfare state provided them with benefits as consumers, just as Fordism provided them with benefits as producers (in terms of higher wages). In both cases, however, they found themselves unable to control the processes involved. Under these circumstances, the postwar settlement could work only so long as the working class was enjoying these clear material benefits in terms of rising standards of living, and it was the latter that were undermined by globalisation.

As Clarke and Newman recognise, the dispersal of state power under managerialism represents an expansion of ruling power overall, which is to be expected in view of the decline in the capacity for working-class resistance at a national level. At the same time, however, the nature of this power has changed, because it relies less on direct control through bureaucratic state apparatuses, and more on what Foucault (1980) has called 'productive subjection' through new discourses and practices (Clarke and Newman 1997: 30). The emphasis is now on public entrepreneurship in contrast to bureaucratic rule-following, adaptation rather than stability, innovation instead of repetition, responsiveness rather than consistency, performance as against hierarchy, and people as opposed to rules (Clarke and Newman 1997: 45). Clarke and Newman argue that this discourse becomes hegemonic by being articulated with New Right radicalism, which is ostensibly concerned with 'rolling back' the state but is in fact directed at increasing state power by changing its character (from monarchic to disciplinary):

> This discourse has set the agenda of change, defining its meaning, its direction and the means of its accomplishment. It is the core discourse that other contending positions must negotiate in attempting to articulate their projects. In particular, it has established the need to remake organisational forms of the state around the managerial prerogative: the 'right to manage'.
>
> (Clarke and Newman 1997: 55)

The disciplinary power of the managerial state has been described by other writers more firmly located in a Foucauldian perspective. For example, M. Dean (1999: 171) has noted that: 'Government . . . has become more multiple, diffuse, facilitative and empowering. It is also, however, strangely more disciplinary, stringent and punitive.' This author also links Foucauldian analysis with the theories of reflexive modernisation developed by Giddens (1991) and Beck (1992) by conceptualising a broad distinction between the 'governmentalisation of the state' and the 'governmentalisation of government' (M. Dean 1999: 194). In the former, government is conceived as acting on processes external to and independent of the state, producing the classical liberal and social forms of government. In the latter, government is reflexive, acting on processes internal to the state itself, for example by using 'technologies of performance'. The latter is clearly identifiable with managerialism. Dean (1999: 179) also recognises the importance of reflexive government for achieving decisions that fit more closely with the rational choices of individuals: 'reflexive government means the rejection of a welfarist regime and its reconfiguration as a series of markets in services and provision that relies upon the rational choices and calculations of individuals within various collectivities and forms of indigenous government.'

Clarke and Newman's analysis is concerned with what they take to be a new organisational settlement. This settlement involves a reworking of the place and power of bureau-professionalism such that the old public service ethos of professionalism is subordinated to managerial discipline. For example: 'Where "need" was once the product of the intersection of bureaucratic categorisation and professional judgment, it is now increasingly articulated with and *disciplined* by a managerial calculus of resources and priorities.' (Clarke and Newman 1997: 76). There is a sense in which the message of managerialism is that 'we are all professionals now', because we are all supposed to be self-motivated and self-disciplined, responsible for our own self-development. The overall effect of this change in hegemony has been described as follows:

> we are witnessing the creation of a bureaucratic monoculture spanning the public and private domains. . . . A managerial stratum is being created, relatively homogeneous in attitudes, working methods and aspirations. Its members are able to move between the public and the private sectors, and as they do so the interests and expectations of this stratum begin to interlock.
>
> (Hirst 1996: 104)

Clarke and Newman are at pains to point out that managerialism has not gone unchallenged, and there are also major gaps between managerial rhetoric and reality. Nevertheless, it is their contention that all challenges are now framed within a field of discourse that is dominated by managerialism itself. The collapse of the national organisational settlement has resulted in a situation where: 'The dominant tendency has been to depoliticise decision-making through the dispersal of power to managerially controlled organisations in both the private and public spheres' (Clarke and Newman 1997: 144). They give a number of examples of this such as large-scale transfers of council housing stock to housing associations, the introduction of grant-maintained schools, and the shift from institutional to community care in health services.

There are some problems with Clarke and Newman's analysis, in that it relates only to the organisational form of settlement. It is not clear, for example, why managerialism should be politically accepted, since it appears to imply a decline in the importance of political parties (in order to minimise interference with the manager's 'right to manage'). It is also unclear why managerialism should maintain the old social settlement of 'Family, Work and Nation' when, as Clarke and Newman (1997: 152–3) recognise: 'the unresolved nature of the crisis in the social settlement cannot be solved within the new organisational regime.' A third problem is that Clarke and Newman never really explain what was wrong with the old

Fordist welfare regime which made a transition to managerialism seem appropriate and even desirable – in other words, what were the factors that caused governments to become more reflexive, what essentially brought about the 'governmentalisation of government'.

Since the publication of Clarke and Newman's book, events have occurred which could be interpreted as indicating the emergence of a managerialist political settlement. This has been christened as the 'Blair–Clinton orthodoxy' (Jordan 1998). The argument is that the old bipartisan political settlement began to disintegrate in the later 1970s, as Keynesian methods of demand management were seen to be incapable of dealing with the new phenomenon of mass unemployment caused by structural changes in the global economic system. The welfare state itself came to be seen by an increasing number of critics as part of the problem, because it supported 'lame ducks', was at least no more productive or efficient than the market, and imposed too great a tax burden on the working population. From a rational choice perspective, the actions of politicians and government officials were to be explained in terms of their own rational self-interests rather than in terms of ideology or democratic values. Political leaders and bureaucrats were seen as maximisers of utility, where the utility concerned was political power and organisational power: they were viewed as 'bureau-maximisers', whose activities therefore needed to be monitored and who needed to be continually held to account for what they did.

The new emerging political settlement is therefore based on an acceptance of this critique of the limitations of state power, requiring a response in terms of democratic renewal, a new role for political parties, and new cultures of responsiveness, accountability and empowerment. The discourse of this settlement is essentially managerialist, with emphasis being placed on innovation, entrepreneurship and partnership. There is a difference, however, between this settlement and the organisational settlement described by Clarke and Newman: here the talk is of public rather than private entrepreneurship, and this is associated with a radical agenda for constitutional change, involving ultimately a disciplinary political regime in place of the current monarchical one. Like the new organisational regime, this new political managerialism has not gone unchallenged, but it is already becoming difficult to mount any challenge except within the framework of the discourse itself. The 'active citizen' simply becomes the counterpart in the political realm to the 'manager' in the organisational realm. Indeed, because of the 'rolling out' of state power as described by Clarke and Newman, the two become one and the same, or at least collaborate closely together in a continuous working partnership.

There is evidence, therefore, to suggest that a managerialist political settlement may be emerging, although the precise character of this settlement is still a matter of debate. Hirst and Khilnani (1996: 3), for example, have gone so far as to claim that: 'Politicians are now the apex of a managerial class that, whether in the public or the private corporate sector, enjoys greater capacities for top-down control and less countervailing power from organised interests like trade unions than ever before'. It has been argued that the form of this settlement has already become clear in the field of law and order, and this form accords precisely with that described by Clarke and Newman, namely a dispersal of power to crime control agencies, legitimated through a new discourse of 'responsibilisation' of individuals and communities, which nevertheless succeeds in retaining, and even reinforcing, a centralised and highly punitive criminal justice system (Garland 1996; Hughes 1998). From a Foucauldian perspective, this process is exactly what one would expect, with the deployment of 'technologies of agency' in order to achieve a disciplined governmentality (M. Dean 1999: 196), involving the linking up of different institutions for punishing, curing, relieving poverty, etc, in specific regimes of practices (M. Dean 1999: 21).

The issue of a changing *social* settlement is a more thorny one. The old Fordist settlement was based on the male breadwinner role (see Chapter 2) and was inherently sexist (Williams 1989), racist (Gilroy 1987) and disablist (Oliver and Barnes 1998). Entitlement to benefits, free health care and other public goods depended mainly upon having made appropriate insurance contributions and/or upon being deemed to be in 'need' as measured by some bureaucratic means. This social settlement therefore involved the creation of vast bureaucratic structures such as the National Health Service and the National Assistance Board (later renamed the Supplementary Benefits Commission), providing security 'from the cradle to the grave' for those who were fortunate enough to be 'inside' the settlement, namely British citizens, or at least those British citizens whose contributions and needs were recognised by the authorities. Interestingly also, the settlement involved a major status distinction between contributors, who were entitled to more generous levels of benefit as of right, and non-contributors, whose benefits were subject to means-testing. Some writers have referred to these groups as the 'productive' and 'non-productive' populations (Gough 1979), thus devaluing the contribution of domestic labour and reflecting the 'workerist' bias of the settlement itself.

The postwar social settlement began to unravel mainly because the male breadwinner role became less monolithic than it used to be, although it remained dominant and remarkably resilient. This slight weakening of the male breadwinner role was associated with the rise in female employment, the rise in numbers of lone parents, and the emergence of long-term mass male unemployment. Other important factors responsible for its disintegration were the growing costs of welfare provision and the difficulties that large bureaucracies experienced in attempting to meet a multiplicity of individual needs. Since the 1970s, governments have attempted to re-engineer the social settlement so that people's expectations of the welfare state will more closely correspond with what that state can deliver. Here again the 'rolling out' of the state as described by Clarke and Newman is a crucial part of the process, but the agenda involved is rather different. In the case of the new organisational and political settlements, power seems to increase as a result of an ever-widening and deepening managerial discipline and democratic self-actualisation; in the case of the attempted new social settlement, however, the concern seems to be to use the old themes of Family, Work and Nation to 'lock' people within old sites of monarchical and disciplinary power. Whereas the new organisational and political settlements can look radical and innovative, the new social settlement, such as it is, looks conservative and even reactionary. But what exactly does it involve, and why should this have come about?

First, Family. Any movement away from the old settlement based on the traditional two-parent family carries a risk of greatly increased costs for the state. Under this settlement, the parents bear the brunt of the cost of bringing up children, with only a small (though important) contribution from the state in terms of child benefit, health care and educational provision. In the case of lone parents, however, the parent is generally less able to bear that cost, so the contribution from the state tends to be higher on the whole, either to enable the parent to look after the child at home or to pay her (as it typically is) child-care costs while she is out at work. Any 'normalisation' of lone parenthood would increase the pressure on state expenditure. This could be incompatible with the traditional assumption that the primary responsibility for a child rests with its parents. The politically preferred responses to dealing with lone parenthood have therefore been to impose greater responsibilities on errant fathers (for example, the Child Support Act) and to encourage greater labour market participation (for example, through the New Deal). The former is reactionary because it attempts to return lone parenthood to the status quo ante, namely effective two-parenthood, while the latter involves reforming the social settlement to one in which 'Family' is more clearly subordinated to 'Work'. This reform only works, however, to the extent that it involves lone parents coming off benefits into more lucrative paid employment, and this in turn depends upon such suitable employment being available. As already noted, such availability is likely to be very limited because of the persistence of mass unemployment. It could be concluded that a new social settlement around 'Family' is emerging, involving a greater acceptance of 'non-traditional' family forms, but the extent of change in welfare policy is likely to be modest, at least for the foreseeable future. Managerialism is not inherently familist and indeed is potentially destructive of family life of all kinds but, for the time being, it appears to be attempting to reinforce traditional family forms. This attempt is unlikely to be successful, for the reasons explained in earlier chapters.

Over the course of time, the state will develop new partnerships with parents in relation to the care and education of children, but it is unlikely that basic relations of power and exploitation within the home, which are already fundamentally shaped by state power as we saw in Chapter 2, will be substantially changed. This means that the 'rolling out' of state power to the family is likely to be minimal, because there is a sense in which such power is well rolled out already. What is likely to change is that parents are increasingly co-opted as active participants in the settlement itself rather than being taken for granted as happened in the old settlement. In this sense, the new settlement promises to be more inclusive, but nevertheless based on an extension of hegemonic disciplinary power. And again, the discourse of this hegemony looks managerialist, with the emphasis on parental leadership, commitment, responsiveness and adaptation, as well as on the self-actualisation of the child. In fact, since the latter is a traditional ideology of education itself, it can be seen that managerialism harmonises particularly well with educationalism.

Second, Work. As mentioned above, the onset of long-term mass unemployment undermined the postwar social settlement based on permanent, full-time male participation in the labour market. Without such participation, the working class loses its capacity to bargain with management, unemployment becomes a means of depressing wage levels, and with the consequent expansion of the unwaged household population the problem of exclusion from the settlement altogether grows. The state response to this undermining of the social settlement has largely been one of attempts to reconnect the long-term unemployed to the labour market, and the emphasis has increasingly been on what are known as 'active' labour market policies, that is policies which do not merely train people up to perform certain types of jobs but which actively seek to create or modify jobs for which unemployed people could be suitable. Policies of this type still have a long way to go, as can be seen from the large number of people in the UK claiming incapacity benefit, but they are in line with the general managerialist tendency to re-assert the value of paid work. Their undeveloped character, which exists in spite of the priority attached by the European Union to tackling unemployment and social exclusion, may well be related to the fact that they can come into conflict with the new political-economic settlement. This happens because the latter involves an acceptance of the limitations of state power in influencing the labour market, whereas active labour market policies appear to imply an expansion of that power. According to the new political and organisational settlements, the 'normal' way for employment to be created is through backing 'winners' in international competition, but the employment created by the victors in this global market is not necessarily that which is suitable (in terms of type or location) for long-term unemployed people.

In fact, this tension between interference in the labour market and acceptance of its discipline can be overcome by ensuring that active labour market policies precisely reinforce that discipline rather than weaken it. For a new social settlement to work, the jobs to which unemployed people are being matched must be 'real' jobs, and this means that they must be jobs which are sustainable in the face of market competition. Under the old settlement, the state could and did create jobs of its own, but these jobs were not sustainable in the longer term, mainly because of competition from the private sector (for example they could undercut the public sector in terms of wages and prices). As a result, under the new settlement the state works more organically in partnership with the private sector. The 'rolling out' of state power has meant that the boundary between public and private sectors has become less rigid and more permeable (though still of fundamental importance for a non-monarchical political order – M. Dean 1999: 206), and the disciplinary power of the state has become more firmly tied to the discipline of the labour market. The new social settlement around work involves a managerialist emphasis on self-development and self-actualisation through paid employment for all those people who are able and permitted to compete in the labour market.

This social settlement has not yet been achieved, for two main reasons. One is that there remains a huge gap between the requirements of the unemployed themselves and the demands of large employers (hence the inevitability of continuing tension and conflict). The second is that access to welfare provision has become increasingly dominated by means-testing, which not only undermined the old settlement (by effectively penalising labour market participation, which is the main source of the means that are tested), but also hampers the efforts to reach a new settlement because of the inevitability of 'poverty traps'. For these reasons alone, a managerialist social settlement is still a long way off. Perhaps realising this, some proponents of such a settlement (such as New Labour) have opted to use compulsion to speed up the process, thus running the risk that the managerial power involved will be monarchical rather than disciplinary. Jordan (1998) shows most vividly how such an approach can be counter-productive and lead to destructive forms of resistance and criminality.

Finally, Nation. The old settlement involved the provision of entitlements to welfare on the basis of national citizenship. Originally defined in terms of the British Empire and Commonwealth, the definition of citizenship was narrowed by successive legislation to include only those whose families had a history of residence in the UK. This settlement was based on essentially national (and nationalistic) solutions to national problems, with politics and administration being dominated by national organisations. With the growth of international competition and globalisation, it became increasingly difficult and inappropriate for economic policy, as well as social policy and welfare, to be determined on a purely national basis. The creation of welfare states in some countries but not others, for example, tended to encourage immigration from the latter to the former, and this in turn tended to lead to the imposition of immigration controls in host countries, which added considerably to the rigidities of labour supply. A relatively free market in capital, therefore, was not matched by a free market in labour, and this served to undermine the settlement between capital and labour: crudely speaking, capital was able to move to countries where wage rates were low, but workers in low wage countries were less able to move to countries where wage rates were high. For these and other reasons (for example, in order to institutionalise the postwar international peace settlement) many countries, especially in Europe, moved increasingly towards supranational settlements such as the European Union. The overall shape of the new settlement, however, is still far from clear, in particular its articulation with the changing military settlement (for example, the expansion of NATO). If we are indeed now moving towards settlements in which national power is counterbalanced by continental power above and regional power below, who exactly is being included in and excluded from such settlements, and on what basis? In the absence of any common agreement on European citizenship among EU countries, or even compatibility of immigration and citizenship policies, the social charter alone looks too weak as a foundation for any new social settlement. Perhaps surprisingly, therefore, in view of the apparent progress being made on this issue, the social settlement around Nation continues to maintain its nationalist form. Indeed, the political settlement in Britain explicitly involves a reworking of this nationalist settlement around the constituent nations of England, Scotland, and Wales, and the only concrete transnational settlement has been with the Republic of Ireland specifically concerning the North.

The argument in this chapter so far can be summarised as follows. The postwar hegemony in Britain and other advanced capitalist countries involved three kinds of settlement: a bipartisan agreement on Fordist means of control in a 'mixed' economy; an institutionalised favouring of able-bodied native white males as breadwinners and as citizens; and a military settlement based on outright Allied victory in the war itself. The first two of these settlements, but not the third, have fallen apart because of the inherent defects in Fordist power, the decline of the patriarchal family, and the erosion of national authority in the sense of the capacity of a nation to determine its own destiny. All three of these latter sources of decline relate to problematic features of the monarchical power involved – that is, the centralised top-down character of each particular settlement or institutional regime. In the case of Fordist power, monarchical power is expressed through bureaucratic control dominated by elites of capital owners and managers. In the case of the patriarchal family, monarchical power clearly rests in the person of the father as 'head of household'. In the case of national authority, monarchical power rests in the state itself, understood as sovereign in the sense of able to command obedience from its subjects.

In response to the demise of these settlements, a new hegemony has arisen whose discourse is essentially managerialist, but the progress of this discourse has been uneven. Its fundamental characteristic is its disciplinary power, understood here as the capacity to mobilise individuals to act willingly so as to (re)produce their own domination. Under disciplinary power, an individual voluntarily submits himself or herself to a myriad of physical routines in the pursuit of self-actualisation. Managerialism is therefore a 'trick' which secures such submission. This 'trick' is accomplished by new forms of settlement. The first is a 'rolling out' of state power that moves away from Fordist solutions, blurs the distinction between public and private institutions, and seeks a wider, stronger and more flexible consensus. The second is a new constitutional settlement, in which democratic renewal is led by political entrepreneurs whose values and practices reflect the new managerialist agenda. The third is a social settlement, in which more democratic forms of family structure emerge, individual differences are more explicitly recognised and tolerated, the 'rolling out' of state power is used to promote managerialist solutions to social problems, and the limitations of national power are to some extent compensated for by recourse to supranational arrangements. It should be noted, however, that the new hegemony is quite compatible with the continuation of forms of sexism, racism, disablism and other types of institutional discrimination.

The new hegemony is not just a new discourse, because it involves fundamental changes in power relations, the reality of which is only beginning to become apparent. Under this new hegemony, not only is power being used in a different way, but the character of the protagonists under the old hegemony and the relationships among them have also changed. For example, the former role of the trade unions as resisters to Fordist monarchical regimes, or as institutionalised bargainers within those regimes (corporatism), has effectively disappeared, as managerial authority has reasserted itself and trade union membership has declined. On the other hand, the new managerial class appears to be distinctive in many ways from the bureau-professional-business class which it is now superseding. The precise character of this new class, however, is not yet clear, and its formation is still strongly contested.

Rational choice theory reconsidered

The first part of this chapter was devoted to a historical description of current changes in state–citizen relations. The nature of these relations, however, remained unanalysed, and in particular the rational basis for these relations was left unexplored. The aim of this section, therefore, is to consider the contribution that rational choice theory can make in this area. The final section of the chapter will then offer a critique of managerialism and other ideologies from a rational choice perspective, and will provide the outline of an alternative approach.

First of all, we need to remind ourselves that the conduct of national politicians is very far removed from the everyday life of most individual citizens, so the connection between the two is inherently complex and poorly understood. This means that all state policy is liable to be misguided, with many substantial consequences that cannot be foreseen by policy-makers. From a rational choice perspective, every state policy needs to be thoroughly justified before it can be accepted by its citizens. In practice, however, this is the exception rather than the rule.

But why do we need the state at all? We saw in Chapters 2 and 3 that households and communities were capable of reproducing themselves in the absence of a state, and indeed the effect of state action was typically to change the nature of the exploitation within these sets of social relations rather than meeting the needs of the individuals concerned. In Chapter 4, however, we found that when it came to relationships going beyond those of personal acquaintance such as market relations, a framework of law seemed to become necessary in order to ensure the discharge of contractual obligations. Rational choice theorists, however, have suggested that even here it may be possible to establish a system of agreements which do not have the force of law but which remove the incentive to free-ride. The main argument used is that continuous interaction gives rise to conditional strategies of the form: 'I will co-operate with you today if and only if you co-operated with me yesterday', and combinations of such strategies are capable of solving the free-rider problem (Taylor 1976; Axelrod 1984; Ostrom 1990). Unfortunately, however, this argument has the corollary that where continuous interaction does not exist, which is often the case once we move beyond households and small communities, the free-rider problem cannot be solved by such anarchistic means.

Laver (1997: 61) has shown how in larger groups it is rational for an individual to co-operate only when such co-operation is 'pivotal' to the action required, in the sense that the individual's choice of strategy makes a difference in future interactions between whether or not enough of the rest of the group will co-operate to make continued interaction worthwhile. Laver's argument is concerned with the collective production of goods that are collectively consumed, but by extension it can be seen to apply to all market interactions between people who are effectively strangers to one another. Essentially, in larger groups strategies of conditional co-operation fail because members of such groups for whom co-operation is not pivotal will tend to defect until the group has shrunk to a size at which free-riding is no longer rational. The only possible solution to this collective-action problem is to introduce clear incentives to co-operate and/or sanctions against non-co-operation. This itself raises second-order collective-action problems, for example how to introduce such a system and get it generally accepted by the people.

The rational choice theorist's argument that some form of legal or quasi-legal framework or other external authority is unavoidable in order to ensure co-operation in groups larger than small communities is an important one. This legal framework needs to embody power and authority which will be sufficient to deal with free-riding by individuals and small groups, but not enough to result in the subjugation of the group as a whole (Laver 1997: 68). Rational choice theorists have therefore appeared to favour either a limited form of monarchical power (a political executive), or some kind of disciplinary regime (involving a 'rule of law'). As it turns out, however, as indicated in Chapter 4 and shown further below, only disciplinary power is consistent with individual rationality.

Second-order collective-action problems arise in relation to the selection of the legal/political authority, the limitation of its coercive power, and its accountability for its performance. To solve the first problem, there must be a sub-group or faction or alliance of factions which is able to prevail over the rest of the group. This can happen, for example, if this faction has superior means of coercion, or if the rest of the group cannot agree on an alternative. Free-riding among faction members can be reduced because of the potential rewards of winning in competition with other factions (the spoils of office, power and prestige). The process of selection can then be conducted by ballot, in which in principle the vote of each individual (for one or other faction) carries the same weight. Solving the second problem requires a system of law to which the authority itself will be subject: otherwise, for example, the authority's access to military might (required for defence of the realm, etc.) will enable it to impose its will in a Hobbesian fashion. In order to avoid military dictatorships, therefore, a democratic culture must be supplemented by a discipline of respect for the law, and the law itself must be drafted on the basis of the equality of free individuals. The third problem arises because the authority will tend to act in the interests of the members of its faction rather than to the benefit of the group as a whole, but monitoring and (if necessary) removing authorities is a difficult and expensive business. Hence the importance of maintaining oppositional factions, as well as exercising 'voice' more generally, which creates costs for incumbent factions.

The question remains as to why a free individual should choose to obey the law if it is not in his or her interest to do so (for example if by not doing so he or she can enjoy a free ride), and for a rational choice theorist the answer has to be because that law is backed by force or (which amounts to the same thing) the individual lacks the resources or power to do otherwise. Incentives rather than sanctions will not do the trick, because it is not possible to reward exclusively only those who obey the law. Furthermore, in order for the trick to really work, the force backing the law must itself be subject to the same law, and this can only be the case if its subjection is supported by an alternative force. Hence Montesquieu's doctrine of the separation of powers (executive, legislature and judiciary), where the law is made by the legislature but implemented and enforced by the executive and judiciary, where the power of the executive is subject to judicial review, and where the power of the judiciary is constrained by executive appointment (or by direct election in more democratic countries). The obligation to obey the law arises from the rational maximisation of value (see Chapter 1), which involves the systematic avoidance of disorder. This also, however, justifies a form of military settlement, in order to maintain this disorder avoidance.

Beyond small communities, therefore, a framework of law is essential in order to sustain both private exchange and public interaction. From a rational choice perspective, however, what general form should such law take? As already shown, law is required in order to ensure fair dealings in market exchange and respect for the autonomy of others. Although there is considerable disagreement as to the proper scope and sanctions of the legal system, many people would agree in principle that in order to be legally responsible for their actions an individual must have a capacity for self-determination (see Chapter 1). The principle of autonomy therefore requires that individuals should be as free as possible to pursue such rational, self-critical strategies. This in turn implies that, as far as possible, all unnecessary constraints on such self-determination should be removed. The law required by a society composed of such individuals is then one which coerces only to the extent required to prevent free-riding and interference in the autonomy of others. But what exactly does this involve?

Liberal thinkers such as Hayek, Giddens and Jordan have typically misrepresented the nature of individual freedom because of their failure to address collective-action problems. Against Hayek in particular it needs to be pointed out that individuals are subject to different degrees of constraint (for example, depending upon exploitation relations and bureaucratic relations), and therefore the realisation of the principle of autonomy requires that collective action be taken that will remove more constraints from some individuals than from others. It is only by such action that constraints overall will be minimised and individual freedom maximised. 'Negative' law such as the criminal law is therefore not enough: 'positive' redistribution is also required in order to secure self-determination for all. The undertaking of such collective action, however, itself involves coercion, because the removal of constraints from some individuals can be achieved only by the imposition of constraints upon others (for example through the tax and benefits system). There are then second-order collective-action problems in achieving such an undertaking, and in ensuring that it does indeed minimise the total amount of constraint upon individuals.

The argument being propounded here is that the principle of autonomy requires the equalisation of the constraints upon individual freedom. Specifically, among other things, this means the abolition of exploitation relations. It is simply not acceptable, from a rational choice standpoint, that relationships should exist that deny to people the control over their everyday lives that they require for self-determination. The constraints that need to be imposed, therefore, are first of all those that prevent people from denying such self-determination to others, and then those second-order constraints that are necessary to enable the imposition of the first-order constraints. The articulation of these constraints, however, is a complex matter, and it is understandable that it would have caused difficulty for political philosophers and theorists. Let us therefore explore some of the ways in which such an articulation can be made, and how it can be distinguished from alternative justifications of allocation and redistribution.

First, formal equality of opportunity or *'merit'*. Liberal theory has traditionally been associated with the idea that the legal/political authority should promote equality of opportunity, that is it should attempt to bring about an equalisation of the constraints upon individuals entering into exchange relations, so that outcomes are determined on the basis of individual merit rather than, say, class privilege. Liberal theory, however, has nothing to say about exploitation as discussed in earlier chapters of this book, and therefore nothing to contribute to solving the problem of the gap between free exchange and unequal outcomes that is characteristic of both domestic and capitalist exploitation. This is a more fundamental point than that commonly made about liberal theory, namely that it leads to a 'meritocracy' (Young 1961), where those with greater capacity to take advantage of opportunities gain at the expense of the rest. Rather, it is saying that even where the capacities of individuals are equal, outcomes will be largely determined by divisions of private and social capital. So long as exploitation exists, the outcomes of production and consumption processes will continue to be divided along class lines. A rational choice theorist can have no principled objection to outcomes being based on 'merit', provided only that the judgment of 'merit' reflects real individual differences in talents and effort. In a capitalist society, however, too many talented and hard-working people go inadequately rewarded.

Second, *need*. A needs-based approach to allocation and redistribution has the advantage of justifying the application of coercive power on the basis of some allegedly objective and universal determination (Braybrooke 1987). From a rational choice perspective, the approach is suspect because of the risks of paternalism, bureaucratic elitism, and enforced dependency (Drover and Kerans 1993: 5). We cannot dispense with the approach altogether, however, because rational choice theory itself postulates a fundamental human need for self-determination. We therefore need to make a distinction of some kind between those individuals who have the means to meet this need for themselves and those who lack such means. Examples of such means would include effective capacity for communication, a basic level of education, a reasonable standard of health, a minimally adequate income, decent affordable housing, and the opportunity to use and build on all of these things in order to fulfil one's desires. Those who lack such means can be regarded as suffering unacceptable constraints which therefore need to be removed – hence the collective-action problem referred to above.

Third, substantive *equality*. The capacity for self-determination is not the same for different individuals, so equality of outcomes cannot be a rational goal. However, as mentioned above, the equalisation of constraints upon individuals, not only in entering into exchange relations but throughout their everyday life, could be argued to be a fundamental assumption in order for rational choice to be effective. In this sense, equality and liberty can, and indeed must, be reconciled in order for either one to be achieved: the principle of individual freedom requires that individuals be equal in terms of not being subject to unnecessary constraints, and this in turn requires a deep equalisation of the constraints placed upon them. This position is compatible with the marxist view of human emancipation, which is commonly misinterpreted as involving equality of outcomes but in fact advocates abolition of alienation and exploitation and the creation of real individual freedom. But what does it mean in practice, and how is it to be achieved?

First, abolition of exploitation has to come from the bottom up, because collective-action solutions that are imposed from above will only produce new forms of unnecessary constraint. The principle of autonomy implies that individuals have equal rights to participate in collective decision-making (Beetham 1992: 46), and therefore to decide which constraints on them should be removed and which should be retained or newly imposed. Further, the fact that collective-action problems can be solved without coercion in small groups, but only with coercion in large groups, suggests that as far as possible decision-making for large groups should be delegated to smaller sub-groups of the large groups. This is the well-known principle of subsidiarity, but it can be realised only through a detailed framework of law, whose realisation itself presents a considerable collective-action problem. Even with such a legal framework, however, small groups will vary in terms of the degree of constraint placed upon their members, resulting in continued inequalities of outcome which cannot be justified in terms of the 'merit' of the individuals concerned. Even within small groups such as households and communities, as we saw in Chapters 2 and 3, exploitation and unjustifiable inequality are well entrenched. Subsidiarity is therefore an important principle, essential in order to minimise the use of coercion, but the application of this principle does not do away with the reality which makes coercion necessary in the first place.

The direction of the argument here raises a dilemma. We cannot attempt to equalise constraints upon individuals from the top downwards without committing ourselves to oppressive forms of monarchic or bureaucratic coercion which fail in any case to achieve the desired equalisation. On the other hand, it seems that neither can we succeed in equalising constraints from the bottom upwards, because small group interactions on their own do not seem to be capable of abolishing established systems of exploitation and unequal capital ownership. This dilemma can perhaps only be resolved by means of a suitable combination of top-down and bottom-up approaches, for example a particular form of disciplinary leadership, establishing a new rule of law from the top, and working in close partnership with a radical libertarian practice which rebuilds social institutions from the bottom. In short, what is required is a new regime of governance, whose principles are outlined below. The final section of this chapter will then attempt to show how this regime can deliver constraint equalisation and solutions to related collective-action problems.

The first principle, as already suggested, must be that of *democracy*, understood as equality of individual rights to participate in decision-making processes. This principle is not restricted, however, to the formal decision-making bodies of the political system, but is to be applied to all institutions and organisations in which individuals have a 'stake'. Families, communities, businesses, voluntary sector agencies and state bureaucracies all should be subject to the democratic control of their 'stakeholders'. Of course there are considerable obstacles to the realisation of this principle in practice, and this is precisely why on its own the principle would be utopian.

Nevertheless, the implications of the principle for different institutions can be expressed in general terms. The issue is of particular relevance for social relations where the individual is subject to coercive authority – for businesses, for example, where there is a clear need for worker voice to counter the oppression implied by such authority, just as it is generally accepted in a democracy that citizen voice is essential to counteract the oppressiveness of state authority. Archer (1996: 88) argues that a process of reform could be introduced whereby workers in a particular firm could gradually accumulate control of the business through a series of trade-offs in which they exchange profit-threatening goods (like excessive wage rises or restrictive work practices) for incremental increases in control enterprise decision-making. He points out that the flexibilisation of work (involving the decline of Fordist regimes) provides an opportunity for greater worker choice and control. However, British employers have not initiated any real redistribution of decision-making authority, not necessarily because it decreases profitability (because there is some doubt about this – Fernie and Metcalf 1995), but because it would threaten managerial status and power (Archer 1996: 93).

Economic democracy is a necessary but not sufficient condition for stakeholder democracy. In order to prevent workers' control from becoming a worker monopoly, it is necessary also to provide for influence by consumers on production processes. Hirst (1994) has argued that this can be achieved through what he calls 'associative democracy', whereby the different groups to which individuals belong become associations that are controlled by their members and regulated by the state. This view, however, takes no account of collective-action problems, and therefore requires substantial qualification before it can be taken seriously. Additional or alternative means must therefore be devised for ensuring accountability to consumers and to the public generally. The most straightforward approach would be to reform political democracy so as to achieve the required representation of consumer interests. This leads us to the second principle of our proposed new governance regime: *partnership*.

Partnership was defined earlier in this book in terms of informal reciprocity within sets of organised collectives. The idea is that networks of private and public sector organisations can provide models of working together to the mutual benefit of all those concerned. The problem of free-riding by individual organisations can be overcome mainly by means of appropriate external regulation, and the appropriateness of the regulation can be secured through effective forms of democratic control. Partnership therefore cannot work on its own – this would result in exclusionary corporatism – but needs to be democratically accountable. For example, at local level, Burns *et al.* (1994) favour an arrangement where a democratically

130 *Social relations and social exclusion*

controlled local authority works in partnership with democratic collectively accountable or controlled provider organisations. The introduction of such partnership arrangements, however, raises new issues for democratisation and new collective-action problems in achieving such democratisation. In order for exploitation and social exclusion to be abolished, intra-organisational democracy needs to be supplemented by both consumer democracy and citizen democracy. This is because consumers have a direct 'stake' in the cost and quality of services and goods provided by producers, while the general public has a 'stake' in the system of regulation that ensures the accountability of both producers and consumers to their fellow citizens. But how are these different forms of democracy to be achieved? This question leads us to our third and final principle, which I call *citizenship*.

What is required to bring about triple democracy (economic, consumer and political) is essentially a 'bootstrap' solution to collective-action problems. Individuals have to internalise a discipline of 'active citizenship' in order to minimise the adverse effects of free-riding. Each citizen then participates in decision-making as far as she or he is free to do so, and alienation and social inequality are soon abolished. From a rational choice theory perspective, however, this appears fanciful and utopian. According to this theory, individuals will tend to participate only to the extent that it is in their interests to do so, and if they can gain the same benefits by free-riding on the efforts of others then this is what they will tend to do. Critics of the theory point out that individuals do sometimes act for wider social benefits, not just their own, and offer alternative explanations in terms of ideology or legitimation. Such alternative explanations, however, themselves need to explain why certain courses of action come to be seen as legitimate, and this returns us to the argument about the basis for the rule of law discussed earlier. There it was argued that a framework of legal and moral constraints will tend to be accepted by rational individuals provided that it promotes a minimisation of constraints more generally. A rational individual may have limited knowledge, but s/he will usually be able to see that a 'free-for-all' is likely to run counter to the fulfilment of her/his desires.

The principle of citizenship is therefore essentially a means by which individuals are constructed as active participants in all aspects of their everyday lives, in order to achieve most effectively the satisfaction of their aspirations. If they choose not to participate in any given aspect, however, they will have to bear certain costs in relation to that particular aspect, for example the costs of employing a representative on their behalf. For each aspect, then, a combination of direct and representative democracy can in principle be developed which will be context-sensitive and context-variable.

Building citizenship

The last part of this chapter will be concerned with articulating this argument in a national context, by way of a commentary and critique of managerialism. For now, however, it is important to explain how citizenship can be built from the bottom up, in order to show how the constraints on individual freedom can be equalised at each institutional level. At the level of the household, for example, means must be devised to prevent free-riding by husbands and by children, putting an end to the double exploitation of domestic labour. This can only succeed, however, if carried out in combination with attempts to abolish the exploitation of labour outside the home, because as we saw in Chapter 2 the free-riding of husbands in the home is dependent upon their 'breadwinning' role in the labour market. The equalisation of constraints upon individuals in the workplace, to be achieved through forms of economic democracy, will then in turn help to redress the imbalance of economic power within the home. Beyond the individual household, local communities can act as seed-beds of citizenship, in which free-riding is minimised through the exertion of pressure from neighbours, relatives and friends. As we saw in Chapter 3, local networks can communicate strong expectations and disapproval if such expectations are not met. Mutual trust can build up on a personal basis, and this can be extended into partnership arrangements, again minimising free-riding and facilitating a mutually beneficial equalisation of constraints upon the individual participants. The development of such communities can then form one basis for institutions of local government.

Ostrom (1990) has argued that democratic control can be achieved through long-term continuity in institutional structures at the level of local communities. These structures are said to facilitate the definition of property rights, assist in monitoring free-riding, and encourage reciprocity. If this is the case, then the problem is not only how to recreate these local institutional structures, but how to ensure that they work together to the benefit of the parties concerned. This problem goes beyond that of community development which was discussed in Chapter 3 because it is concerned with what is the form of political authority that is most conducive to individual freedom. It is important to remind ourselves here that collective-action problems cannot all be solved by means of conditional co-operation within communities, even if incentives are introduced to encourage such co-operation. External public power is sometimes required to enforce solutions, and is perhaps generally indispensable in order to achieve constraint equalisation (Goodin 1992). Herein lies a role for government, and for local government in particular.

Anarchist theorists, communitarians and Green political theorists have envisaged a situation where the pattern of conditional co-operation at the level of a local community is repeated at an inter-community level, an inter-regional level, and an international level – a form of globally generalised reciprocity. The idea is that this would enable the achievement of solutions to collective-action problems without the need for legal regulation in the long term. Rational choice theorists, however, have argued that this is not a realistic prospect, for a number of reasons, some of which have already been discussed above. Therefore, 'as the number and size of communities grows, the probability of . . . breakdown of all-round conditional co-operation . . . becomes higher and higher' (Ward 1996: 138).

One of the strongest arguments against the introduction of an external public power is that it will tend to undermine the capacity of communities to solve their own collective-action problems by destroying informal political processes operating at the local level (Ward 1996: 140). Hence the need to ensure that that power is subject to control by the communities themselves – citizen governance must first and foremost be democratic community governance. Also, for Greens as well as for liberals, the state is as much a *cause* of collective-action problems as part of the solution (Carter 1993), and this again highlights the need for genuinely democratised subsidiarity, that is decentralised political units based on communities with extensive autonomy and rights of self-government, and a high level of direct citizen participation in decision-making (Die Gruenen 1983). All this serves to show the relevance of the principles of democracy, partnership and citizenship.

The democratisation of political authority, partnership with and among such authorities, and the cultivation of citizenship all raise second-order collective-action problems. These have been dealt with indirectly by theorists of local government under the heading of 'citizen governance' (Box 1998), although oddly enough there have been few empirical studies. One such (Abelson *et al.* 1995) found that randomly selected members of the public were *least* likely to think of themselves as appropriate participants in any aspect of decision-making, but the strongest levels of support were for decisions to be made by a combination of groups including elected representatives, experts, randomly selected citizens and those with particular interests in the services concerned. This finding suggests that individuals recognise that equal participation in decision-making is neither realistic nor even desirable, and that effective accountability of public powers is best achieved by means of a suitably heterogeneous decision-making assembly. Such heterogeneity has a distinct advantage of reducing the likelihood of monopoly by one faction. The assembly itself needs to include elected representatives of the people but also individuals who are experts in this particular policy area. This reduces the likelihood of errors based on inadequate knowledge or understanding, or based on lack of awareness of unintended consequences of different courses of action. Not surprisingly, the finding is in complete agreement with the expectation of rational choice theory that individuals will decide whether or not to participate, and who should participate, on the basis of judgments as to which courses of action are most beneficial to themselves. People who say with Burton and Duncan (1996: 13) that: 'If we are to further the debate about democracy we need to better understand why people do or do not participate and on what terms' need to be directed to the rational choice literature.

So, building democracy, partnership and citizenship from the bottom up leads to a renewed emphasis on the importance of local government, and therefore on the need to reform that government in order to abolish oppression and exploitation. The most rational form of local government would then be one in which citizens participate directly as much as they choose, in which its institutions work in close partnership with others in the local area and outside, in which decisions are taken at the lowest possible level and by bodies on which both local people and specialists are represented, and in which free-riding and constraint inequality are minimised through appropriate forms of regulation. In addition, higher levels of government would be required to redress the inequality of constraints upon individual freedom from one local government area to another.

Public choice theory, which is essentially a regional theory within the rational choice paradigm, has suggested that the arrangement which would be most effective in achieving these aims would be a pattern of small, irregularly sized, overlapping functionally based local authorities (Ostrom *et al.* 1988). Bennett (1989) has also argued that the efficiency, effectiveness and accountability of public bodies require flexible decentralisation plus flexible aggregation, with small governmental units joining together as and when necessary for specific tasks. Similarly, Box (1998: 119) has expounded a model of citizen governance in which decision-making is devolved to citizen boards, and the local authority acts as a 'community co-ordinating council' with the power to review board decisions, and council officers or consultants ('experts') act as 'helpers', informing and advising citizens, and ensuring that they have opportunities to participate in decision-making. Collective-action problems would therefore largely be resolved by ensuring that key decisions were all taken within small groups. Problems of inequality among and within groups, however, would remain, and for this reason alone local government is not sufficient to counter exploitation and oppression.

The current reality of local government is very far from that envisaged by public choice theorists. A considerable amount of empirical research, however, has shown that the geographical extent of local authorities does not correspond with citizens' views concerning what would be an appropriate area for local government functions. For example, Hampton (1970) found that people's 'home area' was very localised and rarely larger than an electoral ward, and the Redcliffe-Maud Commission (1969) similarly found that about two-thirds of respondents were oriented to an area the size of their ward or parish. Clearly, it is this localised community that could form the most rational basis for devolved local government such as neighbourhood management (Hampton 1987) or parish councils (Boaden *et al.* 1982). More recently, Hedges and Kelly (1992) have again concluded that an individual's 'home area' is typically smaller than that of current local authorities, and Young *et al.* (1996: 27) went so far as to say: 'the principal implication of our analysis is that community identification . . . provides a wholly inadequate basis for the construction of any feasible system of local government, at least at the levels of presently-existing local authorities, with their current roles and responsibilities'.

It is therefore the perceptions of individual citizens which are closer to rational choice expectations (for a devolved system of citizen governance), and it is existing local government structures which are inappropriate. Unfortunately, however, the Labour government's proposals for modernising local government (DETR 1998a) do not address these issues, although they are aimed at increasing openness, responsiveness and accountability, and encouraging greater citizen participation. The main reason for this neglect is probably that under a unitary (English) national government 'a smaller number of easily monitored and regulated local authorities' (Barnett and Chandler 1997: 154) is required, and this inevitably means the creation of excessively large, complex and inefficient local authorities. The needs of individual citizens are effectively subordinated to the demands of the nation-state.

Returning to the themes of Chapter 3, it could be argued that a form of local government devolved to local communities could have a major role in channelling technical assistance for community development. Decisions on the distribution of this technical assistance could be taken by citizens' boards, and the governing body of the local authority would co-ordinate the activities of the partners involved. As J. Smith (1997: 176–7) has said: 'Whether a community regeneration partnership works . . . depends above all on the attitude of the local authority', and a supportive attitude will be much more likely under a more devolved system of local government. Regulation will be necessary to ensure that the provision of technical assistance is conditional upon constraint equalisation, so that broadly speaking greater assistance goes to those individuals and groups who have greater constraints placed upon them, that is those who are lacking resources of human or social capital. The precise extent of resource redistribution required to equalise constraints will need to be debated within the citizens' boards as well as the governing body of the local authority.

Returning also to the point made in Chapter 4 about the development of partnerships among local communities, there is once again the difficulty that in such larger groupings sanctions are required in order to prevent free-riding, and also to reduce the inequalities among the partners concerned. The means for applying such sanctions are already concentrated in the hands of national governments, and this concentration has occurred as a consequence of long histories of war and conquest. Legal constitutions therefore already exist according to which the necessary coercive power is legitimated. These then form the disciplinary background against which crime and punishment, and citizenship rights and duties, are debated. There is a sense, then, in which if we wish to live in societies larger than small communities, the existence of coercive power of some kind is inevitable, so our task is to make such power as accountable as possible, and that requires the application of the three principles discussed above, namely democracy, partnership and citizenship. But what does this mean, exactly?

Recreating governance

Essentially, building citizenship from the bottom up needs to be accompanied by the recreation of governance from the top down. In the real world, existing hegemonies cannot be wished away, nor is it realistic to imagine that the coercive power of the state will wither away. Having recognised the legitimate role of the state from a rational choice perspective (as a punisher of free-riding and an equaliser of constraints upon individual freedom), therefore, the task is to ensure the democratisation of state power, its linkage with countervailing sources of power, and its 'ownership' by an active citizenry.

Ideally, the way forward would be for the principles of local community governance, as outlined above, to be applied at the level of interaction among communities. This would mean, for example, that local authority governing bodies would function like citizens' boards, whose activities would be co-ordinated with one another and with those of other bodies such as firms, with the nation-state acting as a higher-level co-ordinating council. Within such a larger grouping, however, even if all the bodies being co-ordinated were democratically controlled and accountable to a wide constituency, sanctions would still be necessary to prevent free-riding, and therefore a system of enforceable legal regulation would be indispensable. Even in utopia, therefore, there would be a problem of how to ensure that sanctions were used appropriately, and that the laws governing the application of such sanctions were just.

In reality, we have to deal with a particular form of hegemony, with its own forms of democracy, partnership and citizenship. Let us therefore look at each of these in relation to the changing hegemony discussed earlier in this chapter. First, *democracy*. The postwar hegemony originally involved a form of Schumpeterian democracy, understood in terms of the right of elected representatives to govern as they saw fit, in which the right of citizens to participate equally in decision-making extended only to voting. This form of democracy corresponded with the discipline of a Fordist regime in which the state provided services for the masses, because it represented political parties as agencies which were responsible for the provision of mass political services, such as health, housing, welfare and wealth redistribution. With the dispersal of state power under managerialism, this traditional Schumpeterian democracy has become increasingly inappropriate, and there has been growing concern about the resulting so-called 'democratic deficit'. With the new managerialist political settlement, therefore, there is a burgeoning concern for 'democratic renewal' which is intended to address this problem. Under New Labour, for example, the emphasis is on new forms of subnational government, new kinds of elected bodies, and new types of test of electoral opinion.

Second, *partnership*. Originally, the postwar hegemony involved a clear separation of the command structure of the state from the looser interconnections of the market and civil society, reflecting the wartime concentration of power in large-scale bureaucracies. The continuation of the Cold War justified the long-term maintenance of Fordist power structures, but over the course of time the grip of state bureaucracy gradually loosened, and militarised discipline began to decline. The dispersal of state power eventually leads to a new organisational settlement in which public and private organisations co-operate with one another on the basis of a common discipline and methods of working. This discipline is embodied in the techniques and discourses of managerialism, as described at the beginning of this chapter. The original rigid demarcation of the public from the private sector has become blurred, and it is no longer the case that we must necessarily look to the state to solve our collective-action problems. Partnerships which traditionally existed wholly within the state, such as those in state education between schools, parents and the local education authority, are now increasingly expected to include private sector agencies. Under the new organisational settlement, it is suggested that managerialist forms of regulation, spanning both public and private sectors, are capable of solving collective-action problems by inculcating self-discipline among the key actors, namely the managers.

Third, *citizenship*. Hill (1994) has identified three traditions of citizenship, namely liberal-individualist, civic-republican, and Marshallian (based on social rights). According to the liberal conception, individuals should be free from interference but have basic duties in terms of respecting the rights of others, defending their country against enemies, and paying taxes in return for the provision of law and order; beyond this, obligations arise only on a contractual basis (Hill 1994: 12). This is essentially the concept of citizen as 'nightwatchman'. In contrast, the civic-republican concept sees citizenship as based on membership of a community, arising from norms of reciprocal interaction and common experiences and values, and giving rise to duties of collective participation and action (Hill 1994: 13–14). Finally, the Marshallian concept is based on rights going beyond the ability to reciprocate or participate, involving a right to minimum economic welfare and security up to a right to live according to the prevailing social standards. According to this conception, the state has a general duty to make services available to all citizens, and in return the citizen has a general duty to serve the community where possible and to work (Hill 1994: 15–16).

The liberal definition of citizenship has already been criticised in this chapter on the grounds that it actually reinforces the oppression of those who are exploited or socially excluded. In its more thoroughgoing libertarian versions, it also fails to recognise the need for collective action in order to relieve such oppression as well as to solve collective-action problems such as pollution and crime. The civic-republican definition is essentially an attempt to generalise and legitimate the peer pressure that is placed on individuals to participate in community life. As we have seen, within small communities such pressure can be very effective, but the extension of such a practice to larger groups is problematic. As is also the case in smaller groups, it is potentially oppressive and totalitarian, but it is also liable to be undermined by free-riding. The Marshallian definition is the one that most closely corresponds to the postwar hegemony. It incorporated elements of the liberal definition, in making access to welfare dependent upon the possession of individual citizenship rights, but extended the concept of welfare to something close to the concept of constraint minimisation developed earlier in this chapter – that is, it construed individual freedom as requiring an element of redistribution of wealth and income and enjoyment of a certain standard of living through access to health, education, housing and other service provision. It also incorporated elements of the civic-republican definition, through its emphasis on solidaristic forms of provision, for example through public ownership and nationally-based services such as the National Health Service and the National Assistance Board, as well as its emphasis on the citizen's duty to serve her or his community and country, for example through National Service.

The Marshallian concept of citizenship is therefore the one associated with the postwar social settlement. The character of this settlement, and the factors that have led to its decline, have been discussed earlier in this chapter. The framework of a new managerialist social settlement, however, is only just beginning to emerge. A central concept of such a settlement would appear to be that of the 'active citizen', and this concept has new resonances with those of liberals and communitarians. With the liberals, the active citizen is one who maximises their welfare, involving active health rather than passive undergoing of treatment for illness, positive lifelong learning rather than negative abolition of ignorance, and responsible risk-taking rather than enforced idleness. With the communitarians, the active citizen is actually said to have a duty to be active, to contribute their labour to the common good (within households, communities and the labour market), and to be patriotic. The managerialist social settlement, therefore, appears to involve a unique combination of liberal and communitarian ideals which has been termed the 'Third Way' (Giddens 1998). Its distinctive difference from Marshallian citizenship is strongly debated, but it would appear that it has to do fundamentally with the social basis of welfare entitlements and how welfare services are to be provided. Whereas under the postwar settlement unemployed people (for example) were entitled to state support to enable them to reach a minimum acceptable standard of living, under the new managerial settlement support from the dispersed state (which includes private as well as public sector organisations) is increasingly made conditional upon claimant performance, such as attendance on training courses and the active pursuit of job opportunities.

Before criticising managerialism, it is first necessary to recognise its strengths. From a rational choice theory perspective, managerialism has actually much to commend it. First of all, it assumes that the relationships between states and their citizens should take account of the autonomy and self-development of individual human beings, free from monarchical regimes of patriarchy, racism and centralised bureaucracies. Second, through the dispersal of state power it avoids the Hobbesian danger of absolute monarchy or dictatorship – collective-action problems can be solved not through the invocation of an all-powerful sovereign but through the intercession of essentially limited public or private agencies with circumscribed and specialist functions. Third (although this argument cannot be regarded as convincing by rational choice theorists), managerialism provides a rational justification of why people should obey the law, in that the internalisation of legal regulation is seen, in Hegelian fashion, as the essence of freedom itself. Fourth, managerialism has considerable potential for solving second-order collective-action problems through the formation of like-minded groups of managers whose activities cut across a number of different partner organisations. To some extent, these formations enable the reduction of large-group problems to small-group ones, thus facilitating the non-coercive removal of free-riding. Fifth, and in a similar way (with like-minded groups of politicians), the managerialist emphasis on democratic renewal could help to reinvigorate institutions of representative government which also translate problems of large groups (the citizenry) into problems for small groups (of citizens' representatives). Sixth, a managerialist regime seems more likely than most to produce outcomes for individuals which are related to their competence and hard work rather than to accidents of birth, serendipity, or irrational prejudice. Finally, managerialism responds to criticisms of needs-based redistribution (for example, that such redistribution involves stigma and the undermining of personal autonomy) and establishes a potentially more inclusive system through a more contractual relationship between the individual and the state, moving away from the bureaucratised feudalism of much of traditional state welfare, where the receipt of benefits depended to a great extent on the largesse of Her Majesty's Government.

Managerialism therefore has many important advantages. Unfortunately, however, it also has considerable drawbacks. These can be grouped together under the usual headings of democracy, partnership and citizenship. First, *democracy*. New Labour's democratic innovations, for example, however welcome they may be in themselves, are far removed from the concept of 'stakeholder democracy' espoused by the Labour Party when it was in opposition (Driver and Martell 1998), let alone from the concept of 'triple democracy' outlined earlier in this chapter. What New Labour proposes is essentially a limited reform of political democracy only, with little or no consideration for economic democracy or consumer democracy. Future innovations, such as a Freedom of Information Act, could help to improve the situation by allowing for greater stakeholder influence on decision-making processes, but as it stands the present programme is likely to make little difference to the current grossly unequal balance of power. The dispersal of state power to other bodies has not been followed by processes to make such bodies democratically accountable, so overall managerialism has tended to weaken democracy rather than strengthen it. The inevitable consequence is to strengthen the hold on political power of a relatively small and exclusive elite group.

Perhaps the key issue here is one of public accountability (Rouse and Smith 1999: 236): 'The fundamental controversy concerns which set of stakeholders should be given prominence and in what way their interests are best represented'. What Rouse and Smith (1999: 237) refer to as the 'public administration paradigm' of democratic legitimacy associated with the postwar settlement has given way to a more privatised accountability based on market efficiency. As Walsh (1995: 250) has put it: 'Politics is replaced by management, which, in turn, is replaced by audit.' The Conservatives' rationale for this transition had been that accountability to the individual citizen as consumer was seen as 'a more direct, more democratic form of accountability which would restore the democratic deficit of the discredited public administration paradigm with its attenuated electoral chain of command' (Rouse and Smith 1999: 240–1). The problem was, however, that the 'new managers' were not prepared to share power with their 'consumers', leading to a decline in equity, participation and openness (Painter *et al.* 1995), and culminating in a new culture of sleaze and managerial irresponsibility (Rouse and Smith 1999: 243). New Labour in opposition was vociferous in its criticisms of this lack of accountability, and proposed the devolution of political power and increased public participation in order to restore democratic legitimacy. However, New Labour in power has retained the essence of managerialism such as the performance management ethos, with its emphasis on technical rather than democratic accountability, and 'the decentralisation espoused by the government appears to be at odds with the same government's firm centralised control to contain public spending and promote efficiency through strict performance management' (Rouse and Smith 1999: 255). This shows clearly the disadvantages of what could be called political managerialism.

Second, *partnership*. Here again, accountability seems to be crucial. It is clear, as Clarke and Newman (1997) have pointed out, that managerial networks lack accountability: to their own workforces, to consumers and to the public at large. Under managerialism, partnerships constitute a way of by-passing democratic processes in order to reinforce managerial discipline. While ostensibly critical of traditional monarchic power, therefore, and advocating partnership working as being more flexible, responsive and therefore more in tune with the real demands and needs of the people than traditional bureaucratic provision, managerialism is in fact less publicly accountable, potentially if not actually elitist, and fundamentally anti-democratic. This paradox remains largely hidden, however, because managerialism involves a change in the nature of power (from monarchic to disciplinary) which makes it appear less oppressive and more democratic. Power becomes increasingly dispersed to autonomous, self-governing units, who appear to act freely in markets for public goods and services. The alienation of labour appears to be overcome, and even exploitation seems to disappear. The reality, however, is that for those who are not managers, the rate of exploitation may well be increased, as is evident in the continuing debate on low pay and the minimum wage. Even for those who are managers, the degree of 'ownership' that they have over the fruits of their labour is typically very limited. Their 'freedom' to act on their own initiative is bought at the cost of increased risk and uncertainty about their own survival.

New Labour's managerialism here is more corporatist than that of the Conservatives. Corporatism has been defined as:

> the tendencies to be found in advanced welfare societies whereby the capacity for conflict and disruption is reduced by means of the centralisation of policy, increased government intervention, and co-operation of various professional and interest groups into a collective whole with homogeneous aims and objectives.
>
> (Unger 1972, cited in Hughes 1998: 91)

New Labour does not share the New Right's fetishism of market forces, and is more pragmatic, experimental and collaborative in its general approach (Rouse and Smith 1999: 253). This means that New Labour's managerialism is likely to prove more effective, and therefore potentially even more oppressive, than the Conservatives' commercialised version. The boundary between managers and managed, and therefore between social classes, may become less clear, but the disciplining of *all* groups is likely to become harsher and tighter as time goes by. This new form of political managerialism has been described by Muncie (1999: 169) as 'coercive corporatism'.

Finally, *citizenship*. The managerialist construction of the 'active citizen' is an expression of an ideologically driven transition from monarchic to disciplinary power. Managerialism envisages a society in which citizens freely choose to be exploited (though of course the 'managers' do not see it like that) rather than having exploitation thrust upon them. Fortunately, however, individuals are peculiarly resistant to such constructions (because rational individuals do not choose to be exploited!), and in this respect managerialist hegemony is likely to be contested on an on-going basis. Where oppressed citizens do become 'active', they are likely to press for greater democracy and accountability, and no doubt new forms of struggle will emerge in due course. This is therefore a consequence of managerialism which gives cause for hope for the future.

Managerialism depends explicitly on human agency for its power, and for the reproduction of that power. The question is: what happens if the agents fail to act according to managerialist expectations? Essentially, this counts as a disciplinary failure, triggering the imposition of appropriately coercive sanctions. In principle, rational choice theory can be applied in order to determine the desirability of different courses of action, both for individual agents and for 'enforcers'. The overall consequence is a 'disciplined citizenry'.

Managerialism is therefore defective in its conceptions of democracy, partnership and citizenship. The effects of untrammelled managerialism would be an entrenched political elite, a strengthened coalition of ruling groups, and a more thoroughly disciplined citizenry. A good illustration of the consequences of this is to be found in the Labour government's Green Paper on Welfare (DSS 1998). There the discourse is framed in terms of poverty relief rather than redistribution, economic independence rather than abolition of exploitation, and a strong and cohesive society rather than a free and just society. This discourse is also prevalent in other government publications (DETR 1998b, c; Social Exclusion Unit 1998). The unspoken agenda here is clearly that of the maintenance of the status quo in terms of corporate power and class divisions (see Chapter 4). Individual rights are matched by individual responsibilities, and state duties are matched by individual duties, but what is missing from the whole approach is a matching of state power by state duties. Managerial power, therefore, which now encompasses state power, is left unchecked and virtually absolute.

How, then, is managerialism to be reformed, and new forms of governance to be created? This question will be considered in detail for housing governance in Chapter 6, but the basic principles to be followed are set out below. First of all, credit should be given to liberal critics such as Jordan for emphasising that every element of compulsion within the existing hegemony should be challenged. I would add only that such compulsion needs to be justified in terms of rational choice theory, as politically necessary in order to resolve collection-action problems, abolish exploitation and equalise constraints upon individual freedom. Next, what could be called the core system of tax and benefits needs to be restructured on the basis of answers to two questions: (1) are the tax and benefits in question required in order to prevent free-riding? and (2) how far are the tax and benefits in question actually used to equalise constraints upon individual freedom? Although it will not be possible to determine precise and comprehensive answers to such questions, they can be used to guide processes of tax and benefit reform. A third principle would be that governance should be as democratic as possible, and this involves devolution of power to the lowest possible level. Redistributive systems of tax and benefits therefore need to be combined with more radical dispersal of power to local communities and co-operatives, regulated through a system of partnership agreements. The realisation of this principle will clearly involve the empowerment of grass-roots organisations through the provision of new legal rights, resources and direct power transfers. In this way, the real democratic deficit which is the legacy of managerialism will be gradually overcome.

It seems appropriate to conclude this chapter with a discussion of how public policy might begin to be reformed on the basis of the above principles. One possibility would be to consider a typical example of public coercion such as taxation and outline the ways in which it might be justified. The first way, as mentioned above, is as a means of preventing free-riding, for example to pay for collective defence or for the upkeep of a system of criminal and civil justice or for forms of environmental infrastructure. A second way could be in terms of the form of taxation, for example as a progressive tax on income or a tax on sales or on profits. The distribution of the tax burden could be justified in terms of reducing exploitation (a tax on profits would seem to be most relevant here) or equalising constraints upon individual freedom (as with progressive income tax). Even on the basis of such a rudimentary analysis, it is not difficult to conclude that value-added tax cannot be justified in rational choice terms, so this suggests that our approach has considerable evaluative potential.

Perhaps the most compelling argument against using public power to achieve any kind of redistribution is that it tends to be counter-productive. The history of the postwar hegemony, however, suggests that this claim may have been overstated, because over this period major improvements in the health, housing and education of the nation were achieved through direct state provision. A more realistic verdict is that it is the unaccountable, undemocratic use of power that is more likely to be misdirected, and therefore once again the solution to the problem lies in an extension and deepening of democracy throughout the polity.

Another common argument against using public power is that it tends to undermine individual autonomy, creating 'dependence' on the state and 'trapping' people on benefits. This is an inevitable consequence of relating levels of benefits directly to 'need' instead of 'merit', but it is also the result of excessive marginal rates of tax on lower income groups. The solution is not to remove the benefits on which individuals depend but to increase the income disregards or tax credits for those in paid employment. The Working Families Tax Credit does this to some extent, although it also tends to reinforce the male breadwinner role of the old social settlement. One advantage of managerialism is that by constructing individuals as active citizens it has potential for encouraging their self-development – hence active labour market policies which create real jobs. Problems may arise, however, in relation to those who are less capable of taking advantage of the opportunities that are 'actively' presented. *This is the key source of social exclusion under the new settlement.* Assistance programmes therefore need to be more sensitive to the specific situations of the individuals being assisted. This in turn suggests that locally controlled and managed programmes would be most appropriate, with more liberating aims, involving the redistribution of opportunities and the minimisation of constraints.

Conclusion

This chapter has covered a considerable amount of ground. Postwar changes in state–citizen relations were explained in terms of concepts of hegemony and settlement. The main argument was that key political, social and organisational settlements have broken down due to a variety of economic, social and political factors, and we are currently witnessing the rise of a new, managerialist hegemony. The postwar capitalist military settlement, however, remains firmly in place, especially with the collapse of the Warsaw Pact, and the articulation of managerialism within this settlement is a source of great, global uncertainty – hence the repeated confusion over armed conflicts in different parts of the world (Somalia, Rwanda, the former Yugoslavia, and so on).

Rational choice theory was introduced in order to see if it could throw some light on current changes in state–citizen relations, and if so whether it had implications for the evaluation of how the world might be changed for the better. In this chapter, rational choice theory was identified with a libertarian position, in terms of the minimisation of constraints for all. Arguing against both liberal and state-based approaches to social justice, it was suggested that when this position took account of the realities of exploitation and institutionalised oppression, it came closer to a marxist interpretation.

Returning to the discussion at the end of Chapter 4, it can be seen that a hegemony can be represented as a form of rule in which state coercion receives legitimation, though the extent of this legitimation is limited. Further, in modern capitalist societies, a key factor in securing legitimation, and therefore in establishing and maintaining hegemony, is the neutralisation or accommodation of working-class resistance. Just as we saw in Chapter 4 that this is accomplished through managerialism in the workplace, so in the field of state–citizen relations it is achieved through managerialist forms of democracy, partnership and citizenship. In Foucauldian terms, the latter represents a more comprehensive governmentalisation of government which at the same time actively promotes a more thoroughly self-disciplined citizenry.

The principles of rational choice theory therefore indicate some possible ways forward, and these have been discussed in this chapter under these headings of democracy, partnership and citizenship. These principles were argued to be necessary in order to achieve a workable system of governance in which constraints upon individuals generally would be minimised, and yet at the same time free-riding would be discouraged. These principles were then applied experimentally to the question of the best forms of government at local and national level. In the real world, this requires the following: a focus on the current form of hegemony; an interpretation of it in terms of concepts of democracy, partnership and citizenship; and a critique of it on the basis of rational choice principles. The chapter concluded that such a critique had the potential for giving rise to a programme of political reform. The following chapter attempts to provide an illustration of these arguments in relation to housing policy.

6 Policy implications

The case of housing

Much of the argument in this book has been pitched at an abstract general level. This has been necessary in order to make sense of the systems of social relations within which individuals operate and make their choices. The purpose of this chapter is to relate the abstract generalisations of rational choice theory to policy and practice in everyday life, via the medium of the hegemonic discourses discussed in the previous chapter.

There are a number of reasons for choosing housing policy in particular to illustrate the arguments developed in this book. One is that housing relates so obviously to the themes of household and community discussed in Chapters 2 and 3. A second is that housing is a strong focus for ownership and individuality that are dear to the hearts of most rational choice theorists. A third reason is that policy processes in housing, perhaps more than in any other field, involve well-developed examples of the types of social relations analysed in earlier chapters: voluntary interactions, market relations and state–citizen relations. Indeed, these social relations are so well developed in British housing that they are usually represented as three 'sectors': the voluntary sector, the private sector and the public sector. Historically, these sectors have developed on separate bases and for different reasons, and this in itself presents a challenge for rational choice theory – the prevalence of sector-bound rules and regulations makes it difficult to conceptualise a rational choice among sectors.

The story of housing policy is further complicated by the issue of tenure. Housing is divided not only along sectoral lines, but also in terms of whether it is owned or rented. This leads to a two-dimensional typology of housing regimes (where 'regime' signifies a specific set of legal-institutional arrangements) – see Table 6.1.

This typology is by no means comprehensive (for example, it does not include hybrid forms such as shared ownership), but it contains all the main types of housing regime and has the merit of indicating one which is not so familiar, namely 'social home ownership'. This regime would correspond to a situation where the housing is owned by the individuals concerned but controlled by a state body of some kind. This happens, for example, in the case of the Housing Development Board of Singapore, which develops,

Table 6.1 A typology of housing regimes

Sector/tenure	Owned	Rented
Private	Owner-occupation	Private tenancy
Public	'Social home ownership'	Council tenancy
Voluntary	Ownership co-operative	Housing association tenancy

maintains and improves owner-occupied housing, and allocates it to potential buyers on the basis of strict bureaucratic criteria.

Historical background

Traditionally, the ownership of housing has been very much bound up with the ownership of land. Consequently, in England, for example, when land ownership was concentrated in the hands of a few, most households owned no land at all, and had to rent their homes from a landlord. This was in fact a residue of the feudal system, in which all land was owned by the Crown, and lords of the manor 'held' land from the Crown in return for their allegiance to it. In a similar fashion, the lord's tenants 'held' land from him, hence the expressions 'landlord' and 'tenant' (meaning one who 'holds'). The situation only began to change towards the end of the nineteenth century, with the decline of the large landed estates and the rise of owner-occupation.

Policy on the ownership of land and housing has therefore been crucial for state–citizen relations for many centuries. In the nineteenth century, however, what might be described as the old feudal settlement began to break down under the influence of industrialisation, mass migrations of population and unprecedented urbanisation. These changes presented certain 'problems' that had to be addressed by policy initiatives. The initial response to industrial change, from the mid-eighteenth century onwards, had been to rely on the market to provide housing and other necessities of life, on the basis of at least a century of successful mercantile capitalism. By the mid-nineteenth century, however, there was a growing belief, stimulated by crises such as the Great Famine in Ireland as well as the squalor of the slums in England, that the market alone was not sufficient to provide for the needs of all. Specifically, there was concern about the possibility of revolution to overthrow the grossly unequal pattern of land ownership, about the spread of dangerous diseases such as cholera and typhoid made likely by the overcrowded and insanitary conditions of the slums, and about the mounting cost of poor relief caused by the breakdown of traditional systems of informal and parish support. The policy to address these problems, however, was framed largely in terms of public health – it tackled the question only in terms of insanitary housing, and did nothing to redistribute landed property or to solve the problems of family and community breakdown and destitution.

Selective state action in terms of public health legislation therefore helped to preserve a form of landed hegemony in housing throughout the nineteenth century and into the twentieth century. The consequent removal of the worst housing and the introduction of regulations to ensure the sanitary character of new housing, however, led to new housing problems. Housing shortages, for example, grew as the number of new homes failed to keep pace with the increasing population. Also, as the new housing was of a higher quality than what it replaced, it tended to be more expensive, making it less affordable for poorer households, resulting in problems of rent arrears, moonlighting and evictions.

There were a number of policy responses to this changed situation in the later nineteenth century. First, there was what has come to be known as the voluntary housing movement, which aimed to address the issues of housing shortage and affordability by providing new low-cost rented housing. Many of the pioneers in this movement are still active in the voluntary sector today, for example Peabody Trust, Guinness Trust and William Sutton Trust. Second, there was the birth of professional housing management, in the person of Octavia Hill, where the excess of housing demand over supply was used to justify a system of rationing, in which access to, and continued occupation of, good quality housing was made conditional upon the good behaviour of the tenant. Third, with the Housing of the Working Classes Act 1890 it became possible for local authorities to provide rented housing of their own, for essentially the same purposes as that provided by voluntary agencies.

Considering these three types of policy response today, it can be seen how they prefigured what was to come in terms of both rented housing sectors and management approaches. The philanthropic housing trusts established the voluntary sector as a bastion of paternalistic management, continuing a long tradition of 'enlightened' feudalism. Octavia Hill and her followers reinforced this by accepting uncritically the unequal relationship between tenant and landlord, and emphasising the reciprocal (and therefore apparently equal) duties that each owed to the other. The management of housing thus became reduced to a technical and moral issue, separated from the political question of the distribution of land ownership. Only local authority housing provision appeared to threaten landed property interests, and was therefore strongly opposed by both Hill and the philanthropists.

Until the First World War, then, housing policy was locked within a public health paradigm which left the status quo largely unquestioned, and this status quo could be represented as a form of marketised feudalism. The ownership of land, and consequently of housing, was concentrated in the hands of a small minority of the population, but this minority were very active in the development and management of property for profit, which was a highly competitive business. In a sense, it is correct to say that a free market operated in housing, but it was a market that was fundamentally and systematically distorted by the grossly unequal pattern of land ownership.

The main shifts in housing policy brought about through the First World War were the imposition of rent control in the private sector and the introduction of subsidies for council housing provision. The reasons for these shifts have been well explored elsewhere (Swenarton 1981; Daunton 1987) and need not concern us here. As Bowley (1945) first pointed out, the two shifts were closely linked, because rent control made it unprofitable for builders to provide housing for the working classes, and subsidies became necessary. Clearly, a change in hegemony had occurred, with the state now intervening directly in the market against the interests of landlords, and a decisive decline of landed capital in favour of finance capital. Marketised feudalism appeared to be defeated, and in its place there came a form of state-supported market capitalism. A major symptom of this change was the rise of owner-occupation, which signalled the emergence of a new hegemony. The nature of this new hegemony, however, did not become clear for many decades.

The post-1945 settlement in housing

The settlement after the First World War can be represented as a compromise in response to working-class activism in housing (for example, rent strikes) which effectively sounded the death-knell of the private landlord. This settlement, however, did not manage to solve the traditional housing problems of shortage, lack of affordability and poor condition. Indeed, the policy of rent control, while ensuring that private tenancies remained affordable for lower-income groups, also meant that new private rented housing was unlikely to be provided and existing such housing was likely to deteriorate for lack of investment. Again, the policy of providing subsidised council housing, while addressing the issue of housing shortage, did nothing to improve housing in the private sector. Eventually, in 1930, a 'War on Slums' was declared, which made a significant impact on poor housing conditions, but exacerbated housing shortages and provided replacement housing that was affordable to slum-dwellers only because it was of lower quality. In today's terminology, it can be said that there was a marked lack of 'joined-up thinking' in the inter-war period. Meanwhile, in spite of any specific policy to support it, owner-occupation expanded rapidly over this period: market provision therefore turned out to be more significant, in terms of both quantity and quality, than state provision or state intervention.

The general form of the settlement after the Second World War was discussed in the previous chapter. In relation to housing, this settlement centres on: the role of council housing; the expression of bureau-professionalism in housing; the resonance of housing with the themes of Family, Work, and Nation; and what Ball (1983 1986) has called 'the politics of tenure'. First of all, council housing can be represented as one type of Fordist welfare, an example of bi-partisan agreement on mass social provision. Expenditure on council housing was also viewed in Keynesian terms as a means to bring the country out of recession. All of this contrasted with the situation after the First World War, when council housing was opposed by the Conservatives and was seen as a purely temporary measure to deal with postwar housing shortages. Again, after the First World War, council housing was intended only for the working classes (and even then, only for the 'respectable' working class), whereas after the Second World War it was supposed to be for all social classes.

Second, the growth of council housing involved at the same time a growth of bureaucracy, as local authorities (in contrast with Octavia Hill and her followers) saw housing management in essentially administrative terms as a matter of collecting rent and carrying out repairs. Housing services were to be delivered by increasingly large-scale organisations operating in a centralised, top-down manner. Professionalism was understood not in terms of a personal relationship between professional and client (as, for example, with doctors and lawyers, or even with so-called 'market professionals' such as estate agents), but in terms of technical expertise in finance, construction, surveying or engineering. In the postwar settlement, housing professionals were almost entirely subordinated to organisational regimes.

Third, mass housing provision privileged the traditional nuclear family by providing predominantly three-bedroomed housing, typically on suburban estates often located at some distance from places of paid employment. The assumption was that each home would have two adults, one of whom would go out to work while the other stayed at home and looked after the children (Watson and Austerberry 1986). The needs of large families, joint families, lone parents and single people were systematically ignored under this settlement, and the desirability of linking home with work was implicitly rejected. Just as the social division of welfare was seen as reflecting, but essentially separate from, the social division of labour (Titmuss 1958), so the world of domesticity was regarded as complementary, but entirely unrelated, to the world of paid employment. The 'mixed economy' that the postwar settlement represented was therefore one in which the elements in the mixture remained characteristically distinct.

In relation to the theme of Nation, there is some doubt as to whether housing ever became part of the postwar settlement at all. This is because no citizenship entitlement to housing was granted comparable with that given in health, education and social security. In the terms employed by H. Dean (1999: 214), housing citizenship was only contractarian, not solidaristic. Local authorities were left to decide for themselves whom they would or would not house, and the only safety net provided was through the National Assistance Act 1948, which fell short of keeping families together, let alone providing decent housing. The explanation for this lack of entitlements on the basis of national citizenship is probably that, although council housing became a form of mass provision, it was never a *universal* form in the sense of the National Health Service or state education. Whereas in health and education, public sector provision has always predominated in the postwar period, in housing it has been the private sector that has always contained the vast majority of households. For this reason, it can be said that, in spite of its economic importance, housing never managed to penetrate beyond the fringes of the postwar settlement.

The 'politics of tenure' refers to the fact that the policy debate on housing in Britain since the Second World War, and for some years before that, has been conducted in terms that emphasise ownership rights and systems of housing distribution. This debate has been remarkably stable and enduring, in view of the fact that the tenures concerned have changed substantially over the years. The private rented sector, for example, changed from being the tenure for the overwhelming majority of households to one for only a small minority. From the beginning of the twentieth century until the early 1990s, however, the Labour Party was consistently in favour of control and regulation, while the Conservatives always sought decontrol and deregulation (Balchin 1989: 7). Continuity in the politics of housing policy therefore coincided with major tenure change.

In the case of owner-occupation, there has always been all-party support at national level, albeit with different emphases, with Conservatives extolling the idea of a 'property-owning democracy', especially since 1955, while Labour stressed the importance of people's control over their own housing and freedom from landlords. Partly as a result of this, owner-occupation has become the predominant tenure. Labour itself has never adequately understood the drawbacks of owner-occupation for poorer households. In spite of the collapse of the owner-occupied housing market in the early 1990s, and continuing severe problems of negative equity, mortgage arrears and repossessions, there continues to be a broad acceptance of the basic form of organisation of owner-occupation as a tenure, that is as a set of bureaucratic relations stemming from the power of loan finance capital, exchange relations based on market pricing, and state–citizen relations based mainly on legally conferred rights and fiscal support (Somerville and Knowles 1991). As with private renting, significant change has occurred, with the expansion of owner-occupation among working-class households. Much of this has been made possible, however, by the increased participation of married women in the labour market (Munro and Smith 1989), a development that contradicts the stereotypical nuclear family assumption of the postwar social settlement and points the way towards a different form of settlement altogether.

As for council housing, with the exception of a brief period in the early 1950s, Labour and Conservative policies have been markedly divergent since 1923. On the Conservative side, as Balchin says:

> Over many decades, Conservative policy has been broadly consistent. It has been manifestly antagonistic to the sector in aggregate and to general needs provision in particular. It was only in the 1950s (and under Labour legislation, the 1949 Act) that a Conservative government perceived council housing as a priority.
>
> (Balchin 1989: 177)

Conservative governments have seen council housing either as a necessary but temporary evil (as in the case of rehousing people from the slums) or as providing help for those who cannot satisfy their housing need in other ways – for example, those who can neither afford to buy nor find suitable accommodation to rent privately. This view is of course perfectly consistent with traditional Conservative belief in a property-owning democracy (financed predominantly by private institutions such as building societies) and with Conservative distrust of state monopoly provision. In contrast, Labour has always advocated council housing provision as an important way of solving housing problems of all kinds, but their approach has typically been qualified by bureaucratic and restrictive definitions of housing need – council housing has been deemed to be accessible only to those who are said to be 'deserving' of it. The definitions of 'deserving' and 'undeserving' have varied considerably over the years, and from one (Labour) local authority to another, but there has always been an acceptance on the part of Labour that the 'undeserving' will be left to 'solve their own housing problem'. As with owner-occupation, the social relations of council housing (which Cole and Furbey (1994) have termed 'public landlordism') have not been seriously questioned by Labour. Also, as with the other tenures, the continuity of basic political policy in relation to council housing has co-existed with great changes in the fortunes of the tenure itself, from its heyday in the early postwar period through a long, and accelerating, process of residualisation, associated primarily with the continuing expansion of owner-occupation.

Because of the marginalisation of private renting, and the lack of real political dissension over owner-occupation, the politics of tenure has been concentrated on council housing. In this debate, however, the advocacy of council housing has tended to be weak, because of the Labour Party's acceptance of the superiority of owner-occupation (at least after 1977), and because of council housing's statist and paternalist character – the lack of any real democratic control over council housing provision and management. This helps to explain the lack of any significant national opposition to the Right to Buy for council tenants introduced by the Conservative government in 1980, as well as the Labour Party's later decision (in 1984) to retain this right if it came to power. In general, the lack of Tory support for council housing meant that the postwar settlement in this respect was particularly fragile. This is probably why it was housing, rather than, say, education or health, which became politically most contentious from the mid-1950s until the mid-1980s.

Another aspect of the postwar settlement was the character of bureau-professionalism. For housing, this was rather different from that for other departments of the welfare state, because the professions involved were only loosely associated with 'welfare', being accountants, surveyors, construction managers and estate managers. The balance among these professions also shifted over the years, from a dominance of design and development professions in the early postwar period to an ascendancy of professions concerned with financial and economic regulation and management. The general effect of all this professionalism in housing was to define the postwar housing problem in purely technical terms as one of housing shortage in the early period, with the task of housing policy being seen as one of how to maximise housing output. The provision of council housing in particular was organised as a provision *for* the working classes *by* middle-class professionals and bureaucrats (and their politician partners). The political issue of lack of working-class control over their housing conditions never rose to the surface. Once policymaking in housing became a technical matter, responsibility for it tended to pass to the professional and administrative 'experts', with the politicians' role being reduced to one of setting targets and monitoring efficiency.

The decline of the postwar settlement in housing

Over the course of time, continuing professionalisation, which was partly associated with success in overcoming the most severe housing shortages, led to a progressive weakening of working-class power in the postwar settlement, and a concomitant decline of support for council housing provision. This reduction in working-class pressure for new housing provision, combined with the excesses of the design and development professions in the 1960s (Dunleavy 1981), then brought an end to the dominant perceptions of housing shortage, and saw the rise to prominence of policies based increasingly explicitly on either neo-liberal or social-democratic principles. The fragile consensus embodied in the postwar settlement began to break down, and there occurred a certain revival of political struggle over housing in the late 1960s and through the 1970s. It is this revival which was held in check from the late 1970s onwards by the rise of managerialism, representing a wider and more powerful programme of professionalisation. The result was that by the 1990s housing policy had come once more to be dominated by 'technical' issues such as fund-raising, affordability, service delivery and meeting needs.

Another theme in the decline of the postwar settlement in housing was the growing divergence between the viewpoint of central government and that of many local authorities who continued to give a high priority to the elimination of housing shortages in their areas. This divergence gave rise to open conflict by the end of the 1970s, and this conflict was interpreted by central government as a problem of how to bring to heel these 'overspending' and/or 'inefficient' local authorities. This marked the onset of managerialism as a national 'top-down' project, seeking to replace the so-called 'urban managerialism' (Pahl 1975) which had hitherto existed at local level. The political problem of local working-class resistance to national state power was thus reconstructed as a technical or managerial problem, to be solved primarily in terms of bureaucratic, technical and professional linkages (Houlihan 1988: 78–82, 204). It is these linkages which mainly characterise the long-term process of centralisation of state power referred to by Malpass and Murie (1990: 310). The period since 1974 has seen tightening central control, over aggregate investment, homelessness, area improvement, council house sales and rent levels (Houlihan 1988: 48), with government increasingly by-passing local authorities altogether in order to meet its objectives, most notably through the Housing Corporation and housing associations.

In a sense, the provision of council housing under the postwar settlement was a victim of its own success. The solution to the housing problems of the now 'comfortable' majority led to a diminishing concern with the problems of those who had shrunk to only a minority, and the thrust of housing policy moved decisively away from new build and towards such objectives as control of public expenditure, safeguarding of housing equity and tenure change (from tenancy to ownership). At the same time, this shift meant an end to the postwar consensus and the forging of a new settlement in housing.

The decline of the postwar settlement in housing can be explained in terms of rational choice theory. At a time of severe housing shortages for a substantial proportion of the population, it was to be expected that individuals would be prepared to accept massive public investment in order to meet their needs. Once such needs were met, it was predictable that concerns would be raised about the high level of the expenditure involved, and the implications of this expenditure for levels of taxation. Rhetoric about meeting needs therefore came to be replaced by rhetoric about 'what the country can afford'. The expediency of collectivism in the aftermath of war gradually gave way to the re-assertion of individualism. This change was entirely consistent with the rational interests of the generality of individuals involved.

An interesting point about the decline in the postwar consensus in housing is that the rational choices of 'comfortable Britain' were directly responsible for the continuation of the housing problems which postwar policy was supposed to have solved. For example, the shift away from new build meant that housing shortages continued, though only for the 'uncomfortable' minority. Similarly, the shift away from so-called 'bricks and mortar' subsidy, through which the new build programme had been promulgated, more or less guaranteed that poor housing conditions would continue. And finally, measures to achieve increases in public sector rents, as a way of reducing the overall burden on the public purse, gave rise to a new problem of affordability for lower-income households. All these developments presented potential challenges to the emerging hegemony of managerialism.

In the 1980s, a more strident neo-liberalism took shape in housing policy. This involved not only a continuation of the cuts in public spending initiated by the previous Labour government, but a process of tenure restructuring through the following: the privatisation of council housing, mainly through the Right to Buy, but later on through large-scale voluntary transfers; the expansion of housing associations, through both new build and stock transfer from local authorities; the 'normalisation' of owner-occupation, as the tenure to which all 'normal' households now aspire; and the revival of private renting, as a result of deregulation and increased labour mobility. The details of these changes have been well covered elsewhere (Balchin 1995; Hills 1998; Malpass and Murie 1999), and need not concern us here. The main point to mention is that the changes as a whole can be represented as a dispersal of power away from state bodies, and this is a key link to the argument articulated in the previous chapter concerning managerialism. The period of change is not yet at an end, but the inauguration of a new Labour government has led to a less strident and more pragmatic approach. This has meant, for example, that the persistence of the old housing problems of shortage, poor condition and lack of affordability, for which the previous Conservative government failed to take responsibility, may receive more sympathetic treatment, although so far the evidence in support of this is weak (see below, pp. 163–4; Cooper and Somerville 2000).

The rise of managerialism in housing

The managerialist dispersal of state power in housing has taken a number of forms. These include: the drive to end the direct provision of housing by the state and its replacement by a network of provider agencies, operating in partnership with state organisations; the reform of ownership rights in housing so as to challenge the authority of traditional bureaucratic structures; and the linkage of housing with other areas of public and social policy, for example through community care and area regeneration. Some of these processes are already well established, and will be discussed further below.

Other ways in which managerialism has manifested itself in housing include: the re-professionalisation of housing away from a narrow concern with techniques of housing administration towards the development of more generic managerial skills; the introduction of specific managerial regimes of performance management and Best Value; and the re-moulding of housing organisations in order to increase flexibility, responsiveness and innovation. A further, perhaps unsavoury, aspect of managerialism, particularly under New Labour, has been what could be described as 'remoralisation', whereby individuals are expected increasingly to earn the favours that managers dispose by behaving in the correct manner – so-called 'conditional welfare' (Dwyer 1998). This forms part of a wider programme of 'conditional communitarianism' (H. Dean 1999: 222), according to which the enjoyment of citizenship rights is made to be conditional upon specific performance by individual citizens. So, for example, an applicant for social housing may be required to take an insecure introductory tenancy for twelve months before being permitted to become a secure tenant. Interestingly, rational choice theory suggests that such an approach is unlikely to be successful. On the whole if you want to encourage people to be good, it is better, as Cowan (1999: 494) suggests, to give them something of value which they risk losing if they misbehave. In general, it is more rational to tackle bad behaviour directly rather than indirectly through the rewarding of good behaviour.

The dispersal of state power in housing through inter-organisational networks has been investigated by Reid (1995). The process is clearly well advanced, and some local authorities have been particularly enthusiastic about partnerships generally, but the significance of the shift in power is a matter of some dispute. Has there been a fundamental change in the way the local authority conducts its affairs, or is partnership mere window-dressing, a game that the local authority plays in order to secure funding and achieve its corporate objectives? Available evidence tends to suggest that within local authorities power remains concentrated in a small caucus of senior politicians and chief officers, and decisions then continue to be implemented in an essentially top-down manner. On the whole, therefore, local authorities look to be a long way off from the ideal type of managerialism, where power would be dispersed to front-line staff, acting in partnership with tenants and other stakeholders.

Another point which illustrates the limited character of the dispersal of state power up to now is that a large proportion of the population (nearly one in five) continues to live in council housing. This is nearly twice as many as live in private rented accommodation, and nearly four times as many as live in housing association accommodation. In spite of a process of residualisation going on for over forty years, it remains the case that, of all the tenures, only owner-occupation holds more people than council housing. At the present rate of attenuation, it would take at least another twenty years before the numbers in housing association tenancies overtook those in local authority ones. Up until recently, it was not clear whether this indicated the slow pace of the hegemonic shift or was simply a consequence of the massive extent of the shift involved. Now, with the government's announcement of a stepping up of the stock transfer programme, it looks as if all council housing may be disposed of within fifteen years, so the hegemonic shift is back on course.

On the question of ownership rights, by far the most important change was the introduction of the Right to Buy for secure tenants in 1980, which has resulted in the transfer of 1.7 million homes from local authorities into owner-occupation. The exercise of this right certainly involved a dispersal of power to the new home-owners, as they achieved new freedoms to alter their property and dispose of it as they wished. However, it did not bring with it any serious challenge to existing ways of managing council housing, as the beneficiaries exited the tenure and exercised 'voice' only to the extent of trying to get the local authority to enforce their neighbours' conditions of tenancy. The situation with the Tenants' Choice provisions of the Housing Act 1988 was quite different. Here council tenants effectively gained a right to trigger a transfer of ownership away from the local authority to a landlord of their choice. Unlike the Right to Buy, it appears that this measure had a substantial effect on local authorities' attitudes to tenants, and caused a fundamental review of how housing services were provided in many areas (Birchall 1992). Even though few Tenants' Choice transfers actually took place, from this point on most local authorities attached a high priority to ensuring that their tenants were satisfied with the services they received. In spite of this, the Tenants' Choice provisions were repealed by the Housing Act 1996. This suggests that the government of the time was not, after all, strongly committed to transforming local authority bureaucracy, but was concerned only with demunicipalisation. When the latter failed to materialise, they had no compunction about scrapping the legislation involved.

In community care policy, housing has become linked with other arms of the welfare state such as health and social services. These linkages can be regarded as examples of inter-organisational networks as discussed above, and possibly as involving new forms of disciplinary power in Foucauldian terms (for example, in their emphasis on the 'normalisation' of their subjects). Whether such linkages have led to any substantial changes in power relations or ways of working is again a matter of debate. In relation to housing associations, the issue has been seen in terms of the value of becoming involved in 'housing plus'. Some associations take the view that housing associations should stick to what they are good at, namely traditional housing management, whereas others argue that it is important for associations to be involved on a wider front within the communities they purport to serve. Clearly, at the present time, linkages are in most cases very fragile, so the dispersal of power through these linkages is uncertain, to say the least.

In area regeneration, housing has become involved with a wide range of other agencies, but typically as a junior partner, with lead roles being played by economic development agencies and planners. Here, housing policy has been subordinated to what have been viewed as the more crucial policies of job creation and land-use planning. Consequently, it could be questioned whether any dispersal of state power has taken place at all, particularly as many of the new agencies involved, such as urban development corporations, English Partnerships, and now Regional Development Agencies, are themselves quasi-state organisations or quangos. New inter-organisational networks have been created, which project a facade of power dispersal, but in reality probably amount to a partial nationalisation or regionalisation of local state power configurations. This means that instead of being dispersed horizontally and vertically downwards, power has to some extent been dispersed upwards from local authority level to new quasi-governmental organisations. This in itself could represent a reassertion of bureaucratic power, but in new forms, for which elected regional assemblies could yet provide a measure of legitimacy.

What is housing managerialism?

Housing management has always been a weak profession, representing only a fraction of the workforce in housing, and with little influence over housing policy. This alone is sufficient to explain the low priority attached to housing in the reshaping of the postwar settlement, dependent as that reshaping was on the centrality of professionalisation processes. With the rise of managerialism, however, the profession has tended to place greater emphasis on its management skills and rather less on its specialist housing expertise. In following this approach, the profession hopes to raise its status and reap the benefits to be gained from the emerging new managerial regime. It is not yet clear, however, how successful such an approach is likely to be. There is a risk, for example, that, by losing its distinctive character as a profession, housing may lose its influence on policy altogether.

Another issue in relation to housing management is that there have always existed a variety of competing approaches. Any attempt to evaluate managerialism in housing is inevitably complicated by this variety. Two of the approaches concerned have been discussed already in this chapter, namely the personalised approach of Octavia Hill and the administrative/technical approach of local authorities up to the 1970s. These are the approaches which predominated before the postwar settlement, and were at that time formally organised through the Society of Women Housing Managers and the Institute of Housing respectively. With the rise of managerialism, these approaches have been revisited and rethought, resulting in the decline of the administrative/technical approach and what could be described as the rebranding of the personalised approach. In addition, new approaches have emerged, whose character is only just beginning to become clear.

Somerville and Steele (1999) have distinguished five types of approach, all of which are compatible with managerialism, on the basis of evidence from Britain, Sweden and the Netherlands. They analyse them in terms of the extent to which they disperse power, the degree to which power flows from the top downwards and reciprocally from the bottom upwards, and their effect on increasing residents' independence of action. One of these approaches is the rebranded personalised approach most notably associated with Anne Power (1984 1987), according to which 'good management' is achieved through individual managers having responsibility for a 'patch' or neighbourhood and having control of the delivery of housing (and possibly other) services to people living in that neighbourhood. This approach involves a considerable dispersal of power to managers, though not necessarily to residents because of the possibility that managers might adopt a paternalistic style. Because of its personalised character, however, some influence of residents upon managers is inevitable. The approach has a number of important potential benefits: in theory, if not always in practice, greater account can be taken of the needs and aspirations of individual residents; the drawbacks of remote and arbitrary bureaucratic power are removed; adherence to managerial rule is produced through the forging of personal allegiances, which promotes social cohesion although it can also be discriminatory as managers will tend to have their 'favourites' as well as those they regard as 'pains'; the establishment of a system of 'patches' can help to reduce large-group problems to small-group ones, thus solving the free-rider problem discussed in the last chapter; and the greater freedom for managers can result in more imaginative and innovative solutions to housing problems, particularly solutions that involve and include residents in substantive ways. The general benefits of neighbourhood management are now well established by research (Gregory 1998).

Personalised management, however, also has a number of limitations. The success of the approach depends crucially on the personality and competence of the individual manager. Where such a person has outstanding qualities, the results can be spectacular (Seabrook 1984). Unfortunately, however, this is unusual, and in any case most housing organisations have shown themselves to be remarkably reluctant to devolve power to such managers to the extent which is required for the approach to work. There is also an issue concerning the accountability of such managers. Their accountability down to their residents is not formalised in any sense, so residents cannot be effectively used to monitor and evaluate their performance. On the other hand, the form of their accountability to senior management, which typically relies on traditional bureaucratic means such as reports on voids, arrears and so on, risks undermining the autonomy which lies at the heart of the whole approach. A further issue concerns the potential lack of linkage of such individual managers into supportive managerial networks. In practice, such managers may be operating in splendid isolation, making them vulnerable to destructive influences in some cases, and generally resulting in a growing divergence of practice from one neighbourhood to another – a fragmentation which may or may not be justifiable in terms of real differences among neighbourhoods. A final issue concerns the reactions of residents themselves to the wholesale adoption of a personalised approach to housing management. As envisaged by managerialism, the dispersal of power to individual managers of local offices will encourage residents in these areas to press more strongly for improvements in the area and in service delivery generally. Personalised management alone, however, is unlikely to be able to respond effectively to the demands arising from such 'active citizenship'. The consequence will therefore be continuing conflict, which may or may not be healthy, depending on how well the local office is linked into wider social networks.

The second type of approach identified by Somerville and Steele (1999) is what they term 'market-oriented'. According to this approach, housing services are to be reorganised so as to be more flexible and closer to their customers (what could be described as more 'market-sensitive'), but the reorganisation is essentially a 'top-down' process, and does not increase tenants' independence or freedom of action. In spite of increased resident (or customer) involvement, the housing organisation retains directive control over the whole process, and there is no effective dispersal of power. Strictly speaking, therefore, this is not an expression of managerialism according to the definition developed in the previous chapter, but is rather a bureaucratic response to a situation of increased uncertainty or threats in the external environment. Uncertainty arises because of an increased incidence of management problems such as rent arrears, difficult-to-let properties, anti-social behaviour, and run-down estates, and threats come from, for example, central government in terms of enforced privatisation, year-on-year reductions in housing investment and subsidy and the compulsory competitive tendering of housing management. One reaction of local authorities to such attrition has been to reform their organisational structures into more effective defences against attack from outside, and in some cases this has meant a process of retrenchment whereby the power and autonomy of front-line staff has been curtailed 'for the greater good of the organisation'. The resulting reassertion of bureaucratic line management, however, tends to run counter to the managerialist opening up of the organisation to new, more flexible ways of working. In the long run, such an approach is likely to be self-destructive, as disgruntled staff depart to more congenial organisational environments, and the life-blood of the organisation gradually drains away.

The third type of approach identified by Somerville and Steele (1999) is 'partnership'. Essentially, this means an arrangement where the housing organisation enters into processes of negotiation and agreement with groups of residents in order to achieve outcomes that are beneficial for both parties. Examples of a partnership approach include estate agreements in England, where landlord and tenants agree on the priorities for an estate and the targets for management performance across a range of indicators (Steele *et al.* 1995). A more recent example of such an approach is the Labour government's proposal for Tenant Participation Compacts which sets out in a more detailed form how such partnerships could be developed and monitored (DETR 1999). Partnership approaches therefore appear to involve a real dispersal of power, although the extent of this dispersal is a matter of debate, as it is generally recognised that the partnerships concerned are unequal. They also have the merit of starting from where the residents are at, rather than attempting to impose solutions upon them from outside, even though the housing organisation, as the stronger partner, can always prevail in the end. Like personalised approaches, partnerships can promote the internalisation of managerial objectives and the reduction of large-group problems to smaller-group ones. They can also stimulate democratic renewal through the encouragement of representative negotiating bodies at estate level, thus facilitating more effective resolution of collective-action problems. Finally, if negotiations are undertaken in good faith, and negotiating bodies are reasonably representative of the interests involved, partnerships are capable of producing original solutions that are productive for residents as well as for housing organisations.

On the down side, it has to be said that partnerships have major shortcomings in practice. Just as personalised management is crucially dependent upon the personal power exercised by individual managers, so partnership arrangements are largely at the mercy of individual housing organisations.

Just as there are problems around the accountability of individual managers, so there are problems with the accountability of individual housing organisations. Systems of monitoring and regulation, such as that carried out for registered social landlords in England by the Housing Corporation, or for local housing authorities by the Department of Environment, Transport and the Regions (DETR), cannot yet be said to be adequate to ensure that these organisations play fair by their tenants and do not abuse the superior power which they enjoy in relation to them. The regime of Best Value being introduced by the Labour government holds out the prospect of more effective accountability in the future, mainly because it builds in a measure of evaluation by those who are the recipients of the public services involved. At the present time, however, it is not clear whether this degree of accountability is sufficiently democratic, in the sense of allowing for an evaluation beyond that which is available to service users. There is a risk that the evaluation will be a purely 'internal', and indeed 'technical', matter, with the result that the housing organisation will be able to continue to get its own way in the face of resident opposition. Best Value represents a new stage in the development of managerialism in housing and other public services, involving more sophisticated techniques of performance appraisal, but it is not yet clear whether the development of these techniques will serve to strengthen democracy or weaken it. At a guess, because the system is designed from the top and is intended to be accountable upwards, to DETR and the Housing Corporation, it is likely that the accountability at grassroots level will be a secondary consideration, and therefore any additional dispersal of power, to front-line staff and residents, will be limited. Where conflicts arise between groups of residents and a housing organisation, the odds will continue to be stacked heavily in favour of the housing organisation. This new managerialist formation has been described as 'corporatist managerialism' (Cooper and Somerville 2000).

The other two types of approach identified by Somerville and Steele (1999) are forms of tenant management: that is, arrangements where the tenants collectively control the management of their properties for themselves. Clearly, these arrangements involve a considerably greater dispersal of power than any of the other types. They are indeed the only examples of managerialism in housing where the residents themselves are specifically included in the prevailing hegemony: that is, residents individually and as a group actually become managers, and receive special training in order for them to develop the necessary managerial skills. So long as the collectivity concerned is not too large, management at this level is capable of incorporating many of the advantages of personalised approaches such as responsiveness to the feelings of individual residents and promotion of social cohesion. It also has the potential to avoid some of the problems associated with partnership approaches, because the tenant management body enjoys greater independence than, for example, a tenant group that is a party to an estate agreement. Whether the form of tenant management is a co-operative or a representative tenant-led board, it is fully accountable to the residents, and the local authority is accountable to it through the management agreement. On all criteria, therefore, tenant management approaches look to be a significant managerial advance on the other approaches to housing management.

Still, tenant management has problems. As with personalised management, it runs the risk of favouring its own people and effectively excluding others. This problem is related to the 'freedom' that tenant management bodies have to act on their own initiative which can be associated with increased isolation and uncertainty. Such bodies lack the degree of power that comes with full ownership, but in partial compensation for this they may have more opportunity to tap into networks mediated by their parent organisation. Thus, tenant management approaches incorporate individual residents more explicitly into managerialist rule, and this incorporation can be beneficial for the residents affected, but it could at the same time leave other residents worse off. This could happen either because residents in the same area are not sufficiently included in the arrangement or because residents in other areas are left behind by the 'active citizenship' of the tenant managers rather than being taken forward by them.

This discussion of housing management approaches, while perhaps throwing some light on what managerialism in housing might mean, nevertheless reveals how complicated the situation is. One could go on to ask: what is the nature of managerialism in housing in relation to the themes of Family, Work and Nation? and: how has the shift from monarchical to disciplinary power manifested itself in housing processes?

In relation to Family, there has been some shift away from dealing exclusively with nuclear families and towards dealing with a range of 'non-traditional' forms of household such as joint families and single people, although this shift has not been very significant (Anderson 1999). On the other hand, policies on benefit entitlement from 1988 onwards have tended to make young single adults more dependent on their parents, and for longer periods. These developments, symptomatic of the selfishness and parsimony of the majoritarian 'comfortable Britons', are also consistent with the managerialist co-option of parents as active participants in their own exploitation (see Chapter 5). This also signals one of the mechanisms whereby power relations are changed, from the monarchical rule of the bureaucratic state to the disciplinary regime of responsible parenthood. Dispersal of state power is at the same time a promotion of disciplinary responsibility.

With regard to Work, managerialism in housing is primarily concerned to enhance the role of housing in 'active' labour market policies. A good example of this is the foyer movement, which links the provision of housing for young people with training and assistance to access paid employment. This also links neo-liberal managerialism (equipping people to compete in the free market) with the corporatist managerialism of the New Deal (partnerships with social housing and other organisations to achieve improved 'joined-up' performance). With the support of government funding through the New Deal programme, foyers could be argued to be a positive aspect of managerialism, although to date they have benefited only a small fraction of homeless young people without jobs or qualifications (Quilgars and Anderson 1995; Fearn 2000). Again, the transition to disciplinary power is apparent from the emphasis being placed on the responsibility of the young person to take a proactive role in their own self-development, with the state providing 'a hand-up, not a hand-out'.

Finally, in relation to Nation, the processes of tenure restructuring described earlier in this chapter can in a sense be represented as involving an internationalisation or at least a Europeanisation of the British housing system. For example, the growth of owner-occupation has opened up more of the housing stock to potential overseas purchasers (and vice versa, it has enabled more British citizens to purchase housing abroad), and the transfer of local authority stock to housing associations has opened up the rented housing market to foreign competition. In the future, it is likely that increasing numbers of housing associations will operate on a transnational basis or become part of larger transnational conglomerates such as SERCO or Générale des Eaux. National settlements in housing will therefore gradually fade in importance over the course of time, eventually to be replaced by new Continental settlements. The power of nation-states is already on the wane, but the character of new supranational settlements is emerging only very slowly.

The critique of managerialism in housing

As recognised in the previous chapter, managerialism has considerable strengths. In housing in particular, a major potential advantage has been the dispersal of power to front-line staff and residents. In practice, however, this dispersal has not gone very far or very deep within most housing organisations. In this sense, it can be said that managerialism is not very well established in these organisations, which continue to operate on largely bureaucratic principles. It seems a little speculative, therefore, to criticise something that does not yet exist. Nevertheless, it is possible to indicate some of the paths which managerialism is likely to follow, and then to point out some of the pitfalls that are to be found along these paths.

First of all, to return to rational choice theory. It is often assumed by liberals (for example, Saunders 1990; King 1996, 1998) that owner-occupation is the most rational choice of free individuals, because it gives most control to the individual over their housing. Certainly, owner-occupation confers a major advantage over other tenures in terms of freedom from landlords, and this alone is sufficient to explain its popularity. There are two difficulties with this liberal position, however. One is that in certain circumstances owner-occupation can be a burden rather than a benefit, for example involving huge debts over long periods, or expensive and/or discomforting repair responsibilities, or assets which the owner may not be able to dispose of when they want to. The other is that the choice in question is made on behalf of an entire household, and therefore may not be the most rational from the point of view of less powerful members of that household. For example, in a lower-income household, owner-occupation may be affordable only if at least two members of the household are in paid employment, and as we saw in Chapter 2 this can result in disproportionately greater burdens for the female partner in such households compared with their counterparts in renting households.

Tenure choice is therefore first and foremost a matter of negotiation within any given household, and the pattern of such negotiation was discussed in Chapter 2. Household decisions are then made on the basis of an evaluation of the benefits of owner-occupation (or whatever) relative to the risks. The precise balance of benefits and risks will vary according to the individual household and their situation, in terms of income, job prospects, family connections, community networks, long-term goals, specific skills and preferences, and so on. Individuals will also be affected, however, by the prevailing hegemony, through liberal and managerial discourses of self-reliance, self-management and self-actualisation. Through owner-occupation, managerialism successfully incorporates individual householders as managers of their own destiny, subject only to the discipline of the market. Even when the market fails, as in Britain in the early 1990s, faith in owner-occupation is not lost, either by housing consumers or by politicians. Rather, the anarchy of the market is accepted as part of the risk that is inevitable in a free society. Perhaps the real significance of owner-occupation, then, lies in its disciplinary power.

This discussion prompts the question of under what circumstances individuals within a household will negotiate a choice of tenure other than owner-occupation. The general answer has to be that renting will be considered only if for some reason owner-occupation is unobtainable, perhaps because it is not affordable or is too great a burden to bear in the household's current situation (for example, they may be too young or too old). Under managerialism, there is no possibility of owning and renting having the same status – managerialism itself is far more advanced in the owner-occupied sector, as we have seen. This differentiation between tenures, however, has negative effects for the rented sectors, and thereby for those who 'choose' to rent generally.

In the previous chapter, it was argued that in order for individuals to be able to exercise free rational choice, the constraints upon them must be equalised, and this was to be achieved through forms of democracy, partnership and citizenship. This argument immediately suggests a problem with owner-occupation, because the latter tends to reproduce and reinforce inequalities among households (and perhaps also within households). This is of course a characteristic of market relations generally (see Chapter 4), and suggests a need to introduce, by democratic means, a measure of redistribution among owner-occupying households, for example through capital gains tax (from which owner-occupation is currently exempt) and mortgage benefit (to assist poorer owner-occupiers). The imbalance between owning and renting as a whole also needs to be corrected, for example through greater state assistance to renting in combination with greater democratic rights and empowerment of tenants at grass-roots level. In order to negotiate on an equal basis with their landlords, tenants need to have the right to pursue a path towards democratic legal ownership of their estates, and they need to have access to the support required for them to exercise such a right. This in turn means that they need to develop the capacity to choose their own partners in order to meet their democratically agreed aspirations. Finally, in making their choices, the tenant group needs to have practices, rules and sanctions in place whereby free-riding by members of the group is minimised, for example by making participation particularly attractive or by penalising non-participation socially and/or financially.

The system of governance that would result from such reforms has already been described in Chapter 5. Box (1998)'s model of citizen governance could be reinterpreted at the level of a housing estate. The residents of the estate could be given the right to elect their own representatives to a board which would be responsible for the general management of the estate. The decisions of these boards could be reviewed at the level of the local authority or housing association. The residents would also have the right to trigger the transfer of ownership of the estate to the board, subject to the approval of the majority of them. Finally, the estate boards would have the power to command assistance as necessary, to develop themselves and their estate, from the local authority, central government or the Housing Corporation. In this way, subject to regulations to ensure the good conduct of affairs and equalisation of constraints within the board (these would include policies to ensure fair and non-discriminatory treatment, the promotion of equality of opportunity and the valuing of diversity), individual and community capacity could be developed that would promote an equalisation of constraints on a wider basis.

Managerialism, however, falls well short of such a system of governance. The Labour government, for example, has no plans for the democratisation of housing organisations or for a widespread empowerment of tenants at the estate level. The proposals for Best Value in housing and tenant participation compacts, although an advance on what already exists, are strictly managerialist proposals designed to improve the performance of local housing authorities and housing associations. They have some potential for greater inclusiveness within authorities, for example through compacts at the estate level, and greater fairness among authorities, for example through processes of benchmarking, but at bottom, to use the terminology of Somerville and Steele (1999), they are reformist rather than radical measures, and will serve to consolidate the power of managers rather than put tenants in the driving seat. Compacts in particular signify a new form of partnership between local authorities and voluntary groups (Craig *et al.* 1999), but the relationship continues to be one in which the local authority is the senior partner, and can largely choose for itself how it wants to play the government's game. Finally, and more encouragingly, the government's managerialist use of tenant participation compacts to promote more 'active citizens' could actually lead to a situation where tenants offer resistance to managerialist hegemony on a more wide-ranging, more organised, and systematic basis. In the absence of more radical rights and resources for residents, however, it seems that such resistance is likely to prove ineffective in most cases. Once again, the key flaw in managerialism is shown to lie in the inadequacy of its democratic accountability. This same flaw leads the critic to question how inclusive are its programmes, for example with regard to homeless people, disabled people, black and minority ethnic groups, and poorer households generally.

In relation to New Labour's variant of managerialism in particular, it could be concluded that it is more thoroughgoing than under the Conservatives. It is more pragmatic (with its emphasis on 'what works') than ideological (in terms of a rigid political 'line'), and it is corporatist (with a stress on 'joined-up' policy) rather than laissez-faire or social darwinist. The decline in anti-municipal prejudice is to be welcomed, as is the abandonment of doctrinally driven 'market' solutions to management problems. At the end of the day, however, the managers' 'right to manage' remains fundamental to the approach, and the existing deeply unequal pattern of power relations in housing goes unchallenged.

7 Conclusion

This book has been wide-ranging and ambitious in its scope. It has attempted to apply rational choice theory to what could be argued to be key sets of social relations: domestic relations, communal relations, exchange relations, bureaucratic relations and state–citizen relations. It has consciously avoided currently fashionable discussions of modernity and postmodernity, opting instead for an approach that reaffirms the universality of human nature and uses materially derived general categories to improve our understanding of human action.

The author is aware that this approach is likely to be misunderstood by many readers. It seems sensible, therefore, to set out some of the most common misunderstandings that may arise and try to make the argument as clear as possible. First of all, rational choice theory is based on the assumption of the rationality of individual human action, but this does not mean that people always behave rationally or individualistically. As with many other social theories, the assumption relates to a basic *tendency* in human behaviour, not a universal truth. Essentially, what the theory says is that it will be assumed that people act rationally and in their own self-interest unless there is evidence to show otherwise, and where it is shown that they act irrationally and against their own interests this will be highlighted as a problem that needs to be explained. This was the approach that was followed in particular in Chapter 2, where it appeared that women acted irrationally by being in partnership with men who exploited them, and again in Chapter 4, where it seemed irrational for workers to enter freely into relations of exploitation with employers. In both of these cases, the apparent irrationality of action was explained by reference to the character of the social institutions that had developed so as to structure the opportunities available to the individuals concerned. In other words, it was shown that it was not so much the individuals who were acting irrationally or selflessly – rather, it was the institutions, such as the family and the labour market, which were operating unreasonably by restricting individual choices in ways that could be judged to be oppressive.

A second misunderstanding of rational choice theory is to identify it with a right-wing political position. This misunderstanding arises because of the uncompromising individualism that lies at the heart of the theory, which is contrasted with the collectivism that is said to be characteristic of a left-wing position. Certainly, there is a libertarian strand within the political right that believes strongly in individual freedom and is resolutely anti-collectivist. Rational choice theory, however, is not anti-collectivist at all – rather, it can be regarded as an aid to collective action because it points out some of the obstacles that must be overcome in order for such action to be effective. Far from rational choice being a right-wing theory, this book has attempted to show, following 'analytical marxists' such as Elster, that the theory is more compatible with a left-wing perspective. The most convincing critiques directed at right-wing libertarians are not those which deny the possibility or legitimacy of individual freedom, subsuming it under some collective will, but precisely those that assert the primacy of such freedom and then go on to point out how right-wing programmes always and inevitably undermine such freedom and frustrate its effective exercise. These themes were covered most explicitly in Chapters 5 and 6, where it was argued, among other things, that the assumption of universal human freedom requires that the constraints upon this freedom should be equalised. Far from being a denial of human freedom, therefore, as Hayek believed, a redistribution of opportunities (for example, through a system of taxation and benefits) is a precondition for the maximisation of that freedom.

A third misunderstanding of rational choice theory is to presume that it is saying that everybody is the same, so in any given situation we should be able to predict how someone will act, and since we cannot do this the theory must be wrong. This misunderstanding is complex. In one sense, at least, it is true that the theory does say that all human beings are the same, namely that they all have the capacity to act rationally. This does not mean, however, that how someone will act in a given situation is predictable, for three reasons: first, because individuals do not always act rationally, and we may not know enough about the person concerned to tell whether or not he or she will act rationally in this particular situation; second, we can never know enough about the situation or the context of the individual action to tell precisely what a rational course of action might be; and third, in any given situation, there is likely to be a variety of possible courses of action, all of which might equally appear to be rational. There are inevitable uncertainties concerning both the actor and the arena of action. Rational choice theory is therefore not an exact science, in spite of impressions to the contrary, but nevertheless since on the whole individuals do behave rationally, and often in a publicly accessible form, the theory still has much to offer. This was demonstrated in particular in Chapter 2 where, in spite of considerable diversity from one household to another, many common and enduring features were identified, which could largely be explained in terms of rational choice principles. In another sense, in any case, the theory implies that individuals can be very different from each other, in terms of culture, class, gender, age, nationality, and so on, and therefore calls into question the validity of many traditional sociological categories. This point was explored to some extent in Chapter 4, where traditional explanations of human action in terms of structure and culture were criticised. In their place, it was suggested that what was required was a combination of rational choice theory and dynamic historical analysis: rational choice theory to deal with the position of the actor, and historical analysis to explain the derivation of the institutions that form the context within which choices are made. Chapters 5 and 6 then attempted such historical analyses at the level of state policymaking and implementation.

A fourth misunderstanding of rational choice theory concerns its epistemological status. This book has argued that the theory is not a 'Grand Narrative' like marxism or liberalism or feminism, but merely a set of provisional postulates. The distinction between Grand Theory and what Berkeley (1962) called 'serviceable fictions', however, is not as clear-cut as one might wish. Many adherents of 'Grand Narratives' are also at pains to claim that their theories are no more than working hypotheses, which are to be discarded if the evidence points towards more convincing explanations. This book has therefore attempted to distinguish between the presuppositions of rational choice theory and what might be taken to be more declamatory concepts such as those of exploitation, non-reciprocal obligation, hegemony and disciplinary regime. The key difference between the two sets of ideas is that the former relate to the potentialities of human action whereas the latter are used to make sense of the institutions within which, or in relation to which, action takes place – for example, the family, the workplace and the state. It has been argued in this book that the combination of rational choice theory with appropriate analysis of the institutional 'bounding' of individual choice is sufficient to explain a wide range of social relations. This in turn raises the epistemological issue of what counts as a sufficient or adequate explanation in social science. This book has taken the view that such an explanation is one which generates a range of hypotheses and models that then survive a variety of tests from evidence in different social contexts. Comprehensiveness and critical power are regarded as key criteria for explanatory adequacy.

In Chapter 2, individual action was examined in the context of gender and generational relations within the family. For gender relations, the discussion focused primarily on the domestic division of labour and the management and control of domestic finances, which could be argued to be crucial issues for the governance of this particular institution. On the basis of Carling's Exchange Model of rational choice, the chapter was able to explain much of the research evidence on the domestic division of labour; for example, the longer hours typically worked by the lower-earning partner, the general sexual specialisation of domestic tasks, the tendency for domestic labour time to reduce as participation in the labour market increases, the tendency for partners with more equal employment status to divide domestic work more equally, the common predominance of the husband's occupation in dual-career families, the greater power within the household of wives with independent income, and the tendency over the course of time for husbands to do more domestic work as their wives participate more in the labour market.

Some evidence, however, appeared to be inconsistent with the Exchange Model: for example, the finding cited by many studies that increased participation by wives in the labour market does *not* lead to their husbands doing more domestic work, that husbands' reduced participation in the labour market does not lead to their increased participation in household work, that role reversal hardly ever occurs where the wife's income exceeds that of her husband, and that some husbands continue to be opposed to their wives going out to work at all. All this evidence was explained on the basis of Carling's Chicken Model, which is a classic rational choice scenario where the husband plays chicken with his wife and typically enjoys a free ride on her domestic efforts. The explanatory success of the Chicken Model, however, is possible only on the assumption of the existence of certain norms, in particular norms of reciprocity and utilitarianism. Acting according to norms is perhaps not strictly rational: in Hume's terms, such action arises on the basis of the unjustifiable psychological expectation that the future will resemble the past (Hume 1962). Nevertheless, the adoption of a norm-following strategy can yield considerable benefits for the individual (Laver 1997), so it may be argued to be rational at a second-order level, provided only that individual trust is not broken by the defection of other individuals from the norm. The norm of reciprocity in particular is a precondition for the operation of both the Exchange and Chicken Models, being understood as a rule of conditional co-operation based on a repeatedly reinforced affirmation, by the actions of others, of the trust one has placed in them. This norm therefore appears to be rational at a second-order level, although based on an immeasurable level of risk associated with the uncertainty that any individual inevitably has concerning the motivations and decisions of others. The individual constructs their own 'serviceable fictions' in relation to those with whom they interact, and these fictions are always in danger of being contradicted by the facts of experience.

The norm of utilitarianism, in contrast, appears quite irrational, because it involves an individual in making a contribution to the good of the group (a household, a community, an organisation, a nation, or whatever), irrespective of the costs and benefits to themselves. Thus, in the context of the family, we find utilitarian norms of the male breadwinner and female homemaker. There is a sense in which these norms pre-exist the individual members of families today. The whole force of the family as an institution (and similarly with other social institutions such as bureaucracies and states, and even language) is bound up with the existence of such norms. Such norms therefore already exist as part of the context within which individual action takes place. Family members do not choose whether or not such norms should exist, but only whether or not they will follow them. Following a norm of domestic responsibility, however, seems irrational, because a breadwinning role confers more power and status. Nevertheless, rational choice theory shows that it may still be rational, particularly for a woman, to enter into such an unequal partnership (using the Exchange Model), even though within the relationship itself this inequality can be a source of conflict. Utilitarian norms therefore define a form of hegemony within institutions, serving to shape the regulatory boundaries within which action takes place. Patterns of resistance to such hegemony (which in the case of the family is called patriarchy) are constructed on the basis of specific interpretations of the normative regime.

In relation to the management and control of household finances, Chapter 2 considered the main types of financial management system, and suggested that female-managed systems were most rational (on the basis of the Exchange Model) in low-income households, but as the opportunities for choice grew with increasing income, the (more powerful) husband became more involved, resulting in male-managed systems. A clear shift to joint management occurred only where the wife was in full-time employment, and even then it might not lead to full equality in decision-making. This was again explained in terms of the prevailing normative regime and the application of the Chicken Model in relation to that regime. In general, rational choice theory confirmed the conclusions of feminist theorists on this subject, but also provided an independent explanation of how sexual inequality is institutionalised in the household and thence reproduced from one generation to the next. Analysis of the literature in this area also threw some light on how the distribution of responsibilities between husband and wife is a matter of dispute, with negotiations proceeding over a considerable period of time. Dialectics of sexual power and resistance are highly complex here, and far from being fully investigated.

The section on gender relations concluded with suggestions as to how a rational choice approach could be used to improve the position of women relative to men in the household. It was also pointed out that there are many features of domestic life that rational choice theory is not capable of explaining – for example, the formation of sexual ties and the development of forms of intimacy and lifelong obligation. It was suggested that such features are more effectively explained on the basis of phenomenological theories such as attachment theory. Given the desire for intimacy, however, the formation of long-term non-reciprocal ties could be argued to be the product of rational choice. What then appear to be irrational, or at least non-rational, acts of selfless devotion to duty and the welfare of others could be explained by reference to the routinisation and strong legitimation of past rational choices made by the individuals concerned.

The section on generational relations took up this theme of the rationality of strategies aimed at the long-term preservation of primary group relationships and ties. Structural explanations of kinship relations were specifically criticised on the grounds that they assumed that people formed families as a result of being driven by forces beyond their control, thus implicitly denying the causal efficacy of individual human choice. If having children is primarily a matter of choice, especially these days, however, there seems to be a serious problem for rational choice theory, because the costs of bringing up children appear greatly to outweigh the benefits, and therefore it is difficult to understand why any rational person would choose such a course of action. In considering this problem, the chapter limited itself to demonstrating only the plausibility of rational choice theory as a way of improving our understanding of it. The basic argument was that people want to maximise their resources not only for themselves but also for those whom they regard as their own, and this can involve the maximisation of value even beyond the lifespan of any particular individual. In this way, parents can be represented, through their actions in sharing their lives and goods with their children, as buying into a more permanent source of value. Such a strategy, however, is highly risky, and the chances of inter-generational conflict are considerable. In combination with the greatly increased net costs of bringing up children in modern societies, this high level of risk helps to explain why, considered over a long historical period, the birth rate in these societies continues to fall.

The chapter commented further on the significance of demographic transition, whereby the traditional direction of inter-generational exploitation, in which parents exploit their children, was reversed, resulting in new, and generally unrecognised, forms of exploitation of parents as a result of state intervention, for example in the regulation of child labour and the compulsory provision of education. The chapter criticised the recurrently fashionable idea that there is a form of long-term reciprocity between parents and children, whereby children are expected to care for their parents in return for the care they themselves received when young. All available evidence suggests that this is not the way in which reciprocity develops. The concept of reciprocity is essentially concerned with conditional co-operation and cannot be used to make sense of the character of parental obligation. This is because such obligation is not conditional upon reciprocal action by the child. The myth of long-term reciprocity is a good example of the muddled thinking which is highly prevalent in the area of family relations and family policy. People who argue in this way are essentially confusing norms of reciprocity with utilitarian norms, and the norm of parental responsibility is an example of the latter, not the former.

The chapter concluded by considering such issues as short-term reciprocity between parents and children and young people leaving the parental home. It was pointed out that available evidence concerning these processes supported rational choice theory because it showed that the parties involved adopted strategies of maximising their value within the context of the family as an institution. For example, the child's goal is (eventually) to achieve a measure of independence from their parents, whereas the parent's goal is to 'keep the child close' so as to ensure the continuation of the family unit.

Because these goals are potentially conflicting, growing up and leaving home involves a complex process of negotiation. This process is highly emotive, but also inherently rational.

Chapter 3 considered voluntary social relations going beyond the individual household. A distinction was made between contractual and non-contractual forms of such relations, and the chapter then concentrated on the latter, leaving the former to be examined in Chapter 4. The literature on community and neighbouring was comprehensively reviewed, and it was argued that the dynamics of community beyond the family could be explained largely in terms of the outworking of the norm of reciprocity and the three assumptions of rational choice theory listed in Chapter 1, with the common resource being that of the community itself. The recurring importance of boundary definition and maintenance found in the literature was then explained in terms of the rational desire to establish clearly and publicly the nature of the common resource, in order to minimise the vulnerability to free-riding of routinised practices of mutual aid. The differences in degree of exclusivity from one community to another were then explained largely in terms of the degree of significance of kinship and occupational relations within communities. This is essentially because the latter types of relations give rise to forms of attachment and coercion that are potentially far more exclusionary and cannot be entirely explained in terms of reciprocity. In contrast, the strictly voluntary character of community life can be fully accounted for on the basis of rational choice theory.

An important theme in this chapter was that the dynamics of social exclusion by communities take the same form, whether the socially excluded are minority ethnic groups, 'foreigners', 'roughs', or other groups deemed to be 'deviant' by the standards of the community. In every case, the process is one of assimilation of incomers (and similarly of members of new generations) if they are seen to be capable of adding to the value of the community, or one of exclusion or encapsulation if their potential contribution to the community is viewed negatively. The difference in power between the two groups is crucial. Assuming that the two groups are quite alien to each other, the more powerful one group is (whether 'natives' or 'immigrants'), the more likely it is to encapsulate the other.

Another theme in the chapter is the remarkable resilience of communities in the face of sometimes fundamental economic and social change. This is explained partly in terms of the way in which norms of conditional co-operation have the effect of channelling new generations into traditional gender and familial roles. Although rational at the level of local community interaction, this process can be in tension with developments in the labour market, and this can make it unreasonable for young people to expect to perform these roles. Rational choice at the level of one institution, (in this case, a local community) therefore, does not imply that the choice is rational at other levels.

The chapter went on to consider the nature of community development, arguing that this could be explained in terms of three types of actions: innovations within the community, interventions from outside the community, and interactions between the community and the outside world that produce new incentives or sanctions for collective action. In the literature, these three types of action characterised three main types of approach to community development: self-help, technical assistance and conflict approaches. In the chapter, these approaches were evaluated on the basis of rational choice theory. The success of technical assistance was argued to depend upon whether the 'assisters' are seen by the community as being a net benefit to them rather than a net cost. Similarly, the success of self-help was viewed as dependent upon capacity to maximise internal value and to access benefits outside the community. Finally, the success of conflict approaches was seen to depend very much on solidarity within the community in combination with resourcing from outside the community – a balance which is difficult to achieve and consequently often problematic in practice. Rational choice theory suggests that failure might be more avoidable if more attention were paid to the desires and aspirations of individual residents. This in turn means that divisions and differences within communities need to be taken much more seriously and weighed properly in the balance rather than being glossed over for the sake of putting on a unified front.

The chapter discussed in detail research and publications that have addressed this latter issue, summarising the lessons that have been learned and highlighting a number of problems. One problem, for example, is: how does a community acquire the capacity to know when to ask for assistance and what sort of assistance it needs? Consideration of this problem suggested possible further limitations of rational choice theory, as organisations which have developed, arguably rationally, at other institutional levels (such as the state) intervene in local communities in ways that cannot be foreseen and may not make any strategic sense. There is therefore an irreducible element of contingency here, which places community development always tantalisingly beyond the grasp of rational choice theory. Nevertheless, communities are capable of learning from such interventions and other interactions with outside bodies, with the result that their capacity does develop, at least in some cases, and there do exist established techniques that help them to do this. Not surprisingly, such techniques involve the extension of reciprocity (for example, partnerships between residents and assisters), the increase of net inward capital flows and the application of appropriate sanctions designed to ensure that benefits from these interactions are distributed widely within the community: that is, processes which express the key assumptions of rational choice theory. It is also recognised, however, that rational choice theory may not be the whole story – for example, phenomenological theory may be required in order to explain the depth of commitment that people have to their home area and the outcome of this commitment in terms of the quantity and quality of their voluntary activity.

The chapter continued with a closer examination of the techniques required for community development. This included an assessment of skills and roles that different individuals needed to have and play in order for community development to be sustained. It was pointed out how the adoption and re-enactment of these roles could be understood from a rational choice perspective, in terms of the strategies that different individuals articulate in order to achieve the fulfilment of their desires. In addition to rational choice, however, the discussion brought out the importance of developing a shared culture within the community, enriching the meaning of community life and providing a source of motivation for communal action. This led to a reconsideration of the role of community organisations, in terms of maximising the effectiveness of informal cultures and sustaining the achievements of informal community action. The chapter looked briefly at ways in which such organisations can be made inclusive, accountable, responsive and representative, a theme which was revisited and further developed in Chapters 5 and 6. In general, it was argued that community development essentially involves the development of *all* sections of the community.

The chapter concluded by re-examining what counts as success in community development and asking why such success is so rarely accomplished. Following Jerry Smith (1997), it was suggested that the main conditions for success are legal ownership, psychological ownership and neighbourhood management, and it was argued that it is these conditions that are most conducive to the free exercise of rational choice, best enabling the maximisation of utility for every community member. What frustrates this, however, are entrenched power blocs at national and local level, whose character is both economic and political. These power blocs are the subject of succeeding chapters, and rational choice theory teaches us that in spite of their overwhelming dominance they are not all-pervasive: they can be resisted and even transformed if people see it is in their interest to do so. What is required is a critique that links rational choice within a community with rational choice at a bureaucratic and political level. The initiation of such a critique was attempted in Chapters 4–6.

Chapter 4 focused on contractual relations. The advantages of such relations for individuals were emphasised, but it was also pointed out that they were a key source of social inequality, because of the way in which they have developed historically. In order to exercise free rational choice in the present, the dead weight of the effects of past (possibly) rational choices has to be resisted and overcome. Where, for example, individuals have become locked, through capitalism, into oppressive and exploitative bureaucracies, there is a need for them to have the freedom to 'exit' from such bureaucracies without making themselves significantly worse off (the other option, of 'voice' – in this case, economic democracy – is discussed in Chapter 5).

The crucial question for rational choice theory here is why individuals should freely choose to enter into contracts that involve their exploitation and oppression. The chapter explains this largely in terms of two factors: the system of property ownership established by conquest and law, which institutionalises the inequality between haves and have-nots, making the latter dependent upon the former, for example for providing them with work; and techniques of domination that ensure effective surveillance and supervision of the have-nots, neutralising their opposition and overcoming their resistance. The apparent irrationality of individual choices is therefore largely explained by reference to the ways in which the capacity for choice is bounded by the constraints of specific historically derived institutional arrangements.

The chapter went on to consider the issue of class divisions in detail, as crystallisations of such institutionally constrained patterns of interaction, for example between employers and employees. It started from the premise that if people were able to determine their own career paths (and hence life courses) then there would exist a high degree of social mobility. In fact, however, the evidence in favour of free movement across class boundaries, taken from a number of advanced industrial countries, is not very convincing. The chapter looked at two major approaches to explaining this social rigidity, namely 'structural' and 'cultural' approaches, and concluded that neither approach is compatible with rational choice theory. Essentially, by emphasising the effects of past socialisation and current beliefs and mores, the 'cultural' approach underplays the significance of institutional constraints. Contrastingly, by attributing causal primacy to abstract and non-human (possibly inhuman) social forces, the 'structural' approach implicitly devalues the role of individual human agency. The key rational choice concept of a free agent acting within the already existing context of an institutional arrangement is therefore absent from these perspectives: in the 'structural' approach, human agency is not conceived as free, and in the 'cultural' approach, human agency is not sufficiently or accurately contextualised. In marxist terms, the former is economistic and the latter is voluntarist.

In contrast with such approaches, the chapter put forward the concept of a duality of interrelated labour processes set within a long history of class-differentiated possession of private and social capital. The dynamics of the processes involved gave rise to an ongoing struggle between competing class 'strategies' of inclusion and exclusion, which in turn produced, and continue to produce, a range of forms of ownership of capital and 'assets'. This combination of labour process theory and historical analysis was then used to explain the origins and maintenance of characteristic patterns of social division and exclusion based on class, sex and skill.

Just as Chapter 3 considered community development as well as community formation, so Chapter 4 discussed the combating of social divisions as well as their creation. It was pointed out how private capital is responsible for the exclusion of communities and their individual members by denying their autonomy of action, and therefore one way for communities to develop is for them to create and build private capital of their own. The limitations of trade unions were underlined by comparing them with the self-help or cooperative approach in community development. This argument suggests that more radical approaches might be appropriate, involving the dissolution of complex hierarchical organisations and the promotion of genuine self-employment. Traditional socialism, in the sense of a collectivisation of private capital, was rejected on the grounds that it failed either to address the free-rider problem or to recognise the value of individual legal ownership for human freedom. The argument could no doubt have been strengthened by a detailed examination of the effects of globalisation, but it was judged that this would have made the overall argument too unwieldy. Instead, the chapter continued the analogy with community development, suggesting that the empowerment of the workforce, and thence the elimination of employment-related social divisions, could be achieved through judicious combinations of technical assistance, self-help and conflict approaches. In general terms, it was argued that the way forward, both for communities and for workplaces, was to forge partnerships and alliances with other communities and workforces, on as wide a basis as possible. Given the acknowledged limitations of trade union action, however, the prospects for any major victory here must be regarded as remote.

The chapter considered briefly why workplaces are typically sexist and racist as well as oppressive and exploitative of their workforces generally. From a rational choice perspective, both sexual and racial discrimination can be explained by reference to what could be called sexual and racial inequalities of constraints, whereby the choices made by women and people from minority ethnic groups leave them at a systematic disadvantage in relation to men and people from the majority ethnic group. This in-built disadvantage is then compounded and reinforced by the exclusionary practices of men and the majority ethnic group, acting to protect their own advantaged position.

The chapter continued with a discussion of Foucault's ideas, as a way of attempting to understand why free individuals should choose to be exploited and oppressed. This question actually derives from Rousseau (1968), but the discussion here provided a more modern interpretation. Drawing on Foucault's (1980) distinction between monarchic and disciplinary power, it was argued that worker acceptance of managerial authority is linked not only to the sanctions that managers have at their disposal to ensure their subordinates' compliance, but also to the workers' internalisation of the values of the organisation itself. This interpretation presents problems from the point of view of rational choice theory, because it seems to imply nothing less than the impossibility of truly free individual action in modern societies. In opposition to this pessimistic view, the chapter argued that managerialist hegemonies at work are not all-powerful, and that there is room not only for resistance but for transformation of prevailing disciplinary regimes. The discussion revealed a paradox, however, in that the internalisation of managerial values can be represented as both liberating (from monarchically based forms of discrimination, for example based on sex, race, age and disability) and enslaving (sacrificing the needs of the individual to the service of the organisation). It was suggested, perhaps controversially, that the historically unprecedented success of capitalist corporations could be due to their capacity to achieve a measure of liberation for sections of their workforces within an overall framework of tight discipline based on the logic of the market and of capital itself.

The chapter concluded with a discussion of further objections to this Foucauldian interpretation. The key question remained: if the contracts which people enter into are found to be oppressive, why do they not break them? Answering this question involved a return to the consideration of sanctions and the importance of an individual's reputation: if an individual wants their labour to be as marketable as possible, they will want to be seen by potential employers as reliable above all, and this means a high level of discipline, whether it be self-imposed or determined by others. This consideration leads on to the issue of who should enforce sanctions and ensure the observance of discipline, and hence to an explanation of the derivation of the state, as the enforcer and oppressor of last resort and as the ultimate auditor of disciplinary rule. This issue was examined in greater detail in Chapter 5, with the state itself being understood as in the process of moving from a more directive to a more reflexive regime, in response to the need to resolve problems of collective action and resistance.

Chapter 5 considered the nature of the relations between the modern state and its citizens. The historical development of this state was briefly described, and Gramsci's concept of hegemony was deployed in order to characterise the institutional context within which the actions of individual citizens take place. The boundedness of rational citizenship was seen to be determined by the specificity of the hegemony prevailing in a particular place at a particular time. The chapter went on to analyse the postwar hegemony in Britain, seeing it as comprising a number of different 'settlements': military, political/organisational and social. The military settlement involved a balance of power between capitalist and communist blocs, the political/organisational settlement involved the establishment of Fordist bureaucratic and professional techniques of domination, and the social settlement involved a division of welfare that largely reproduced and reinforced existing divisions of labour along lines of sex, race, age and ability.

Since the 1960s, this hegemony has undergone major changes, but the extent and depth of these changes is a matter of debate. The military settlement epitomised by NATO remains in place, though its rationale has become more uncertain since the ending of the Cold War. The centralised authority of the political/organisational settlement has been gradually eroded, and state power has been increasingly dispersed under what Clarke and Newman (1997) have called a new hegemony of 'managerialism', involving democratic renewal, new roles for political action, and new cultures of responsiveness, accountability and empowerment. And the postwar social settlement of 'Family, Work and Nation' has been undermined by changes in employment patterns, ever-increasing demands for welfare provision from citizens, and growing understanding of the inherent limitations of massive bureaucratic organisation.

The chapter attempted to explain in particular why the new managerialist social settlement appears in many respects to be reasserting old patriarchal norms of social responsibility, for example relating to the primacy of the breadwinning role within households and the importance of parental responsibility for child development. The crucial difference, perhaps, is that managerialism actively recruits individuals to the new settlement, whereas the old settlement tended to leave them to fend for themselves (for better or for worse). For example, in relation to the family, the old settlement took very much for granted the 'normality' of the two-parent nuclear family and its associated gender division of labour and on the whole did not look too closely at how it actually worked in practice. In contrast, the new settlement starts from an awareness of the widespread breakdown of this traditional family form and actively seeks to recreate it, most notably through the statutory enforcement of parental responsibilities (for example on child support, education and discipline). In relation to employment, the old settlement left it very much up to individuals whether or not they participated in the labour market and, if they did, how they went about their search for work. The new settlement strongly encourages all people of working age to be economically active and increasingly requires those who are not to give an account of themselves to the authorities. Both settlements acknowledge that the state has an obligation to ensure that employment in some form is available for all those with a 'breadwinning' responsibility, but there is lack of clarity within the settlements about what form of employment is appropriate for different individuals and who exactly can be said to have a breadwinning responsibility (for example, lone parents with young children whose father is not on the scene). With regard to the theme of 'Nation', the old settlement had already begun to move from an unreflexive nineteenth-century imperialist notion of (entitlement to benefits on the grounds of) Commonwealth citizenship to a form of citizenship that was defined more explicitly in terms of British nationality. The new settlement that is now emerging appears to involve a more self-consciously English (and Scottish, Welsh and Irish) nationalistic and regionalistic programme as a response to the twin developments of declining nation state power and increasing importance of the European Union.

Having analysed the character of the postwar hegemony and the transition to managerialism, the chapter went on to consider how rational choice theory could throw further light on such changes. It was argued that in groups larger than small communities an element of coercion was unavoidable in order to ensure the co-operation of the individuals concerned. In order to avoid oppression and abuse of power, coercive authority needed to be sufficient to deal with free-riding, but not so great that it led to tyranny. This problem could be solved through appropriate forms of democratic accountability and means to encourage adherence to the rule of law. Law itself should be coercive only to the extent required to prevent free-riding and interference in the autonomy of others.

The chapter took the line that for individuals to be able to act freely and autonomously the constraints upon them need to be equalised as far as possible, and this requires the abolition of exploitation and the substantive reconciliation of the principles of liberty and equality. Secondary principles of democracy, partnership and citizenship were derived and applied in an attempt to develop guidance for law-making that will satisfy the rational political ideal. Such an approach runs the risk of accusations of utopianism but it is necessary in order to establish criteria by which managerialism can be evaluated and which can facilitate its transformation.

The last section of the chapter then applied the reformulated rational choice theory in an intellectual re-engineering of the social institutions examined throughout the book. State power was argued to have a role in enforcing constraint equalisation within households, local communities, markets, bureaucracies and public life generally. The view of liberals, anarchists, communitarians and others that life in complex modern societies can be regulated entirely on the basis of voluntary conditional co-operation was rejected as utopian, and instead attention was concentrated on how individual citizens can ensure that state power is exercised for their benefit. The term 'citizen governance' (Box 1998) was used to summarise the ideal arrangement, whereby sovereign power is vested in heterogeneous decision-making assemblies, which include both elected representatives and acknowledged experts in their field. This leads to a new emphasis on the importance of local government as a key arena for the development of state–citizen relations. The chapter therefore considered the most appropriate form of local government from a rational choice point of view, based on citizens' own perceptions of the boundaries of their local community and the functions over which that community should have control.

At the level of national government, the chapter considered how the principles of democracy, partnership and citizenship were expressed within the current changing hegemony, in terms of devolution, public–private sector co-operation and positive welfare. The strengths of managerialism were explicitly recognised as well as its drawbacks. The latter in particular were summarised as follows: a democratic renewal that is restricted to a limited form of political democracy and does not seriously encompass control by either workers or consumers; a version of partnership that bypasses democratic processes and places power increasingly in the hands of private bodies who are accountable only to relatively privileged elites; and a construction of active citizenship which does nothing to challenge the exploitation and oppression that so many citizens have to suffer in their daily lives but rather seeks the collusion of individuals with those oppressive and exploitative regimes. The chapter concluded by setting out a rational choice approach to the reform of managerialism, applying it to the critique of coercive measures (requiring them to be justified in every case), the reconstruction of the tax and benefits system, and the gradual bridging of the democratic deficit through a root-and-branch dispersal of power to individuals, households, local communities and teams of workers.

Chapter 6 provided a case study to illustrate the arguments developed in Chapter 5. Housing policy was chosen because it was seen to have more resonance with earlier themes of the book such as that of households in Chapter 2 or residential communities in Chapter 3. The chapter provided an overview of the history of housing policy in England, and explained how its specific form fitted into the general postwar settlement described in Chapter 5. It was shown how council housing provided a good example of Fordist mass provision, with growing bureaucratisation and professionalisation, and how it both reflected and reinforced the traditional nuclear family form. At the same time, housing appeared to be less central to the postwar settlement than health, education or social security, as evidenced by the lack of citizenship entitlement to housing and the continuing predominance of private sector provision. Over a long historical period, predating the postwar settlement, housing also had its own peculiar politics, the 'politics of tenure', an analysis of which is essential for understanding housing policy formation and maintenance.

Having analysed the specificities of housing policy, the chapter went on to chart the decline of the postwar settlement in housing and the rise of managerialist approaches. The decline was explained largely in terms that were internal to the housing policy process itself, for example the waning support for council housing provision as a result of continuing professionalisation and its own success in overcoming severe housing shortages. Another important factor was the growing divergence of policy between central government and many local authorities which led the former to reconsider and reconstruct the relationship between the two. The resulting creeping centralisation of state power then gave rise to problems of management and governance which eventually prompted a turn towards managerialism.

The chapter identified the forms that the managerialist dispersal of power has taken in housing, namely: ending direct state provision of housing and replacing it with a network of public–private/voluntary sector partnerships; reforming ownership rights in order to challenge bureaucratic authority; and linking housing with other policy areas. Further evidence of managerialism in housing comes from the re-professionalisation of housing away from housing administrative techniques towards the acquisition of more generic managerial skills, and new and enhanced emphases on performance management, organisational flexibility, responsiveness and innovation. It was noted, however, that the process of managerialisation has not gone as far as some commentators have claimed, and evidence on stock transfer, ownership rights, community care and area regeneration was adduced to show that dispersal of power and the associated progress of managerialism in housing have been strictly limited.

The chapter looked more closely at housing managerialism in an attempt to flesh out the bones of managerialism itself. The discussion revealed a perhaps unexpected degree of complexity, with four or five different types of approach being identified: personalised management, 'market-oriented' management, 'partnership' approaches, and tenant representative or co-operative management. All of these, in different ways, could claim to be variants of managerialism, and each has its own specific advantages and disadvantages from a rational choice point of view. The chapter concluded that, although relatively underdeveloped in housing, the influence of managerialism could be cited to explain the apparently unshakable faith in owner-occupation, and the corresponding loss of faith in renting, that is so widespread in Britain today. In order to achieve an equalisation of constraints within the housing system, it was necessary to redress the existing imbalance between owning and renting, and to introduce new rights and resources for tenants to achieve a measure of equality with their landlords. Managerialism at the level of a housing estate could be harnessed and made fully accountable to tenants through a system of citizens' boards. Current government proposals, however, fall well short of such a thoroughgoing democratisation.

Epilogue

Because this book has been so wide-ranging in its scope, it is difficult to summarise all its achievements. The most important ones, however, are these:

1. A restatement of rational choice theory as a normative theory of agency and a theory of the possibility of collective action. The theory postulates what individuals are likely to do if they behave rationally, sets these postulates in the context of specific social institutions, and then compares what is expected to happen with what actually happens. Where the latter differs from the former, or where further information is supplied about the actor or about the context within which they act, the postulates are modified. The modified postulates can then be tested in the light of fresh evidence about the text and context of human action. In principle, this process of knowledge growth can continue indefinitely.
2. The main problem in understanding the context of human action is its extreme complexity. In order to make this complexity manageable, the book has selected what might be argued to be key social institutions such as the family, community, workplace, and the state, and considered the dynamics of social interaction within these institutions. In each case, the point has been to show how rational choice theory can be used to make sense of observed and recorded patterns.
3. In relation to households, the book has shown how a wealth of evidence about gender and generational relations can be explained on the basis of two simple rational choice models. Even where the models fail, the

reasons for their failure are illuminating. The concept of a patriarchal hegemony in transition to a form of state-sponsored disciplinary power has been introduced in order to make sense of the changes in the household as an institution and to justify policy reforms.

4 The book has comprehensively reviewed the literature on community and community development, explaining community dynamics in terms of implications drawn from basic assumptions of rational choice theory. Patterns of social inclusion and exclusion have been shown to be produced by any one of a limited number of rational strategies of collective action directed at maximising the utility of the community group. On community development, the book has argued strongly for more attention to be given to enabling individual residents to fulfil their own desires and aspirations as they see fit, based on an informed appraisal of their situation. It has also considered what might be the most rational ways to achieve this and concluded that lasting progress can be made only on the basis of community ownership and government of common resources.

5 Turning to issues of exploitation and oppression in society more widely, the book has explained these mainly in terms of property relations and techniques of domination. This hybrid Marxist-Foucauldian theory has been found sufficient to explain why rational individuals might choose to follow courses of action that frustrate their own self-development and self-actualisation. Individuals find themselves up against what seem like all-powerful forces, produced by centuries of economic development, social action and political and military struggle, but the key message of the whole book is that these forces can be defeated because they express only the dead weight of past actions which must always be vulnerable in the face of the determined collective effort of live human beings. For this reason, the book has attacked those writers who assume, or appear to assume, that individuals are at the mercy of impersonal social forces as well as those who neglect to theorise such forces in the first place. The book's own theory employs a new concept of labour process duality which is essentially an embodiment of generations of struggle between capital and labour and explains how this duality is responsible for creating institutional discrimination of all kinds and is durable because of its self-reinforcing and increasingly disciplinary character. The theory also suggests that exploited and oppressed workers, at home and in paid employment, can be emancipated and empowered through judicious application of the techniques of community development.

6 With regard to state–citizen relations, it has been shown how the new global hegemony of managerialism has become increasingly entrenched, and a critique of that hegemony has been developed based on rational choice principles. The key principle here has been argued to be that of the equalisation of constraints upon individuals, in order to maximise the freedom of all citizens. The case has been made for the use of state

power in order to achieve such equalisation and it has been shown how the resulting forms of citizen governance might be instituted at local and national government levels. In order for proposed political reforms to be realistic, however, there is a need for managerialism to be challenged and superseded, and the book sets out a rational choice approach to doing this, through critique, administrative reconstruction, democratisation and empowerment.

7   Finally, the book provides an original account of housing policy in England by way of illustration of the dynamics of state–citizen relations. This clarifies the meaning of concepts that might otherwise appear too abstract, such as managerialism. On the other hand, however, through a discussion of the various forms of housing managerialism, it is suggested that managerialism might be a good deal more complex than has generally been recognised. This could present more substantial problems for the future in securing its supersession.

The main conclusion to be drawn from this book is that rational choice theory has considerable scope for explaining the dynamics of interaction in a wide variety of social institutions, and for shedding new light on a number of puzzles concerning how these institutions work. In combination with concepts of exploitation and hegemony, the book has shown how this theory is capable of a deep explanation of social reality generally, leading to clear prescriptions for social and political reform. It is extraordinary how much our understanding can be enhanced simply by taking seriously the idea that all human beings might be capable of acting rationally and that they have equal rights of autonomy – that is, to develop freely in their own way without some of them being more constrained than others.

Bibliography

Abelson, J., Lomas, J., Eyles, J., Birch, S. and Veenstra, G. (1995) 'Does the community want devolved authority? Results of deliberative polling in Ontario', *Canadian Medical Association Journal* 153, 4: 403–12.
Abrams, P. (1980) 'Social change, social networks and neighbourhood care', *Social Work Service* 22: 12–23.
Adair, J. (1986) *Effective Teambuilding*, Aldershot: Gower.
Aglietta, M. (1979) *A Theory of Capitalist Regulation: The US Experience*, London: New Left Books.
Ainley, P. (1991) *Young People Leaving Home*, London: Cassell.
Alinsky, S. (1969) *Reveille for Radicals*, New York: Random House.
—— (1972) *Rules for Radicals*, New York: Random House.
Allan, G. (1979) *A Sociology of Friendship and Kinship*, London: Allen and Unwin.
Allan, G. and Crow, G. (eds) (1989) *Home and Family: Creating the Domestic Sphere*, Basingstoke: Macmillan.
Allatt, P. and Yeandle, S. (1986) ' "It's not fair, is it?" Youth unemployment, family relations and the social contract', in S. Allen *et al.* (eds), *The Experience of Unemployment*, Basingstoke: Macmillan.
—— (1992) *Youth Unemployment and the Family: Voices of Disordered Times*, London: Routledge.
Allen, J. (1990) 'Localities and social change', in J. Anderson and M. Ricci (eds) *Society and Social Science: A Reader*, Milton Keynes: Open University Press.
Ambrose, P. (1986) *Whatever Happened to Planning?* London: Methuen.
Anderson, I. (1999) 'Social housing or social exclusion? Non-access to housing for single homeless people', in S. Hutson and D. Clapham (eds) *Homelessness: Public Policies and Private Troubles*, London: Cassell.
Anderson, M. (1977) 'The impact on the family relationships of the elderly of changes since Victorian times in government income-maintenance provisions', in E. Shanas and M.B. Sussman (eds) *Family, Bureaucracy and the Elderly*, Durham, NC: Duke University Press.
Anderson, M., Bechhofer, F. and Gershuny, J. (eds) (1994) *The Social and Political Economy of the Household*, Oxford: Oxford University Press.
Anderson, M., Bechhofer, F. and Kendrick, S. (1994) 'Individual and household strategies', in M. Anderson *et al.* (eds) *The Social and Political Economy of the Household*, Oxford: Oxford University Press.
Anwar, M. (1979) *The Myth of Return*, London: Heinemann.
—— (1985) *Pakistanis in Britain: A Sociological Study*, London: New Century.

Apps, P. (1981) *A Theory of Inequality and Taxation*, Cambridge: Cambridge University Press.
Arber, S. and Gilbert, G.N. (1989a) 'Transitions in caring: gender, life course and care of the elderly', in B. Bytheway, T. Keil, P. Allatt and A. Bryman (eds) *Becoming and Being Old: Sociological Approaches to Later Life*, London: Sage.
—— (1989b) 'Men: the forgotten carers', *Sociology* 23, 1: 111–18.
Arber, S. and Ginn, J. (1992) ' "In sickness and in health": care-giving, gender and the independence of elderly people', in C. Marsh and S. Arber (eds) *Families and Households: Divisions and Change*, Basingstoke: Macmillan.
Archer, R. (1996) 'Towards economic democracy in Britain', in P.Q. Hirst and S. Khilnani (eds) *Reinventing Democracy*, Oxford: Basil Blackwell.
Ashford, S. (1987) 'Family matters', in R. Jowell *et al.* (eds) *British Social Attitudes: The 1987 Report*, Aldershot: Gower.
Auletta, K. (1982) *The Underclass*, New York: Random House.
Axelrod, R. (1984) *The Evolution of Co-operation*, New York: Basic Books.
Bagihole, B. (1994) *Women, Work and Equal Opportunities*, Aldershot: Avebury.
Balchin, P. (1989) *Housing Policy: An Introduction*, London: Routledge.
—— (1995) *Housing Policy: An Introduction* 3rd ed., London: Routledge.
Ball, M. (1983) *Housing Policy and Economic Power: The Political Economy of Owner-Occupation*, London: Methuen.
—— (1986) 'Housing analysis: time for a theoretical refocus?', *Housing Studies* 1, 3: 147–65.
Barnett, N. and Chandler, J. (1997) 'Local government and community', in Hoggett, P. (ed.) *Contested Communities: Experiences, Struggles, Policies*, Bristol: The Policy Press.
Baumann, G. (1996) *Contesting Culture: Discourses of Identity in Multi-ethnic London*, Cambridge: Cambridge University Press.
Beck, U. (1992) *Risk Society: Towards a New Modernity*, London: Sage.
Becker, G.S. (1981) *A Treatise on the Family*, Cambridge, Mass.: Harvard University Press.
Beckford, J. (1989) *Religion and Advanced Industrial Society*, London: Unwin Hyman.
Beechey, V. (1987) *Unequal Work*, London: Verso.
Beetham, D. (1992) 'Liberal democracy and the limits of democratisation', in D. Held (ed.) *Prospects for Democracy*, Oxford: Political Studies Association/Basil Blackwell.
Bell, C. and McKee, L. (1985) 'Marital and family relations in times of male unemployment', in B. Roberts *et al.* (eds) *New Approaches to Economic Life*, Manchester: Manchester University Press.
Bender, E.I. (1986) 'The self-help movement seen in the context of social development', *Journal of Voluntary Action Research* 15: 77–84.
Bengtsson, B. (1998a) 'Tenants' dilemma – on collective action in housing', *Housing Studies* 13, 1: 99–120.
—— (1998b) 'Solving the tenants' dilemma: collective action and norms of co-operation in housing', paper presented to ENHR conference on *Housing Futures: Renewal, Sustainability and Innovation*, Cardiff: 7–11 September.
Benhabib, S. (1988) 'Autonomy, modernity and community: communitarianism and critical social theory in dialogue', in A. Honneth *et al.* (eds) *Zwischenbetrachtungen im Prozess der Aufklärung*, Frankfurt: Suhrkamp.

—— (1990) 'Afterword: communicative ethics and current controversies in practical philosophy', in F. Dahlmayr and S. Benhabib (eds) *The Communicative Ethics Controversy*, Cambridge, Mass.: MIT.
Bennett, R. (ed.) (1989) *Territory and Administration in Europe*, London: Pinter.
Berger, R.L. and Kellner, H. (1964) 'Marriage and the construction of reality', *Diogenes*: 1–23.
Berk, S.F. (1985) *The Gender Factory: The Apportionment of Work in American Households*, New York: Plenum.
Berkeley, G. (1962 [1710]) *The Principles of Human Knowledge*, London: Collins/Fontana.
Betzig, L. (1988) 'Mating and parenting in Darwinian perspective', in L. Betzig, M. Borgerhoff Mulder and P. Turke (eds) *Human Reproductive Behavior: A Darwinian Perspective*, Cambridge: Cambridge University Press.
Beynon, H. (1975) *Working for Ford*, Wakefield: EP Publishing.
Binns, D. and Mars, G. (1984) 'Family, community and unemployment: a study in change', *Sociological Review* 32, 4: 662–95.
Birchall, J. (1992) 'Council tenants: sovereign consumers or pawns in the game?', in J. Birchall, (ed.) *Housing Policy in the 1990s*, London: Routledge.
Birklen, D. (1983) *Community Organizing: Theory and Practice*, New Jersey: Prentice-Hall.
Blood, R.O. and Wolfe, D.M. (1960) *Husbands and Wives*, Glencoe, Illinois: Free Press.
Blumin, S.M. (1989) *The Emergence of the Middle Class: Social Experience in the American City*, Cambridge: Cambridge University Press.
Blumstein, P. and Schwartz, P. (1983) *American Couples*, New York: William Morrow.
Boaden, N., Goldsmith, M., Hampton, W. and Stringer, P. (1982) *Public Participation in Local Services*, London: Longman.
Bohman, J. (1992) 'The limits of rational choice explanation', in J.S. Coleman and T.J. Fararo (eds) *Rational Choice Theory: Advocacy and Critique*, Newbury Park, CA: Sage.
Booth, A., Johnson, D.R., White, L. and Edwards, J.N. (1984) 'Women outside employment and marital stability', *American Journal of Sociology* 90: 567–83.
Bostyn, A.M. and Wight, D. (1987) 'Inside a community: values associated with money and time', in S. Fineman (ed.) *Unemployment: Personal and Social Consequences*, London: Tavistock.
Bourdieu, P. and Passeron, J.-C. (1977) *Reproduction in Education, Society and Culture*, Beverly Hills: Sage Publications.
Bowley, M. (1945) *Housing and the State*, London: Allen and Unwin.
Box, R. (1998) *Citizen Governance: Leading American Communities into the 21st Century*, London: Sage.
Boyer, R. (1986) *La Theorie de la Regulation: Une Analyse Critique*, Paris: editions la decouverte.
Braithwaite, V.A. (1990) *Bound to Care*, Sydney: Allen and Unwin.
Brannen, J. and Moss, P. (1987) 'Dual-earner households: women's financial contributions after the birth of the first child', in J. Brannen and G. Wilson (eds) *Give and Take in Families*, London: Allen and Unwin.
Brannen, J. and Wilson, G. (eds) (1987) *Give and Take in Families*. London: Allen and Unwin.

Braybrooke, D. (1987) *Meeting Needs*, Princeton, NJ: Princeton University Press.
Brent, J. (1997) 'Community without unity', in P. Hoggett (ed.) *Contested Communities: Experiences, Struggles, Policies*, Bristol: The Policy Press.
Bretherton, I. (1985) 'Attachment theory: retrospect and prospect', in I. Bretherton and E. Waters (eds) *Growing Points in Attachment Theory and Research*, Monographs of the Society for Research in Child Development 50 (1–2, Serial No. 209).
Brody, H. (1973) *Inishkillane: Change and Decline in the West of Ireland*, London: Allen Lane.
Brownill, S. (1990) *Developing London's Docklands: Another Great Planning Disaster?* London: Paul Chapman.
Bryson, L., Bittman, M. and Donath, S. (1994) 'Men's welfare state, women's welfare state: tendencies to convergence in practice and theory?', in D. Sainsbury (ed.) *Gendering Welfare States*, London: Sage.
Buchanan, J. (1965) 'An economic theory of clubs', *Economica* 32: 1–14.
Buck, N., Gershuny, J., Rose, D. and Scott, J. (eds) (1994) *Changing Households: The BHPS 1990 to 1992*, Colchester: ESRC Research Centre on Micro-Social Change.
Bulmer, M. (1978) 'Social structure and social change in the twentieth century', in M. Bulmer (ed.) *Mining and Social Change: Durham County in the Twentieth Century*, London: Croom Helm.
Burgoyne, C.B. (1990) 'Money in marriage: how patterns of allocation both reflect and conceal power', *Sociological Review* 38: 634–65.
Burns, D., Hambleton, R. and Hoggett, P. (1994) *The Politics of Decentralisation: Revitalising Local Democracy*, Basingstoke: Macmillan.
Burrows, R. and Marsh, C. (eds) (1992) *Consumption and Class: Divisions and Change*, New York: St Martin's Press.
Burton, P. and Duncan, S. (1996) 'Democracy and accountability in public bodies: New agendas in British governance', *Policy and Politics* 24, 1: 5–16.
Cain, M.T. (1985) 'Fertility as an adjustment to risk', in A. Rossi (ed.) *Gender and the Life Course*, New York: Aldine.
Caldwell, J.C. (1981) 'The mechanics of demographic change in historical perspective', *Population Studies* 35, 1: 5–27.
—— (1982) *Theory of Fertility Decline*, London: Academic Press.
Campbell, B. (1993) *Goliath: Britain's Dangerous Places*, London: Methuen.
Cancian, F. (1993) 'Gender politics: love and power in the private and public spheres', in B.J. Fox (ed.) *Family Patterns, Gender Relations*, Oxford: Oxford University Press.
Carey, L. and Mapes, R. (1972) *The Sociology of Planning*, London: Batsford.
Carling, A. (1991) *Social Division*, London: Verso.
—— (1992) 'Rational choice and household division', in C. Marsh and S. Arber (eds) *Families and Households: Divisions and Change*, Basingstoke: Macmillan.
Carter, A. (1993) 'Towards a Green political theory', in A. Dobson and P. Lucardie (eds) *The Politics of Nature: Explorations in Green Political Theory*, London: Routledge.
Cheal, D. (1988) *The Gift Economy*, London: Routledge.
Cherlin, A. (1978) 'Employment, income and family life: the case of marital dissolution', in *Special Report No. 26*, London: National Commission for Manpower Policy: 157–78.
Chigudu, H., Machila, M., Anderskouv, L. and Strobech, U. (1996) *Partnership in Development: A Guide to Partnership Planning, Monitoring and Evaluation*, Copenhagen: MS, Danish Association for International Co-operation.

Church, A. and Hall, J. (1989) 'Local initiatives for economic regeneration', in D. Herbert and D. Smith (eds) *Social Problems and the City: New Perspectives*, Oxford: Oxford University Press.
Clark, D. and Taylor, R. (1988) 'Partings and reunions: marriage and offshore employment in the British North Sea', in J. Lewis, M. Porter and M. Shrimpton (eds) *Women, Work and Family in the British, Canadian and Norwegian Offshore Oilfields*, Basingstoke: Macmillan.
Clarke, J. and Newman, J. (1997) *The Managerial State*, London: Sage.
Clegg, S.R. and Dunkerley, D. (1980) *Organisation, Class and Control*, London: Routledge and Kegan Paul.
Coffield, F., Borrill, C. and Marshall, S. (1986) *Growing Up at the Margins: Young Adults in the North East*, Milton Keynes: Open University Press.
Cohen, A.P. (1985) *The Symbolic Construction of Community*, London: Ellis Horwood and Tavistock.
Cohen, B. and Fraser, N. (1991) *Childcare in a Modern Welfare State*, London: Institute for Public Policy Research.
Cohen, P. (1984) 'Subcultural conflict and working-class community', in E. Butterworth and D. Weir (eds) *The New Sociology of Modern Britain*, London: Fontana.
Cole, I. and Furbey, R. (1994) *The Eclipse of Council Housing*, London: Routledge.
Coleman, J.S. (1990) *Foundations of Social Theory*, Cambridge, Mass.: Harvard University Press.
Colenutt, B. (1991) 'The London Docklands Development Corporation: has the community benefited?' in M. Keith and A. Rogers (eds) *Hollow Promises: Rhetoric and Reality in the Inner City*, London: Mansell.
Collier, J., Rosaldo, M.Z. and Yanagisako, S. (1993) 'Is there a family? New anthropological views', in B.J. Fox (ed.) *Family Patterns, Gender Relations*, Oxford: Oxford University Press.
Collins, C. (1997) 'The dialogics of "community": language and identity in a housing scheme in the west of Scotland', in P. Hoggett (ed.) *Contested Communities: Experiences, Struggles, Policies*, Bristol: The Policy Press.
Conlisk, J. (1996) 'Why bounded rationality?', *Journal of Economic Literature* 34: 669–700.
Connell, J. (1978) *The End of Tradition: Country Life in Central Surrey*, London: Routledge and Kegan Paul.
Connerly, C.E. (1985) 'The community question: an extension of Wellman and Leighton', *Urban Affairs Quarterly* 20: 537–56.
Connidis, I.A. (1989) *Family Ties and Aging*, Toronto: Butterworths.
Coontz, S. (1988) *The Social Origins of Private Life: A History of American Families 1600–1900*, London: Verso.
Cooper, C. and Hawtin, M. (eds) (1997) *Housing, Community and Conflict: Understanding Resident 'Involvement'*, Aldershot: Arena.
—— (eds) (1998) *Resident Involvement and Community Action: Theory to Practice*, Coventry: Chartered Institute of Housing.
Cooper, C. and Somerville, P. (2000) 'Housing policy', in T. Burden, C. Cooper and S. Petrie *Modernising Social Policy: Unravelling New Labour's Welfare Reforms*, Aldershot: Ashgate.
Cornwell, J. (1984) *Hard-Earned Lives: Accounts of Health and Illness from East London*, London: Tavistock.

Corr, H. and Jamieson, L. (eds) (1990) *Politics of Everyday Life: Continuity and Change in Work and the Family*, Basingstoke: Macmillan.
Cowan, D. (1999) *Housing Law and Policy*, Basingstoke: Macmillan.
Cowan, R.S. (1989) *More Work for Mother*, New York: Free Association Books.
Cragg, A. and Dawson, T. (1984) *Unemployed Women*, Department of Employment Research Paper No. 47, London: HMSO.
Craig, G. and Mayo, M. (eds) (1995) *Community Empowerment: A Reader in Participation and Development*, London: Zed.
Craig, G., Taylor, M., Szanto, C. and Williamson, M. (1999) *Developing Local Compacts: Relationships Between Local Public Sector Bodies and the Voluntary and Community Sectors*, York: YPS/JRF.
Crehan, K. (1986) 'Women, work and the balancing act', in E. Scarlett *et al.* (eds) *Women, Work and the Family in Britain and Germany*, London: Croom Helm.
Crow, G. (1989) 'The use of the concept of "strategy" in recent sociological literature', *Sociology* 23: 1–24.
—— (1997a) 'What do we know about the neighbours? Sociological perspectives in neighbouring and community', in P. Hoggett (ed.) *Contested Communities*, Bristol: Policy Press.
—— (1997b) 'Competing approaches to power in theories of community', paper presented to the BSA conference at the University of York, April.
Crow, G. and Allan, G. (1994) *Community Life: An Introduction to Local Social Relations*, Hemel Hempstead: Harvester Wheatsheaf.
Crystal, S. (1982) *America's Old Age Crisis: Public Policy and the Two Worlds of Aging*, New York: Basic Books.
Dale, R. *et al.* (eds) (1981) *Education and the State: Politics, Patriarchy and Practice*, Brighton: Falmer Press.
Daniel, W.W. (1990) *The Unemployed Flow*, London: Policy Studies Institute.
Daunton, M.J. (1983) 'Public place and private space: the Victorian city and the working-class household', in D. Frazer and A. Sutcliffe (eds) *The Pursuit of Urban History*, London: Edward Arnold.
—— (1987) *A Property Owning Democracy?* London: Faber.
David, M. (1980) *The State, the Family and Education*, London: Routledge and Kegan Paul.
Davidoff, L. (1986) 'The role of gender in the "first industrial nation",' in R. Crompton and M. Mann (eds) *Gender and Stratification*, Cambridge: Polity Press, 190–213.
Davidoff, L. and Hall, C. (1987) *Family Fortunes: Men and Women of the English Middle Class 1780–1850*, London: Hutchinson.
Davies, W.K.D. and Herbert, D.T. (1993) *Communities Within Cities: An Urban Social Geography*, London: Belhaven Press.
Davis, H.R. and Salasin, S.E. (1975) 'The utilization of evaluation', in H.R. Davis and M. Guttentag (eds) *Handbook of Evaluation Research*, Beverly Hills, California: Sage.
Day, G. and Murdoch, J. (1993) 'Locality and community: coming to terms with place', *Sociological Review* 41, 1: 82–111.
De Tocqueville, A. (1966) (orig. 1835) *Democracy in America*, New York: Harper and Row.
Dean, H. (1999) 'Citizenship', in M. Powell (ed.) *New Labour, New Welfare State? The 'Third Way' in British Social Policy*, Bristol: The Policy Press.
Dean, M. (1999) *Governmentality: Power and Rule in Modern Society*, London: Sage.

Deem, R. (1986) *All Work and No Play? The Sociology of Women and Leisure*, Milton Keynes: Open University Press.
Delphy, C. and Leonard, D. (1992) *Familiar Exploitation: A New Analysis of Marriage in Contemporary Western Societies*, Cambridge: Polity Press.
Deng, Z. and Bonacich, P. (1991) 'Some effects of urbanism on black social networks', *Social Networks* 13: 35–50.
Dennett, D.C. (1991) *Consciousness Explained*, Harmondsworth: Penguin.
DETR (1998a) *Modern Local Government: In Touch with the People*, London: The Stationery Office.
—— (1998b) *Building Partnerships for Prosperity – Sustainable Growth, Competitiveness and Employment*, London: The Stationery Office.
—— (1998c) *Planning for the Communities of the Future*, London: The Stationery Office.
—— (1999) *Tenant Participation Compacts: Consultation Paper*, London: DETR.
Devine, F. (1992) *Affluent Workers Revisited: Privatism and the Working Class*, Edinburgh: Edinburgh University Press.
Dhooge, Y. (1982) 'Livelihood II: local involvement', in S. Wallman *et al.* (eds) *Living in South London: Perspectives on Battersea 1871–1981*, Aldershot: Gower.
Diamond, J. (1997) *Guns, Germs and Steel: A Short History of Everybody for the Last 13,000 Years*, London: Jonathan Cape.
Die Gruenen (1983) *Programme of the German Greens*, London: Heretic Books.
Dobash, R. and Dobash, R. (1992) *Women, Violence and Social Change*, London: Routledge.
Dominelli, L. (1990) *Women and Community Action*, Birmingham: Venture Press.
Douglas, M. (1987) *How Institutions Think*, London: Routledge and Kegan Paul.
Doyal, L. and Gough, I. (1991) *A Theory of Human Need*, Basingstoke: Macmillan.
Driver, S. and Martell, L. (1998) *New Labour: Politics after Thatcherism*, Cambridge: Polity Press.
Drover, G. and Kerans, P. (eds) (1993) *New Approaches to Welfare Theory*, Aldershot: Edward Elgar.
DSS (1998) *The Welfare Reform Green Paper*, London: The Stationery Office.
Duncan, S.S. and Edwards, R. (1998) *Lone Mothers and Paid Work: Discourse, Context and Action*, Basingstoke: Macmillan.
Dunleavy, P. (1981) *The Politics of Mass Housing in Britain 1945–1975*, Oxford: Clarendon Press.
Dwyer, P. (1998) 'Conditional citizens? Welfare rights and responsibilities in the late 1990s', *Critical Social Policy* 57: 18, 4: 493–517.
Dyhouse, C. (1986) 'Mothers and daughters in the middle class home, c.1870–1914', in J. Lewis (ed.) *Labour and Love: Women's Experiences of Work and Family, 1850–1940*, Oxford: Basil Blackwell.
Edgell, S. (1980) *Middle-Class Couples*, London: Allen and Unwin.
Edholm, F. (1993) 'The unnatural family', in B.J. Fox (ed.) *Family Patterns, Gender Relations*, Oxford: Oxford University Press.
Edwards, R. and Duncan, S. (1997) 'Supporting the family: lone mothers, paid work and the underclass debate', *Critical Social Policy* 53: 17, 4: 29–49.
Edwards, R. and Ribbens, J. (1991) 'Meanderings around "strategy": A research note on strategic discourses in the lives of women', *Sociology* 25: 477–90.
Elias, N. (1974) 'Foreword – towards a theory of communities', in C. Bell and H. Newby (eds) *The Sociology of Community: A Selection of Readings*, London: Frank Cass.
Elias, N. and Scotson, J. (1965) *The Established and the Outsiders*, London: Frank Cass.

—— (1994) *The Established and the Outsiders: A Sociological Enquiry into Community Problems*, 2nd ed., London: Sage.
Elster, J. (1989) *The Cement of Society: A Study of Social Order*, Cambridge: Cambridge University Press.
Emptage, T. (1994) 'Married to the state – mothering on welfare: survival strategies of single mothers in a UK public housing estate', unpublished PhD thesis, University of Hull.
Eriksen, J.A., Yancey, W.L. and Eriksen, E.P. (1979) 'The division of family roles', *Journal of Marriage and the Family* 46: 301–13.
Erikson, R. and Goldthorpe, J.H. (1992) *The Constant Flux: A Study of Class Mobility in Industrial Societies*, Oxford: Clarendon Press.
Esping-Andersen, G. (1993) 'Mobility regimes and class formation', in G. Esping-Andersen (ed.) *Changing Classes: Stratification and Mobility in Post-industrial Societies*, London: Sage.
—— (1994) 'Postindustrial cleavage structures: a comparison of evolving patterns of social stratification in Germany, Sweden and the United States', in D.B. Grusky (ed.) *Social Stratification: Class, Race and Gender in Sociological Perspective*, Oxford: Westview Press.
Etzioni, A. (1995) *The Spirit of Community*, London: Fontana Press.
Evason, E. (1985) *On the Edge: A Study of Poverty and Long-term Unemployment in Northern Ireland*, London: CPAG.
Eyles, J. (1979) 'Area-based policies for the inner city', in D.T. Herbert and D.M. Smith (eds) *Social Problems and the City*, Oxford: Oxford University Press.
Fearn, J. (2000) 'Building solutions to homelessness', unpublished PhD thesis, University of Kent at Canterbury.
Fernie, S. and Metcalf, D. (1995) *Participation, Contingent Pay, Representation and Workplace Performance: Evidence from Great Britain*, Centre for Economic Performance Discussion Paper 232, London: London School of Economics.
Fielding, D. and Clift, C. (1991) *The Balance of Power*, London: Lowe Howard-Spink.
Finch, J. (1985) 'Work, the family and the home', *International Journal of Social Economics* 12.
—— (1987) 'Family obligations and the life course', in A. Bryman, W.R. Bytheway, P. Allatt and T. Keil (eds) *Rethinking the Life Cycle*, Basingstoke: Macmillan.
—— (1989) *Family Obligations and Social Change*, Cambridge: Polity Press.
—— (1995) 'Responsibilities, obligations and commitments', in I. Allen and E. Perkins (eds) *The Future of Family Care for Older People*, London: HMSO.
Finch, J. and Groves, D. (eds) (1983) *A Labour of Love: Women, Work and Caring*, London: Routledge and Kegan Paul.
Finch, J. and Mason, J. (1993) *Negotiating Family Responsibilities*, London: Routledge.
Findlay, P. and Newton, T. (1998) 'Reframing Foucault: the case of performance appraisal', in A. McKinlay and K. Starkey (eds) *Foucault, Management and Organization Theory: From Panopticon to Technologies of Self*, London: Sage.
Firth, R. (1956) *Two Studies of Kinship in London*, London: The Athlone Press.
Fischer, C.S. (1982) *To Dwell Among Friends*, Chicago: Chicago University Press.
Fischer, C.S., Jackson, R.M., Steuve, C.A., Gerson, K., Jones, L., McAllister, M. and Baldassare, M. (1977) *Networks and Places*, New York: Free Press.
Fisher, R. and Kling, J. (1989) 'Community mobilisation: prospects for the future', *Urban Affairs Quarterly* 25: 200–11.
Fletcher, R. (1966) *The Family and Marriage in Britain*, Harmondsworth: Penguin.

Foucault, M. (1977) *Discipline and Punish: The Birth of the Prison*, Harmondsworth: Penguin.
—— (1979) *The History of Sexuality*, Harmondsworth: Penguin.
—— (1980) *Power/Knowledge: Selected Interviews and Other Writings 1972–1977*, ed. C. Gordon, Brighton: Harvester Press.
Fox, B.J. (ed.) (1993) *Family Patterns, Gender Relations*, Oxford: Oxford University Press.
Fox, B.J. and Luxton, M. (1993) 'Conceptualising "family",' in B.J. Fox (ed.) *Family Patterns, Gender Relations*, Oxford: Oxford University Press.
Gallie, D. (1994) 'Are the unemployed an underclass? Some evidence from the Social Change and Economic Life Initiative', *Sociology* 28, 3: 737–57.
Gans, H. (1962) *The Urban Villagers*, New York: Free Press.
—— (1967) *The Levittowners*, London: Allen Lane.
Garland, D. (1996) 'The limits of the sovereign state: strategies of crime control in contemporary society', *British Journal of Criminology* 36, 4: 445–71.
Geerken, M. and Gove, W.R. (1983) *At Home and at Work*, Beverly Hills: Sage.
Georgellis, Y. and Popapanagos, H. (1995) 'The effect of child care costs on UK lone mothers' participation and full-time work probabilities', *Working Paper No. 95: 11*, Stoke on Trent: Division of Economics, Staffordshire University.
Gershuny, J. (1982) 'Household work strategies', paper presented to ISA conference in Mexico City, August.
—— (1998) 'Thinking dynamically: sociology and narrative data', in L. Leisering and R. Walker (eds) *The Dynamics of Modern Society*, Bristol: The Policy Press.
Gershuny, J., Godwin, M. and Jones, S. (1994) 'The domestic labour revolution: a process of lagged adaptation?', in M. Anderson *et al.* (eds) *The Social and Political Economy of the Household*, Oxford: Oxford University Press: 151–97.
Gershuny, J.I., Miles, I., Jones, S., Mullins, C., Thomas, G. and Wyatt, S.M.E. (1986) 'Preliminary analysis of the 1983/4 ESRC time budget data', *Quarterly Journal of Social Affairs* 2: 13–39.
Giarchi, G. (1984) *Between McAlpine and Polaris*, London: Routledge and Kegan Paul.
Giddens, A. (1984) *The Constitution of Society*, Cambridge: Polity Press.
—— (1991) *Modernity and Self-Identity: Self and Society in the Late Modern Age*, Cambridge: Polity Press.
—— (1998) *The Third Way: The Renewal of Social Democracy*, Cambridge: Polity Press/Blackwell.
Gilchrist, A. (1992) 'Struggles for new thinking and new respect', *Community Development Journal* 27, 2: 175–81.
—— (1995) *Community Development and Networking*, London: Community Development Foundation.
Gilchrist, A. and Taylor, M. (1997) 'Community networking: developing strength through diversity', in P. Hoggett (ed.) *Contested Communities: Experiences, Struggles, Policies*, Bristol: The Policy Press.
Gillespie, N., Lovett, T. and Garner, W. (1992) *Youth Work and Working-Class Youth Culture: Rules and Resistance in West Belfast*, Buckingham: Open University Press.
Gilligan, J.H. (1987) 'Visitors, tourists and outsiders in a Cornish town', in M. Bouquet and M. Winter (eds) *Who from their Labours Rest? Conflict and Practice in Rural Tourism*, Aldershot: Avebury.
Gilroy, P. (1987) *'There Ain't No Black in the Union Jack'*, London: Hutchinson.
Goffman, E. (1961) *Asylums*, Garden City, NJ: Anchor Books.

—— (1969) *The Presentation of Self in Everyday Life*, London: Allen Lane.
Goldthorpe, J.H. (with Llewelyn, C. and Payne, C.) (1987) *Social Mobility and Class Structure in Modern Britain*, 2nd ed., Oxford: Clarendon Press.
Goodin, R. (1992) *Green Political Theory*, Cambridge: Polity Press.
Gough, I. (1979) *The Political Economy of the Welfare State*, London: Macmillan.
Gould, C.C. (1988) *Rethinking Democracy: Freedom and Social Co-operation in Politics, Economy and Society*, Cambridge: Cambridge University Press.
Gramsci, A. (1971) *Selections from the Prison Notebooks of Antonio Gramsci*, London: Lawrence and Wishart.
Granovetter, M.S. (1973) 'The strength of weak ties', *American Journal of Sociology* 78: 1360–80.
Gray, A. (1979) 'The working class family as an economic unit', in C.C. Harris (ed.) *The Sociology of the Family*, Sociological Review Monograph 28: 186–213.
Gregory, S. (1998) *Transforming Local Services: Partnership in Action*, York: YPS/JRF.
Gregson, N. and Lowe, M. (1993) 'Renegotiating the domestic division of labour? A study of dual career households in North-East and South-East England', *Sociological Review* 41: 475–505.
—— (1994) *Servicing the Middle Classes: Class, Gender and Waged Domestic Labour in Contemporary Britain*, London: Routledge.
Grieco, M. (1987) *Keeping it in the Family: Social Networks and Employment Chance*, London: Tavistock.
Grusky, D.B. (1994) 'The contours of stratification', in D.B. Grusky (ed.) *Social Stratification: Class, Race and Gender in Sociological Perspective*, Oxford: Westview Press.
Gyford, J. (1991) 'Does place matter? Locality and local democracy, the Local Government Management Board', *The Belgrave Papers* No. 3.
Habermas, J. (1987) *The Theory of Communicative Action, Vol 2*, Cambridge: Polity Press.
Hall, P. (1997) 'Social capital, a fragile asset', in *The Wealth and Poverty of Networks: Tackling Social Exclusion*, Demos Collection Issue 12, London: Demos.
Hallman, H.W. (1984) *Neighbourhoods: Their Place in Urban Life*, Beverly Hills, CA: Sage.
Hampton, W. (1970) *Democracy and Community*, Oxford: Oxford University Press.
—— (1987) *Local Government and Urban Politics*, London: Longman.
Hardhill, I. and Green, A. (1990) *An Examination of Women Returners in Newcastle (Benwell and South Gosforth)*, Newcastle: CURDS, Newcastle University.
Hardin, R. (1982) *Collective Action*, Baltimore and London: Johns Hopkins University Press.
—— (1992) 'The street-level epistemology of trust', *Politics and Society* 21: 505–29.
Harper, D. (1992) 'Small neighbourhoods and community case studies', in C. Ragin and H. Becker (eds) *What is a Case? Exploring the Foundations of Social Inquiry*, Cambridge: Cambridge University Press.
Harris, R. (1972) *Prejudice and Tolerance in Ulster: A Study of Neighbours and 'Strangers' in a Border Community*, Manchester: Manchester University Press.
—— (1987) *Redundancy and Recession in South Wales*, Oxford: Basil Blackwell.
Harrison, L., Hoggett, P. and Jeffers, S. (1995) 'Race, ethnicity and community development', *Community Development Journal* 30, 2: 144–57.
Hart, C., Jones, K. and Burns, M. (1997) 'Do the people want power? The social responsibilities of empowering communities', in P. Hoggett (ed.) *Contested Communities: Experiences, Struggles, Policies*, Bristol: The Policy Press.

Hastings, A., McArthur, A. and McGregor, A. (1996) *Less Than Equal? Community Organisations and Estate Regeneration Partnerships*, Bristol: The Policy Press.

Hayek, F. von (1982) *Law, Legislation and Liberty: A New Statement of the Liberal Principles of Justice and Political Economy*, London: Routledge and Kegan Paul.

Healy, P. (1997) 'City fathers, mandarins and neighbours: crossing old divides in new partnerships', in O. Kalltorp, I. Elander, O. Ericsson and M. Franzen (eds) *Cities in Transformation – Transformation in Cities*, Aldershot: Avebury.

Hedges, A. and Kelly, J. (1992) *Identification with Local Areas: Summary Report on a Qualitative Study*, London: DoE.

Henwood, M., Rimmer, L. and Wicks, M. (1987) *Inside the Family: Changing Roles of Men and Women*, Occasional Paper No. 6, London: Family Policy Studies Centre.

Heraud, B. (1968) 'Social class and the new towns', *Urban Studies* 5(1).

Hertz, R. (1986) *More Equal than Others*, Berkeley: University of California Press.

Hewlett, S.A. (1987) *A Lesser Life: The Myth of Women's Liberation*, London: Michael Joseph.

Hill, D.M. (1994) *Citizens and Cities: Urban Policy in the 1990s*, Brighton: Harvester Wheatsheaf.

Hiller, D.V. and Philliker, W.W. (1986) 'The division of labour in contemporary marriage', *Social Problems* 33: 191–201.

Hills, J. (1998) 'Housing', in H. Glennerster and J. Hills (eds) *The State of Welfare*, 2nd ed., Oxford: Oxford University Press.

Hirschmann, A.O. (1970) *Exit, Voice and Loyalty: Responses to Decline in Firms, Organizations and States*, Cambridge, Mass: Harvard University Press.

Hirschon, R. (ed.) (1983) *Women and Property – Women as Property*, New York: St Martins Press.

Hirst, P.Q. (1994) *Associative Democracy: New Forms of Economic and Social Governance*, Cambridge: Polity Press.

—— (1996) 'Democracy and civil society', in P.Q. Hirst and S. Khilnani (eds) *Reinventing Democracy*, Oxford: Basil Blackwell.

Hirst, P.Q. and Khilnani, S. (1996) 'Introduction', in P.Q. Hirst and S. Khilnani (eds) *Reinventing Democracy*, Oxford: Basil Blackwell.

—— (eds) (1996) *Reinventing Democracy*, Oxford: Basil Blackwell.

Hochschild, A. (1990) *The Second Shift*, London: Viking.

Hockey, J. and James, A. (1993) *Growing Up and Growing Old: Ageing and Dependency in the Life Course*, London: Sage.

Hoggett, P. (ed.) (1997) *Contested Communities: Experiences, Struggles, Policies*, Bristol: The Policy Press.

Hojnacki, W. (1979) 'What is a neighbourhood?' *Social Policy* Sept./Oct.: 47–52.

Holme, A. (1985) *Housing and Young Families in East London*, London: Routledge.

Homans, G.C. (1961) *Social Behaviour: Its Elementary Forms*, New York: Harcourt, Brace.

Homer, A., Leonard, A. and Taylor, P. (1985) 'The burden of dependency', in N. Johnson (ed.) *Marital Violence*, London: Routledge and Kegan Paul.

Horrell, S. (1994) 'Household time allocation and women's labour force participation', in M. Anderson *et al.* (eds) *The Social and Political Economy of the Household*, Oxford: Oxford University Press.

Houlihan, B. (1988) *Housing Policy and Central–Local Government Relations*, Aldershot: Avebury.

Howe, L. (1990) *Being Unemployed in Northern Ireland: An Ethnographic Study*, Cambridge: Cambridge University Press.

Hoyle, C. and Sanders, A. (2000) 'Police response to domestic violence: from victim choice to victim empowerment?', in *British Journal of Criminology* 40, 1: 14–36.

Hughes, G. (1998) *Understanding Crime Prevention: Social Control, Risk and Late Modernity*, Buckingham: Open University Press.

Hume, D. (1962 [1739]) *A Treatise of Human Nature*, Glasgow: Fontana/Collins.

Humphries, J. (1977a) 'Class struggle and the persistence of the working-class family', *Cambridge Journal of Economics* 1, 3: 241–58.

—— (1977b) 'The working-class family, women's liberation and class struggle: the case of 19th century British history', *The Review of Radical Political Economy* 9: 25–41.

Hunt, P. (1980) *Gender and Class Consciousness*, Basingstoke: Macmillan.

Hunt, P. (1989) 'Gender and the construction of home life', in G. Allan and G. Crow (eds) *Home and Family: Creating the Domestic Sphere*, Basingstoke: Macmillan.

Hunter, A. (1975) 'The loss of community: an empirical test through replication', *American Sociological Review* 40: 537–52.

Husband, C. (ed.) (1982) *'Race' in Britain*, London: Hutchinson.

Hutson, S. and Jenkins, R. (1986) 'Family relations and the unemployment of young people in Swansea', in M. White (ed.) *The Social World of the Yong Unemployed*, London: Policy Studies Institute: 37–53.

—— (1989) *Taking the Strain*, Milton Keynes: Open University Press.

Hyatt, J. (1995) *Calling in the Specialist: The Value of Using Consultancy in Community Capacity Building*, London: Community Development Foundation.

Jamieson, L. and Toynbee, C. (1990) 'Shifting patterns of parental authority 1900–1980', in H. Corr and L. Jamieson (eds) *Politics of Everyday Life: Continuity and Change in Work and the Family*, Basingstoke: Macmillan.

Jeffers, S., Hoggett, P. and Harrison, L. (1996) 'Race, ethnicity and community in three localities', *New Community* 22, 1: 111–26.

Jencks, C. and Petersen, P. (eds) (1991) *The Urban Underclass*, Washington, DC: Brookings Institution.

Jenkins, R. (1983) *Lads, Citizens and Ordinary Kids: Working-class Youth Life-styles in Belfast*, London: Routledge and Kegan Paul.

—— (1984) 'Understanding Northern Ireland', *Sociology* 19: 253–64.

Jephcott, P. with Robinson, H. (1962) [1971] *Homes in High Flats*, Edinburgh: Oliver and Boyd.

Jephcott, P., Seear, N. and Smith, J. (1962) *Married Women Working*, London: Allen & Unwin.

Jones, G. (1991) 'The cost of living in the parental home', *Youth and Policy* 32: 19–29.

—— (1992) 'Short-term reciprocity in parent–child economic exchanges', in C. Marsh and S. Arber (eds) *Families and Households: Divisions and Change*, Basingstoke: Macmillan.

—— (1995) *Leaving Home*, Milton Keynes: Open University Press.

Jordan, B. (1996) *A Theory of Poverty and Social Exclusion*, Cambridge: Polity Press.

—— (1998) *The New Politics of Welfare*, London: Sage.

Jordan, B., James, S., Kay, H. and Redley, M. (1992) *Trapped in Poverty? Labour Market Decisions in Low-income Households*, London: Routledge.

Jowell, R. and Airey, C. (eds) (1984) *British Social Attitudes: The 1984 Report*, Aldershot: Gower.

Jowell, R. *et al.* (eds) (1987) *British Social Attitudes: The 1987 Report*, Aldershot: Gower.

Jowell, R. and Topf, R. (eds) (1988) *British Social Attitudes: The Fifth Report*, Aldershot: Gower.
Jowell, R. and Witherspoon, S. (eds) (1985) *British Social Attitudes: The 1985 Report*, Aldershot: Gower.
Jowell, R., Witherspoon, S. and Brook, L. (1989) (1984–90; Annual) *British Social Attitudes*, Aldershot: Gower.
Katznelson, I. (1986) 'Working class formation: constructing cases and comparisons', in I. Katznelson and A.R. Zolberg (eds) *Working Class Formation*, Princeton, NJ: Princeton University Press.
Kempson, E. (1996) *Living on a Low Income*, York: York Publishing Services.
Kempson, E., Bryson, A. and Rowlingson, K. (1994) *Hard Times? How Poor Families Make Ends Meet*, London: Policy Studies Institute.
Keyes, L. (1987) 'The shifting focus of neighbourhood groups', *Policy Studies Journal* 16, 2: 300–6.
King, P. (1996) *The Limits of Housing Policy: A Philosophical Investigation*, London: Middlesex University Press.
—— (1998) *Housing, Individuals and the State: The Morality of Government Intervention*, London: Routledge.
Klein, J. (1965) *Samples from English Culture Vol. 1*, London: Routledge.
Komarovsky, M. (1967) *Blue Collar Marriage*, New York: Vintage Books.
Komendi, E. (1990) 'Time use trends in Denmark', in G.V. Mortensen (ed.) *Time and Consumption*, Copenhagen: Danmarks Statistik.
Kotler, M. (1969) *Neighbourhood Government: The Local Foundations of Political Life*, New York: Bobbs Merrill.
Laite, J. and Halfpenny, P. (1987) 'Employment, unemployment and the domestic division of labour', in D. Fryer and P. Ullah (eds) *Unemployed People*, Milton Keynes: Open University Press.
Land, H. (1969) *Large Families in London*, London: Bell.
—— (1978) 'Who cares for the family?' *Journal of Social Policy* 7(3).
Lash, S. and Urry, J. (1994) *Economies of Signs and Space*, London: Sage.
Laurie, H. and Rose, D. (1994) 'Divisions and allocations within households', in N. Buck *et al*. (eds) *Changing Households: The BHPS 1990 to 1992*, Colchester: ESRC Research Centre on Micro-Social Change.
Laver, M. (1997) *Private Desires, Political Action: An Invitation to the Politics of Rational Choice*, London: Sage.
Le Play, F. (1855) [1877–9] *Les ouvriers Europeens*, 1st ed.: Paris; 2nd ed.: Tours: Alfred Mame et fils.
Leadbeater, C. (1997) *The Rise of the Social Entrepreneur*, London: Demos.
Lee, D. and Newby, H. (1983) *The Problem of Sociology*, London: Hutchinson.
Leiman, M. (1993) *The Political Economy of Racism: A History*, London: Pluto Press.
Leisering, L. and Walker, R. (eds) (1998) *The Dynamics of Modern Society: Poverty, Policy and Welfare*, Bristol: The Policy Press.
Leonard, D. (1980) *Sex and Generation*, London: Tavistock.
Leonard, D. and Speakman, M. (1986) 'Women in the family – companions or caretakers?' in V. Beechey and E. Whitelegg (eds) *Women in Britain Today*, Milton Keynes: Open University Press.
Lewis, C. and O'Brien, M. (1987) *Reassessing Fatherhood: New Observations on Fathers and the Modern Family*, London: Sage.
Lewis, J. (1980) *The Politics of Motherhood*, London: Croom Helm.

—— (ed.) (1986) *Labour and Love: Women's Experiences of Work and Family, 1850–1940*, Oxford: Basil Blackwell.
Lipietz, A. (1985) *Mirages and Miracles: The Crisis of Global Fordism*, London: Verso.
Littrel, D.W. and Hobbs, D. (1989) 'The self-help approach', in J.A. Christenson and J.W. Robinson (eds) *Community Development in Perspective*, Ames: Iowa State Press.
Loney, M. (1983) *Community Versus Government: The British Community Development Project 1968–78 – A Study of Government Incompetence*, London: Heinemann.
Luke, T. (1990) *Social Theory and Modernity*, London: Sage.
Luxton, M. (1980) *More than a Labour of Love*, Toronto: Women's Press.
McCrone, D. (1994) 'Getting by and making out in Kirkcaldy', in M. Anderson *et al.* (eds) *The Social and Political Economy of the Household*, Oxford: Oxford University Press.
McCulloch, A. (1997) 'You've fucked up the estate and now you're carrying a briefcase!', in P. Hoggett (ed.) *Contested Communities: Experiences, Struggles, Policies*, Bristol: The Policy Press.
McKay, S. (1998) 'Exploring the dynamics of family change: lone parenthood in Great Britain', in L. Leisering and R. Walker (eds) *The Dynamics of Modern Society*, Bristol: The Policy Press.
McKee, L. (1987) 'Households during unemployment: the resourcefulness of the unemployed', in J. Brannen and G. Wilson (eds) *Give and Take in Families*, London: Allen and Unwin.
McRae, S. (1986) *Cross-Class Families*, Oxford: Clarendon Press.
Malmberg, B. (1998) 'Housing costs and fertility – Swedish evidence', paper presented to ENHR conference on *Housing Futures: Renewal, Sustainability and Innovation*, Cardiff: 7–11 September.
Malpass, P. and Murie, A. (1990) *Housing Policy and Practice*, 3rd ed., Basingstoke: Macmillan.
—— (1999) *Housing Policy and Practice*, 5th ed., Basingstoke: Macmillan.
Mamdani, M. (1972) *The Myth of Population Control: Family, Caste and Class in an Indian Village*, New York: Monthly Review Press.
—— (1981) 'The ideology of population control', in K.L. Michaelson (ed.) *And the Poor Get Children: Radical Perspectives in Population Dynamics*, New York: Monthly Review Press.
Mann, K. (1992) *The Making of an English 'Underclass'? The Social Divisions of Welfare and Labour*, London: Open University Press.
Mansfield, P. and Collard, J. (1988) *The Beginning of the Rest of Your Life? A Portrait of Newly-wed Marriage*, Basingstoke: Macmillan.
Marris, P. (1987) *Meaning and Action: Community Planning and Conceptions of Change*, London: Routledge.
Marsden, D. (1982) *Workless*, London: Croom Helm.
Marsden, D. and Abrams, S. (1987) ' "Liberators", "companions", "intruders" and "cuckoos in the nest": a sociology of caring relationships over the life cycle', in P. Allatt, T. Keil, A. Bryman and B. Bytheway (eds) *Women and the Life Cycle*, Basingstoke: Macmillan.
Marsh, C. and Arber, S. (eds) (1992) *Families and Households: Divisions and Change*, Basingstoke: Macmillan.
Marshall, G., Rose, D., Newby, H. and Vogler, C. (1989) *Social Class in Modern Britain*, London: Unwin Hyman.

Marshall, S.A. and Mayer, N. (1983) *Neighbourhood Organisations and Community Development*, Washington, DC: Urban Land Institute.
Martin, B. (1984) ' "Mother wouldn't like it": housework as magic', *Theory, Culture and Society* 2, 2: 19–36.
Martin, J. and Roberts, C. (1984) *Women and Employment*, Report on Department of Employment/OPCS Survey, London: HMSO.
Marx, K. (1968 [1849]) 'Wage labour and capital', in K. Marx and F. Engels, *Selected Works*, London: Lawrence & Wishart.
Mason, J. (1989) 'Reconstructing the public and the private: the home and marriage in later life', in G. Allan and G. Crow (eds) *Home and Family: Creating the Domestic Sphere*, Basingstoke: Macmillan.
Mayo, E., Fisher, T., Conaty, P., Doling, J. and Mullineux, A. (1998) *Small is Bankable:* Community reinvestment in the UK, York: YPS/JRF.
Meillasoux, C. (1981) *Maidens, Meal and Money: Capitalism and the Domestic Community*, Cambridge: Cambridge University Press.
Middleton, C. (1979) 'The sexual division of labour in feudal England', *New Left Review* 113/114: 147–68.
Millward, N. (1968) 'Family status and behaviour at work', *Sociological Review* 16: 149–64.
Milofsky, C. and Hunter, A. (1994) 'Where non-profits come from: a theory of organisational emergence', paper presented to the Association for Research on Non-Profit Organisations and Voluntary Action, San Francisco: Oct.
Mollenkopf, J. (1989) 'Who (or what) runs cities, and how?' *Sociological Forum* 4: 119–37.
Moore, R. (1982) *The Social Impact of Oil: The Case of Peterhead*, London: Routledge.
Morris, L. (1990) *The Workings of the Household*, Cambridge: Polity Press.
—— (1994) *Dangerous Classes: The Underclass and Social Citizenship*, London: Routledge.
—— (1995) *Social Divisions: Economic Decline and Social Structural Change*, London: UCL Press.
Morris, L. and Irwin, S. (1992) 'Unemployment and informal support: dependency, exclusion or participation?', *Work, Employment and Society* 6, 2: 185–207.
Morris, L. and Scott, J. (1996) 'The attenuation of class analysis: some comments on G. Marshall, S. Roberts and C. Burgoyne, "Social class and the underclass in Britain and the USA"', *British Journal of Sociology* 47, 1: 45–55.
Morris, L.D. (1984) 'Redundancy and patterns of household finance', *Sociological Review* 32: 492–593.
—— (1985) 'Renegotiation of the domestic division of labour', in B. Roberts *et al.* (eds) *New Approaches to Economic Life*, Manchester: Manchester University Press.
Morris, R.N. and Mogey, J. (1965) *The Sociology of Housing*, London: Routledge.
Mullan, B. (1980) *Stevenage Limited: Aspects of the Planning and Politics of Stevenage New Town 1945–78*, London: Routledge.
Muncie, J. (1999) 'Institutionalised intolerance: youth justice and the 1998 Crime and Disorder Act', *Critical Social Policy* 59: 19, 2: 147–75.
Munro, M. and Smith, S.J. (1989) 'Gender and housing: broadening the debate', *Housing Studies* 4, 1: 3–17.
Murgatroyd, L. (1985) 'The production of people and domestic labour revisited', in R. Close and R. Collins (eds) *Family and Economy in Modern Society*, Basingstoke: Macmillan.

Murray, C. (1984) *Losing Ground*, New York: Basic Books.
Newby, H., Bell, C., Rose, D. and Saunders, P. (1978) *Property, Paternalism and Power: Class and Control in Rural England*, London: Hutchinson.
Newell, S. (1993) 'The superwoman syndrome: gender differences in attitudes towards equal opportunities at work and towards domestic responsibilities at home', in *Work, Employment and Society*: 7, 2: 275–89.
Nissel, M. and Bonnerjea, L. (1982) *Family Care of the Handicapped Elderly: Who Pays?* London: Policy Studies Institute.
North, D.C. (1990) *Institutions, Institutional Change and Economic Performance*, Cambridge: Cambridge University Press.
Nozick, R. (1974) *Anarchy, State and Utopia*, Oxford: Basil Blackwell.
—— (1993) *The Nature of Rationality*, Princeton, NJ: Princeton University Press.
Oakley, A. (1974) *Housewife*, Harmondsworth: Penguin.
Oliver, M. and Barnes, C. (1998) *Disabled People and Social Policy*, Addison Wesley Longman.
Olson, M. (1965) *The Logic of Collective Action: Public Goods and the Theory of Groups*, Cambridge, Mass.: Harvard University Press.
O'Neill, J. (1986) 'The disciplinary society: from Weber to Foucault', *British Journal of Sociology* 38, 1: 42–60.
Osborn, F. et al. (1984) *The Social Life of Britain's Five Year Olds*, London: Routledge.
Ostrander, S.A. (1984) *Women of the Upper Class*, Philadelphia: Temple University Press.
Ostrom, E. (1990) *Governing the Commons: The Evolution of Institutions for Collective Action*, Cambridge: Cambridge University Press.
Ostrom, V., Bish, R. and Ostrom, E. (1988) *Local Government in the United States*, San Francisco: Institute for Contemporary Studies.
Pahl, J. (1983) 'The allocation of money and the structuring of inequality within marriage', *Sociological Review* 31.
—— (ed.) (1985) *Private Violence and Public Policy*, London: Routledge and Kegan Paul.
—— (1989) *Money and Marriage*, Basingstoke: Macmillan.
—— (1991) 'Money and power in marriage', in P. Abbot and C. Wallace (eds) *Gender, Power and Sexuality*, Basingstoke: Macmillan.
Pahl, J.M. and Pahl, R.E. (1971) *Managers and Their Wives*, London: Allen Lane.
Pahl, R. (1975) *Whose City?* 2nd ed., Harmondsworth: Penguin.
—— (1984) *Divisions of Labour*, Oxford: Basil Blackwell.
—— (1988) 'Some remarks on informal work, social polarization and the social structure', *International Journal of Urban and Regional Research* 12, 2.
Painter, C. (1995) 'Management by the unelected state: the rise of quangocracy', in K. Isaac-Henry, C. Painter and C. Barnes (eds) *Management in the Public Sector: Challenge and Change*, London: Chapman and Hall.
Painter, C., Rouse, J., Isaac-Henry, K. and Munk, L. (1995) *Changing Local Governance: Local Authorities and Non-elected Agencies*, Luton: LGMB.
Parkin, F. (1979) *Marxism and Class Theory: A Bourgeois Critique*, London: Tavistock.
Parkinson, M. (1998) *Combating Social Exclusion: Lessons from Area-based Programmes in Europe*, Bristol: Policy Press/JRF.
Parry, G., Moyser, G. and Wagstaffe, M. (1987) 'The crowd and the community: context, content and aftermath', in G. Gaskell and R. Benewick (eds) *The Crowd in Contemporary Britain*, London: Sage.

Pateman, C. (1988) *The Sexual Contract*, Cambridge: Polity Press.
Paterson, F. (1988) 'Schooling the family', *Sociology* 22, 1: 65–86.
Payne, G. (1992) 'Competing views of contemporary social mobility and social divisions', in R. Burrows and C. Marsh (eds) *Consumption and Class: Divisions and Change*, New York: St Martin's Press.
Peach, C. (1996) 'Does Britain have ghettos?', *Transactions of the Institute of British Geographers* 21: 216–35.
Pearson, R. (1993) 'Knowing one's place: perceptions of community in the industrial suburbs of Leeds, 1790–1890', *Journal of Social History* 27, 2: 221–44.
Perlman, J. (1979) 'Grassroot empowerment and government response', *Social Policy* 10: 16–21.
Perri 6 (1997) *Escaping Poverty: From Safety Nets to Networks of Opportunity*, London: Demos.
Phillips, S.K. (1986) 'Natives and incomers: the symbolism of belonging in Muker parish, North Yorkshire', in A.P. Cohen (ed.) *Symbolising Boundaries: Identity and Diversity in British Cultures*, Manchester: Manchester University Press.
Piachaud, D. (1979) *The Cost of a Child*, London: CPAG.
—— (1984) *Round About Fifty Hours per Week*, London: CPAG.
Pleck, J.H. (1985) *Working Wives, Working Husbands*, Beverly Hills: Sage.
Popple, K. (1994) 'Combating racism', in V. Harris (ed.) *Community Work Skills Manual*, Newcastle: Association of Community Workers.
—— (1995) *Analysing Community Work: Its Theory and Practice*, Milton Keynes: Open University Press.
Porteous, J.D. (1989) *Planned to Death: The Annihilation of a Place called Howdendyke*, Manchester: Manchester University Press.
Posner, R. (1977) *Economic Analysis of Law*, 2nd ed., Boston: Little Brown and Co.
Power, A. (1984) *Local Housing Management: A Priority Estates Project Survey*, London: DoE.
—— (1987) *Property Before People: The Management of Twentieth Century Council Housing*, London: Allen and Unwin.
—— (1997) *Estates on the Edge: The Social Consequences of Mass Housing in Europe*, Basingstoke: Macmillan.
Power, A. and Tunstall, R. (1995) *Swimming Against the Tide: Progress or Polarisation on 20 Unpopular Estates*, York: Joseph Rowntree Foundation.
Procter, I. (1990) 'The privatisation of working-class life: a dissenting view', *British Journal of Sociology* 41, 2: 157–80.
Purcell, K. (1996) 'Researching value-loaded issues: the management of food in households', in L. Morris and E. Stina-Lyon (eds) *Gender Relations in Public and Private*, Basingstoke: Macmillan.
Putnam, R.D. (1993) *Making Democracy Work: Civic Traditions in Modern Italy*, Princeton: Princeton University Press.
Quilgars, D. and Anderson, I. (1995) *Foyers for Young People: Evaluation of a Pilot Initiative*, York: Centre for Housing Policy, University of York.
Qureshi, H. and Walker, A. (1989) *The Caring Relationship: Elderly People and Their Families*, Basingstoke: Macmillan.
Rainwater, L. (1971) *Behind Ghetto Walls: Black Families in a Federal Slum*, London: Allen Lane.
—— (1984) 'Mother's contribution to the family money economy in Europe and the United States', in P. Voydanoff (ed.) *Work and Family*, Palo Alto: Mayfield.

Rapoport, R. and Rapoport, R.N. (1971) *Dual Career Families*, London: Robertson.
Redcliffe-Maud, J. (1969) *Report of the Royal Commission on Local Government in England Vol 3*, Cmnd 4040, London: HMSO.
Rees, A. (1951) *Life in a Welsh Countryside: A Social Study of Llanfihangel yng Ngwynfa*, Cardiff: University of Wales Press.
Reid, B. (1995) 'Interorganisational networks and the delivery of housing services', *Housing Studies* 10, 2: 133–49.
Reiger, K.M. (1985) *The Disenchantment of the Home: Modernising the Australian Family 1880–1940*, Melbourne: Oxford University Press.
Rex, J. and Moore, R. (1967) *'Race', Community and Conflict: A Study of Sparkbrook*, Oxford: Oxford University Press.
Richards, L. (1990) *Nobody's Home: Dreams and Realities in a New Suburb*, Melbourne: Oxford University Press.
Rimmer, L. (1981) *Families in Focus*, London: Study Commission on the Family.
Roberts, B., Finnegan, R. and Gallie, D. (eds) (1985) *New Approaches to Economic Life*, Manchester: Manchester University Press.
Roberts, E. (1995) *Women and Families: An Oral History, 1940–1970*, Oxford: Basil Blackwell.
Robertson, A.F. (1991) *Beyond the Family: The Social Organisation of Human Reproduction*, Cambridge: Polity Press.
Robinson, V. (1986) *Transients, Settlers and Refugees: Asians in Britain*, Oxford: Clarendon Press.
—— (1993) 'Ethnic minorities and the enduring geography of settlement', *Town and Country Planning*, March: 53–6.
Rogers, B. (1980) *The Domestication of Women: Discrimination in Developing Societies*, London: Tavistock.
Rosaldo, M.Z. and Lamphere, L. (eds) (1974) *Woman, Culture and Society*, Stanford, CA: Stanford University Press.
Rosen, E.I. (1987) *Bitter Choices*, Chicago: Chicago University Press.
Rouse, J. and Smith, G. (1999) 'Accountability', in M. Powell (ed.) *New Labour, New Welfare State? The 'Third Way' in British Social Policy*, Bristol: The Policy Press.
Rousseau, J.-J. (1968 [1762]) *The Social Contract*, Harmondsworth: Penguin.
Rubin, L. (1976) *Worlds of Pain*, New York: Basic Books.
—— (1983) *Intimate Strangers*, New York: Harper and Row.
Saegert, S. (1980) 'Masculine cities and feminine suburbs: polarised ideas, contradictory realities', *Signs* 5: S96–S111.
Sahlins, M. (1965) 'On the sociology of primitive exchange', in M. Branton (ed.) *The Relevance of Models in Social Anthropology*, London: Tavistock.
Sampson, R.J. (1991) 'Linking the micro- and macro-level dimensions of community social organisation', *Social Forces* 70, 1: 43–64.
Sarre, P., Phillips, D. and Skellington, R. (1989) *Ethnic Minority Housing: Explanations and Policies*, Aldershot: Avebury.
Saunders, P. (1979) *Urban Politics: A Sociological Interpretation*, London: Hutchinson.
—— (1986) *Social Theory and the Urban Question*, 2nd ed., London: Hutchinson.
—— (1990) *A Nation of Home Owners*, London: Unwin Hyman.
Savage, M., Barlow, J., Dickens, P. and Fielding, T. (1992) *Property, Bureaucracy and Culture: Middle Class Formation in Contemporary Britain*, London: Routledge.

Scherer, J. (1972) *Contemporary Community: Sociological Illusion or Reality?* London: Tavistock.
Seabrook, J. (1984) *The Idea of Neighbourhood: What Local Politics Should be About*, London: Pluto.
Sen, A. (1987) *The Standard of Living*, Cambridge: Cambridge University Press.
Shaw, A. (1988) *A Pakistani Community in Britain*, Oxford: Basil Blackwell.
Shaw, M.E. (1976) *Group Dynamics: The Psychology of Small Group Behaviour*, 2nd ed., New York: McGraw-Hill.
Shimin, S. (1962) 'Extra-mural factors influencing behaviour at work', *Occupational Psychology* 36: 124–31.
Simon, H.A. (1982) *Models of Bounded Rationality*, Boston: MIT Press.
Sixsmith, A.J. (1986) 'Independence and home in later life', in C. Phillipson, M. Bernard and P. Strang (eds) *Dependency and Interdependency in Old Age – Theoretical Perspectives and Policy Alternatives*, London: Croom Helm.
Skelcher, C., Mccabe, A. and Lowndes, V. with Nanton, P. (1996) *Community Networks in Urban Regeneration . . . 'It all depends who you know'*, Bristol: Policy Press.
Sklair, L. (1998) 'As political actors', *New Political Economy* 3, 2: 284–7.
Smith, J. (1997) 'Transforming estates', in C. Cooper and M. Hawtin (eds) *Housing, Community and Conflict: Understanding Resident 'Involvement'*, Aldershot: Arena.
Smith, L. (1989) *Domestic Violence: An Overview of the Literature*, London: HMSO.
Smith, S.R. (1999) 'Arguing against cuts in lone parent benefits: reclaiming the desert ground in the UK', *Critical Social Policy* 60: 19, 3: 313–14.
Smith, Y. (1997) 'The household, women's employment and social exclusion', *Urban Studies* 34, 8: 1159–77.
Social Exclusion Unit (1998) *Bringing Britain Together: A National Strategy for Neighbourhood Renewal*, Cm. 4045, London: The Stationery Office.
Somerville, P. (1994) 'Tenure, gender and household structure', *Housing Studies* 9, 3: 329–50.
—— (1997) 'The social construction of home', *Journal of Architectural and Planning Research* 14, 3: 226–45.
Somerville, P. and Knowles, A. (1991) 'The difference that tenure makes', *Housing Studies* 6, 2: 112–30.
—— (1995) 'Making sense of tenant participation', *Netherlands Journal of Housing and the Built Environment* 10, 3: 259–81.
Somerville, P. and Steele, A. (1999) 'Making oneself at home: the mediation of residential action', *International Journal of Urban and Regional Research* 23, 1: 88–102.
Spain, D. (1993) 'Been-heres versus come-heres: negotiating conflicting community identities', *Journal of the American Planning Association* 59, 2: 156–71.
Stacey, M. (1969) 'The myth of community studies', *British Journal of Sociology* 20, 2: 34–47.
Stack, C. (1974) *All Our Kin: Strategies for Survival in a Black Community*, New York: Harper and Row.
Stamp, P. (1985) 'Balance of financial power in marriage', *Sociological Review* 33: 546–57.
Steele, A., Somerville, P. and Galvin, G. (1995) *Estate Agreements: A New Arrangement for Tenant Participation*, Salford: University of Salford.
Strathearn, M. (1981) *Kinship at the Core: An Anthropology of Elmdon, a Village in North West Essex in the 1960s*, Cambridge: Cambridge University Press.

Summers, G.F. (1986) 'Rural community development', *Annual Review of Sociology* 12: 347–71.
Suttles, G. (1972) *The Social Construction of Communities*, Chicago: University of Chicago Press.
Swenarton, M. (1981) *Homes Fit for Heroes*, London: Heinemann.
Tanner, N. (1974) 'Matrifocality in Indonesia and Africa and among Black Americans', in M.Z. Rosaldo and L. Lamphere (eds) *Woman, Culture and Society*, Stanford, CA: Stanford University Press.
Tarrow, S. (1994) *Power in Movement: Social Movements, Collective Action and Politics*, Cambridge: Cambridge University Press.
Taylor, Marilyn (1995) *Unleashing the Potential: Bringing Residents to the Centre of Regeneration*, York: Joseph Rowntree Foundation.
Taylor, Michael (1976) *Anarchy and Co-operation*, London: Wiley.
—— (1987) *The Possibility of Co-operation*, Cambridge: Cambridge University Press.
Taylor, Michael and Ward, H. (1982) 'Chickens, whales and lumpy goods', *Political Studies* 25, 3: 350–70.
Taylor-Gooby, P. (1991) *Social Change, Social Welfare and Social Science*, Hemel Hempstead: Harvester Wheatsheaf.
Tebbutt, M. (1995) *Women's Talk: A Social History of 'Gossip' in Working-class Neighbourhoods, 1880–1960*, Aldershot: Scolar Press.
Teeland, L. (1998) 'Home, sick: how seriously ill residents view and use their home', paper presented to ENHR conference on *Housing Futures: Renewal, Innovation and Sustainability*, Cardiff: 7–11 September.
Thorns, D.C. (1976) *The Quest for Community: Social Aspects of Residential Growth*, London: Allen and Unwin.
Tilly, L. and Scott, J. (1978) *Women, Work and the Family*, New York: Holt, Rinehart and Winston.
Titmuss, R.M. (1958) 'The social division of welfare', in R. Titmuss, *Essays on Welfare*, London: Allen and Unwin.
Treas, J. (1991) 'The common pot or separate purses: a transactions cost interpretation', in R. Blumberg (ed.) *Gender, Family and Economy: The Triple Overlap*, Beverly Hills: Sage.
Unger, R. (1972) *Law and Modern Society: Towards a Critique of Social Theory*, New York: Free Press.
Van Parijs, P. (1987) 'A revolution in class theory', *Politics and Society* 15: 453–82.
Vidich, A. and Bensman, J. (1960) *Small Town in Mass Society*, New York: Anchor Books.
Vogler, C. (1994) 'Money in the household', in M. Anderson *et al.* (eds) *The Social and Political Economy of the Household*, Oxford: Oxford University Press.
Voydanoff, P. and Kelly, R.F. (1984) 'Determinants of work-related family problems among employed parents', *Journal of Marriage and the Family* 46: 881–92.
Walby, S. (1990) *Theorising Patriarchy*, Oxford: Basil Blackwell.
Walker, K.E. and Woods, M.E. (1976) *Time Use: A Measure of Household Production of Family Goods and Services*, Washington, DC: American Home Economics Association.
Walker, R. and Leisering, L. (1998) 'New tools: towards a dynamic science of modern society', in L. Leisering and R. Walker (eds) *The Dynamics of Modern Society*, Bristol: The Policy Press.
Wallace, C. (1987) *For Richer, For Poorer*, London: Tavistock.

—— (1993) 'Reflections on the concept of "strategy",' in D. Morgan and L. Stanley (eds) *Debates in Sociology*, Manchester: Manchester University Press.
Wallman, S. (1984) *Eight London Households*, London: Tavistock.
Walsh, K. (1995) *Public Services and Market Mechanisms: Competition, Contracting and the New Public Management*, Basingstoke: Macmillan.
Ward, H. (1987) 'The risks of a reputation for toughness', *British Journal of Political Science* 17: 23–52.
—— (1996) 'Green arguments for local democracy', in D. King and G. Stoker (eds) *Rethinking Local Democracy*, Basingstoke: Macmillan.
Warren, R.B. and Warren, D.I. (1977) *The Neighbourhood Organizer's Handbook*, Indiana: University of Notre Dame Press.
Warwick, D. and Littlejohn, G. (1992) *Coal, Capital and Culture: A Sociological Analysis of Mining Communities in West Yorkshire*, London: Routledge.
Watson, S. with Austerberry, H. (1986) *Housing and Homelessness: A Feminist Perspective*, London: Routledge.
Weber, M. (1968 (orig. 1922) *Economy and Society: An Outline of Interpretive Sociology*, vols 1–3, ed. G. Roth and C. Wittich, New York: Bedminster Press
Weenig, M., Schmidt, T. and Midden, C. (1990) 'Social dimensions of neighbourhoods and the effectiveness of information programmes', *Environment and Behavior* 22: 27–54.
Wellman, B., Carrington, P. and Hall, A. (1988) 'Networks as personal communities', in B. Wellman and S. Berkowitz (eds) *Social Structures: A Network Approach*, Cambridge: Cambridge University Press.
Wenger, G.C. (1984) *The Supportive Network: Coping with Old Age*, London: Allen and Unwin.
Werbner, P. (1984) 'Middle-class Pakistanis', in E. Butterworth and D. Weir (eds) *The New Sociology of Modern Britain*, London: Fontana.
—— (1988) 'Taking and giving: working women and female bonds in a Pakistani immigrant neighbourhood', in S. Westwood and P. Bhachu (eds), *Enterprising Women: Ethnicity, Economy and Gender Relations*, London: Routledge.
West, A. and McCormick, J. (1998) 'Three steps and beyond: micro-economies for social inclusion', in C. Oppenheim (ed.) *An Inclusive Society: Strategies for Tackling Poverty*, London: Institute for Public Policy Research.
West, P. (1984) 'The family, the welfare state and community care: political rhetoric and public attitudes', *Journal of Social Policy* 13, 4: 417–46.
Wheelock, J. (1986) *Unemployment, Gender Roles and Household Work Strategies on Wearside*, EEC Report.
Whyte, W.F. (1955) *Street Corner Society*, 2nd ed., Chicago: University of Chicago Press.
—— (1966) 'The outgoing life', in E. and M. Josephson (eds) *Man Alone*, New York: Dell Publishing Company.
Wiewel, W. and Gills, D. (1995) 'Community development organisational capacity and US urban policy: lessons from the Chicago experience 1983–93', in G. Craig and M. Mayo (eds) *Community Empowerment: A Reader in Participation and Development*, London: Zed: 127–39.
Wight, D. (1993) *Workers Not Wasters: Masculine Respectability, Consumption and Employment in Central Scotland*, Edinburgh: Edinburgh University Press.
Williams, F. (1989) *Social Policy: A Critical Introduction*, Cambridge: Polity Press.

Williams, M.R. (1985) *Neighbourhood Organisations*, Westport, Connecticut: Greenwood.
Williams, R.G.A. (1983) 'Kinship and migration strategies among settled Londoners: two responses to population pressure', *British Journal of Sociology* 34: 386–415.
Willmott, P. (1986) *Social Networks, Informal Care and Public Policy*, London: Policy Studies Institute.
Wilson, G. (1997) *Money in the Family*, Aldershot: Avebury.
Wilson, W.J. (1987) *The Truly Disadvantaged: The Inner City, the Underclass, and Public Policy*, Chicago: University of Chicago Press.
Witherspoon, S. (1988) 'A woman's work', in R. Jowell and R. Topf (eds) *British Social Attitudes: The Fifth Report*, Aldershot: Gower.
Young, K., Gosschalk, B. and Hatter, W. (1996) *In Search of Community Identity*, York: YPS/JRF.
Young, M. (1961) *The Rise of the Meritocracy 1870–2033: An Essay on Education and Equality*, Harmondsworth: Penguin.
Young, M. and Lemos, G. (1997) *The Communities We Have Lost and Can Regain*, London: Lemos and Crane.
Young, M. and Willmott, P. (1957) *Family and Kinship in East London*, London: Routledge and Kegan Paul.
Zey, M. (1998) *Rational Choice Theory and Organisational Theory: A Critique*, London: Sage.

Index

A VICTORY, community development approach 67–8
added value concept, generational relations 98
affective communities 53, 56, 57
Allan, G. 60, 64
allocation, needs-based approach 127
assimilation, communities 59–60
assistance programmes, role of 142
associations: households as 31; housing 152–3, 154, 155, 163; vs communities 48
associative democracy 129
autonomy: subsidiarity and 128; workforce 107
autonomy principle, and law 126

background communities, community development 74–6, 79
Balchin, P. 149
benefits systems 47, 118, 119, 141–2
Best Value, and housing 153, 159, 163
Blair–Clinton orthodoxy, managerialism 117
Bohman, J. 6
boundary definition issues, communities 57–8
breadwinner role, and postwar social settlement 118–19
breadwinning, vs domesticity 14–15, 17, 19–22, 24, 168–9
British Household Panel Survey 30
bureau-professionalism, and housing policy 150–1
bureaucracies: company 105; growth 90; housing policy 144–5; and individuals 91; labour market 50, 89; social settlement and 118; state 50–1
bureaucratic relations 90, 106–7

capitalism: basis 7; competitive phase 112; development 89, 112–13; education system and 38; and exploitation 6–7, 89, 96–7, 108; Fordist phase 112–13, 122–3; global unity of domination concept 108; liberal phase 112; post-Fordist phase 112, 113–14; rational choice theory 10; transnational class 114
Chicken Model: and domestic violence 32–3; households 18–25, 46, 169; housekeeping allowance system 29–30; rational choice theory 9, 46, 168
child benefit 47, 119
child care, labour market and 31
child development, state intervention 38, 43–4, 46–7
childbearing: and free-riding 44; and generational relations 34–47, 170; lagged adaptation and 38; marginal utility and 38–9; rational choice theory 34–8, 170; state intervention and 38; tax and 44, 47; wealth flows theory 37–9
citizenship: building 130–4, 134–42; collective-action problems and 136–7, 138; governance regime 130; and hegemony 135, 136–7; and managerialism 137–42; principle of 130; traditions of 136–7, *see also* state–citizen relations
civic republican citizenship 136–7
Clarke, J. 115–17

class divisions: contractual relations and 91–2, 174; and private capital 96–7; social capital and 96; underclass positions 94
classes, transnational 114
collective action, contractual relations 110–11
collective ownership 82, 103, 175
collective resistance, to oppression 101–2, 110, 113
collectivism 166
communities: acquaintance networks 61; affective 53, 56, 57; assimilation 59–60; boundary definition issues 57–8; effective 53, 56; ethnic groups in 59–60, 62–3, 80–1; family-based 58, 66; formal organisations 56–7, 69–70; immigrant groups 59–60, 63–4; interactions 9–10; kinship 53–4, 55, 64, 86–7; modern vs traditional 53–4; multicultural 61; polarisation 59–60; rational choice theory 9–10; segregation in 62; social interaction types 56; social network analysis 55; unemployment in 64–5; voluntary relationships 56; vs associations 48
community corporations, community development 70
community development 66–87, 172–3; approaches 67–71; background communities 74–6, 79; charities 73; coercive power 83–7, 134–42; collective ownership 82; community corporations 70; community spirit 82; defined 66; elitism 79–80; empowerment 83–7; formal structures 79–80, 84; funding 70; goals 70; government policy 83–4; inclusiveness 81; and institutional structures 131–2; job opportunities 73, 86; leadership 76–7, 81; local government and 134; networking 75, 79, 84; rational choice theory 69, 71; resistance 70; resource redistribution 134; social divisions 86–7; success 81–3; supporters 77–8, 80; unity issues 71–2; urban regeneration 78; and wider society 104
competitive phase, capitalism 112
complementary reciprocity, rational choice theory 5
conclusion 165–82; main 182

conflict approach, community development 67, 69–71, 85, 86
Conservative Party: and council housing 150; housing policy 149–50
consumptionist approach, social mobility 92, 94
contractual relations 10–11; advantages 88–9; and bureaucratic relations 90; and class divisions 91–2, 174; collective action 110–11; constructive nature 90–1; destructive nature 90–1; employment 89; and empowerment 90–1; and exploitation 110–11; external nature 90; and informality 89; social capital and 49, 89; and social divisions 88–111, 173–6; social mobility and 101–2; and trust 49; vs bureaucratic relations 106–7
controlling behaviours, intimacy and 32–3
Cooper, C. 84–6
council housing: and Conservative Party 150; housing policy and 147–8; and Labour Party 150
crime control agencies, power dispersal 118
Crow, G. 52, 60, 64

Davies, W.K.D. 67
democracy: associative 129; building 132–3, 134–42; democratic deficit 135; economic and stakeholder 129; governance regime 128–9; and hegemony 135; implications 128–9; inter-organisational 130; managerialism and 138–9; property-owning democracy concept 149–50; and public accountability 139; Schumpeterian 135; stakeholder 138–9; triple 130
disciplinary political regimes 117
disciplinary power 106–7, 110; and housing 155; managerialism 115–16, 139–40; retaining 119; state–citizen relations 112, 124–5
discrimination: institutional 107; racism and 106, 107
division of labour: domestic 17–25; and Exchange Model 18–20, 46; future changes 31; rational choice theory 18
division of welfare concept 99
domestic labour, waged 22–4, 29

domestic labour process: exploitation 97–8, 100–1, 119–20; gender relations 105
domestic relations: co-operation and 88; rational choice theory 15–17
domestic social relations 13–47, 51, 167–71
domesticity, vs breadwinning 14–15, 17, 19–22, 24, 168–9

economic democracy 130; and stakeholder democracy 129
education: and generational relations 38; and social mobility 93, 98
education system: and capitalism 38; state intervention 38, 43–4, 47
effective communities 53, 56
emancipation, and marxism 127–8
emotional choice theory, childbearing 36
employment contracts 89
empowerment: community development 83–7; and contractual relations 90–1; domestic violence victims 33; labour empowerment forms 103–4; workplace-based 104–5
encapsulation, communities 59–61, 64
enforcement, rational choice theory and 109–10
equality of opportunity: labour market 31; legal/political authorities 126–7
ethnic groups: in communities 59–60, 62–3, 80–1; social reproduction analysis 99–100
European Union, and social settlement 121–2
Exchange Model: and division of labour 18–20, 46; gender relations 19–20; households 18–25
exploitation: abolishing 126–7, 127–8, 130, 132–3; capitalism and 6–7, 89, 96–7, 108; concept 6–7; contractual relations and 110–11; defined 6; domestic labour process 97–8, 100–1, 119–20; generational relations and 43–4; labour market 96–7, 108; labour processes 97–8; and value 6; vs oppression 7; of wives 31, 97–8

family: and housing managerialism 160; and managerialism 119–20; and patriarchy 122

financial management: households 25–34, 169; systems distribution 26–30
Fordist phase: capitalism 112–13, 122–3; and monarchic power 123
formal organisations, communities 56–7, 69–70
Foucauldian theory: political economy and 8–9; power concepts 11; rational choice theory and 8–9, 106–8, 175–6
Fox, B.J. 34
free collective bargaining 102, 110, 114
free-riding: and childbearing 44; community development 68, 69, 70, 131; households and 20, 21–2, 25, 131; housekeeping allowance system 30; state–citizen relations 124; and taxation 141–2; workplace 110
Freedom of Information Act 138–9

gender relations: division of labour 17–25; domestic labour process 105; Exchange Model 19–20; households 9, 13, 14–34, 46–7; and Industrial Revolution 14; and post-industrial society 17; rational choice theory 169; recursive determination 16; role reversals 24
generational relations: added value concept 98; and childbearing 34–47, 170; education and 38; and exploitation 43–4; households 9, 13, 34–47; inheritance issues 36–7, 39, 40; lagged reciprocity 39–40; parental care 40; phenomenological theory 42; reciprocity 34–5, 37, 39–41, 170–1; value and 36–7
Gills, D. 76
globalisation, effects of 114–15
governance: citizenship and 130; democracy and 128–9; and housing 163–4; new regime of 128–30; partnership and 129–30; recreating 135–42
government: central vs local 151–2; and housing policy 151–2; local 133–4; and managerialism 115–16; reflexive 115–16, 117
Gregson, N. 22–3
Guinness Trust, housing trust 146

Hart, C. 83

Hawtin, M. 84–6
hegemony 8, 11; challenging 141; changing 112–23; and citizenship 135, 136–7; democracy and 135; and disciplinary power 113, 114, 122–3; managerialism 114, 115, 122–3; and partnership 135–6; postwar 122–3, 136–7; settlements 113–14, 116–23
Herbert, D.T. 67
Hill, Octavia 146, 156
Hirst, P.Q. 116
households: as associations 31; Chicken Model 18–25, 46, 169; Exchange Model 18–25; and families 13–47, 167–71; financial management 25–34, 169; formation 17; low vs high income 24–5; normalisation processes 14; and patriarchy 9, 25; and rational choice theory 9, 13–47, 169
housing: and Best Value 153, 159, 163; and capital gains tax 162–3; and community care policy 155; and conditional communitarianism 153; and conditional welfare 153; and governance 163–4; and housing associations 152–3, 154, 155, 163; Institute of Housing 156; and managerialism 151, 152, 153–64; market-oriented approach 157–8; and New Deal 160–1; partnership approach 158–9; and performance management 153; personalised management approach 157; private sector 144–5; public sector 144–5; re-professionalisation of 153; and Regional Development Agencies 155; Society of Women Housing Managers 156; and state power dispersal 154; tenant management 159–60; Tenant Participation Compacts 158, 163–4; tenure choice 162; voluntary sector 144–5, 146
housing associations 152–3, 154, 155, 163
housing costs, and fertility rates 38
housing organisations 158–9; and Labour Party 163; and power 161
housing policy 11; and council housing 147–8; and government 151–2; historical background 145–7; and housing services 148; housing shortage 146, 147, 152; and land ownership 145–7; and local authorities 151–2; and market capitalism 147; and marketised feudalism 145–7; and owner-occupation 147, 149, 153, 161–3; and politics of tenure 147–8, 149; and public health 145–6; and rational choice theory 144; Right to Buy 150, 152, 154; and slums 145, 147; state–citizen relations 144, 145–7
housing regimes 144–5
housing services, and housing policy 148
housing shortage, and housing policy 146, 147, 152
Housing of the Working Classes Act (1890) 146

immigrant groups: communities 59–60, 63–4; exclusion 100–1
inheritance issues, generational relations 36–7, 39, 40
insiders: communities 57–8; labour market 94
Institute of Housing 156
institutional discrimination 107
institutional structures: and community development 131–2; and democratic control 131
interaction variable, neighbourhoods 54
international comparative approach, social mobility 92–6
intimacy: attachment theory 32–4; defined 32

job competence 107–8
joint management, household finances 26–30

kinship communities 53–4, 55, 64, 86–7

labour empowerment: company bureaucracy and 105; competitive markets and 105, 114; constraints 105–6; forms 103–4
labour market: active policies 120–1; bureaucracies 50, 89; and child care 31; cultural issues 95; equality of opportunity 31; exploitation 96–7; insiders-outsiders 94, 100; and lone parenthood 44, 45, 95; and state power 120–1; structural issues 95

Labour Party: and council housing 150; and housing organisations 163; housing policy 149–50, *see also* New Labour

labour processes: analysis 98–9; exploitation in 97–8, 108; state regulation and 99; types 97, *see also* capitalist labour process; domestic labour process

lagged adaptation: domestic work 20, 21–2; household management systems 30

land ownership, and housing policy 145–7

law: autonomy principle 126; enforcing 125–6; obeying 125–6; and self-determination 126

legal framework, state–citizen relations 124–30

legal/political authorities: equality of opportunity 126–7; and liberal theory 126–7; selection 125

liberal theory: and legal/political authorities 126–7; and meritocracy 126–7

link-persons, community development 76, 77

local authorities: and housing policy 151–2; public choice theory and 133

local government: and community development 134; modernising 134; and public choice theory 133–4

lone parenthood 42–3, 44–5; and labour market 44, 45, 95; normalisation 119; and patriarchy 45; state intervention 45

Lowe, M. 22–3

Luxton, M. 34

managerialism: Blair–Clinton orthodoxy 117; bureaucratic monoculture 116; and citizenship 137–42; and democracy 138–9; democratic accountability 164; disciplinary power 115–16, 139–40; and educationalism 120; and family 119–20, 160; government and 115–16; hegemony 114, 115, 122–3; homogeneous 116; and housing 151, 152, 153–64; and monarchic power 139–40; and New Labour 140, 164; and partnership 138, 139–40; political 117–18; political settlements 117–18; and power 140–1; private/public 116;

and rational choice theory 161–2; and state power 136; untrammelled 141; and welfare state 117

market exchange, contractual relations 48–9

market-oriented approach, housing 157–8

marketised feudalism, and housing policy 145–7

markets, social evolution and 112–13

marriages 29, 31–2, 88

Marshallian citizenship 136–7

means-testing, welfare and 121

meritocracy, and liberal theory 126–7

migration, and welfare 121–2

monarchic power 106–7, 110, 114, 115; and Fordism 123; and managerialism 139–40; problematic features 122; retaining 119; and state–citizen relations 124–5

monarchical political regimes 117

nation: and housing managerialism 161; and social settlement 119, 121–3

National Health Service: and citizenship 137; social settlement and 118

neighbour-based communities 66, 86–7

neighbourliness 48, 51–2; and co-operation 88; rational choice theory 52–3

networking, community development 75, 79, 84

New Labour: democratic innovations 138–41; and managerialism 140, 164

Newman, J. 115–17

Northern Ireland: communities 62; unemployment 65

opportunities, redistribution of 166

opportunity, equality of 126–7

oppression: abolishing 132–3; capitalist 113; collective resistance 101–2, 110, 113; vs exploitation 7

organisational settlements: collapse of 116; hegemony 113–14, 116

outsiders: communities 57–8, 75; labour market 94, 100

owner-occupation, and housing policy 147, 149, 153, 161–3

ownership: collective 82, 103; communal facilities 88; land 145–7

parenthood: lone 42–3, 44–5, *see also* generational relations
partnership: building 132–3, 134–42; governance regime 129–30; and hegemony 135–6; managerialism and 138, 139–40
partnerships: community, defined 104; worker 105
patriarchal marriages 29
patriarchy: and family 122; and households 9, 25; and lone parenthood 45
performance management, and housing 153
phenomenological theory: generational relations 42; marriages 31–2
political economy, and Foucauldian theory 8–9
political managerialism 117–18
political regimes: disciplinary 117; monarchical 117
political settlements, managerialism 117–18
political/economic settlements, hegemony 113–14
politics, and rational choice theory 165–6
politics of tenure, and housing policy 147–8, 149
post-1945 housing settlement 147–53
post-Fordist phase, capitalism 112, 113–14
postwar hegemony 122–3, 136–7
postwar settlement in housing 151–3
postwar social settlement 118–19, 137
power: community development 83–7, 134–42; family 119–20; Foucauldian theory 11; and housing organisations 161; and managerialism 140–1; mechanisms 102; monarchic *see* monarchic power; and rational choice theory 6; resource theory 18, 20, 26–7; and social capital 101–2; social class and 100–1; state 119–20; victim empowerment 33
prisoner's dilemma, households 20
private capital 49, 50; and class divisions 96–7; power and 101–2; socialism and 103, 175; way forward 103
production vs reproduction, gender relations 14–15, 17
property-owning democracy concept 149–50

public administration paradigm 139
public choice theory 1–2; and local authorities 133; and local government 133–4
public powers: external 131–2; redistribution 142

racism: capitalist labour process 100; discrimination and 106, 107; workplace 105–6
rational choice theory 1–10; assumption 165; capitalism 10; Chicken Model 9, 46, 168; childbearing 34–8, 170; and collectivism 166; communities 9–10; community development 69, 71; constraints system 2; contractual relations 10, 108–9; criticisms 11–12, 22–5; defending 11–12; described 165–8; Exchange Model 9, 167–8; and Foucauldian theory 8–9, 106–8, 175–6; gender relations 169; generational relations 34–8, 40–1, 169–70; and households 9, 13–47, 169; and housing policy 144; and individuals 166–7; and institutions 5–6; and managerialism 161–2; misunderstandings 11–12, 165–8; neighbourliness 52–3; and politics 165–6; problems 22–5, 34–5, 90, 108–10; and reciprocity 4–5, 168; reconsidered 123–30; sanctions 109; self-determination 1–2, 3, 127; shortcomings 6; social division theory 101–2; social exclusion theory 101–2; and state–citizen relations 123–30, 143; state's role 135
reciprocity: balanced 48; communities 47–9; generational relations 34–5, 37, 39–41, 170–1; households and 9; intimacy and 33–4; rational choice theory 4–5, 168; and the state 50–1
redistribution: landed property 145–6; needs-based approach 127, 134, 138; of opportunities 166
Regional Development Agencies, and housing 155
resource redistribution, community development 134
resource theory of power 18, 20; household financial management 26–7
Right to Buy, housing policy 150, 152, 154

role reversals, gender relations 24
ruling class, working class relations 113

sanctions 109
SCELI *see* Social Change and Economic Life Initiative
Schumpeterian democracy 135
self-determination: and equality 127–8; and law 126; rational choice theory 1–2, 3, 127
self-development, workplace 108
self-help approach, community development 67, 68–9, 85
Skelcher, C. 84
slums, and housing policy 145, 147
Smith, J. 80–1, 82
social capital: community development 69, 74; and contractual relations 49, 89; power and 101–2; and social class 96; trade unions 102
Social Change and Economic Life Initiative (SCELI) 26
social class: analysis 98–9; assets 99–100; characterised 99–100; power and 100–1; social capital and 96
social divisions: combating 101–6, 174–5; community development 86–7; contractual relations and 88–111, 173–6
social evolution, markets and 112–13
social exclusion theory, rational choice theory 101–2
social justice, state–citizen relations and 112–43, 176–9
social mobility: approaches to 92–7; and class closure 92–3; and class system 101–2; consumptionist approach 92, 94; and contractual relations 101–2; dynamic approach 92, 96–7; and education 93, 98; international comparative approach 92–6
social relations: domestic 13–47, 51, 167–71; informal group 48–87; theory of 1–12; types 51
social settlement: and breadwinner role 118–19; and bureaucracies 118; changing 118; and European Union 121–2; and family 119–20; hegemony 113–14, 116–23; managerialist 137–8; and nation 119, 121–3; National Health Service and 118; non-achievement 121; postwar 118–19, 137; transnational 121–2, 123; undermining 120–1; and unemployment 120–1; and work 119, 120–1
socialism: and collective ownership 103, 175; private capital and 103, 175
state intervention: bureaucracies 50–1; child development 38, 43–4, 46–7; and childbearing 38; education system 38, 43–4, 47; lone parenthood 45; and reciprocity 50–1
state power: dispersal 136, 138–9, 154; and labour market 120–1; and managerialism 136; productive subjection 115; rolling out 121, 123
state–citizen relations 11, 50–1, 58; co-operation 124; current changes 112–23; disciplinary power 112, 124–5; free-riding and 124; housing policy 144, 145–7; legal framework 124–30; and monarchic power 124–5; and rational choice theory 123–30, 143; and social justice 112–43, 176–9; and state policy 123–4

tax: capital gains 162–3; childbearing and 44, 47
tax and benefits systems 141–2
technical assistance approach, community development 67–8, 71, 73, 82–3, 85
tenant management, housing 159–60
Tenant Participation Compacts, housing 158, 163–4
Tenants' Choice, Housing Act 154–5
tenure, and housing policy 144–5, 147–8, 149
text–context interaction: rational choice theory 1–3, 8; socialisation 8
trade unions: decline 123; free collective bargaining 102, 110; social capital 102
transnational classes 114
transnational social settlement 121–2, 123
trust: and contractual relations 49; state–citizens 50–1

unemployment: in communities 64–5; mass 114, 120; and social settlement 120–1
Unger, R. 140

unicity, community development 72
urban regeneration, community development 78

value: context-dependent 3; and exploitation 6; and generational relations 36–7; and groups 8; and households 31; maximising 4–5
victim empowerment, domestic violence 33
violence, and intimate relationships 32–3
voluntary relationships, communities 56

waged domestic labour 22–4, 29
wealth flows theory, childbearing and 37–9
welfare: division of 99; Green Paper (1998) 141; means-testing and 121; and migration 121–2; social division of 148
welfare state 114–15, 115–17
Wiewel, W. 76
women: double exploitation 97–8; and independence 24–5; and social/political change 16–17
work: flexibilisation 129; and housing managerialism 160–1; and social settlement 119, 120–1
workers' collectives 103, 110
working class, ruling class relations 113
workplace: Foucault and 106–7; gender relations 105; racism 105–6; workplace-based empowerment 104–5